For Sam to enjoy and read about, a very proud part of the country I live in.

Best wishes
Eddie.

© The Northern Echo

ISBN 0-9536984-3-2

December 1999

Design by: Tim Murphy Creative Solutions

Published in Great Britain by leighton in association with The Northern Echo

The Teleport
Doxford International
Sunderland
SR3 3XD
Tel: +44 (0) 191 525 2400
Fax: +44 (0) 191 520 1815
www.leighton.com

British Cataloguing-in-Publications Data

*A catalogue record for this book is available from the British Library*

The publisher has made every effort to obtain permission to reproduce material in this book from the appropriate source. If there are any errors or omissions please contact the publisher who will make suitable acknowledgement in the reprint.

Printed and bound in Great Britain by Butler & Tanner Limited, Somerset.

# Contents

| | | |
|---|---|---|
| 1. | **The Roman Conquest** 43AD to 122AD | Page 001 |
| 2. | **Hadrian,s Wall** 122AD to 303AD | Page 007 |
| 3. | **Roman Sites in the North East** | Page 013 |
| 4. | **The Anglian Invasions** 306AD to 593AD | Page 021 |
| 5. | **The Rise of Northumbria** 598AD to 633AD | Page 029 |
| 6. | **Oswald and Aidan** 633AD to 655AD | Page 035 |
| 7. | **Wilfrid and Cuthbert** 657AD to 688AD | Page 041 |
| 8. | **The Age of Bede** 690AD to 735AD | Page 047 |
| 9. | **Kingdom at War** 736AD to 854AD | Page 053 |
| 10. | **Jorvik** 866AD to 900AD | Page 059 |
| 11. | **The Irish-Norwegians** 900AD to 945AD | Page 063 |
| 12. | **Eric Bloodaxe** 946AD to 989AD | Page 069 |
| 13. | **The Birth of Durham** 990AD to 1031AD | Page 075 |
| 14. | **The Norman Conquest** 1031AD to 1066AD | Page 081 |
| 15. | **Conquest of the North** 1067AD to 1080AD | Page 087 |
| 16. | **The Prince Bishops** 1081AD to 1135AD | Page 093 |
| 17. | **Two Great Cathedrals - Durham and York** | Page 099 |
| 18. | **The Monastic Revival** 1080AD to 1536AD | Page 105 |
| 19. | **A Part of Scotland** 1135AD to 1157AD | Page 113 |
| 20. | **Bishop Pudsey** 1154AD to 1198AD | Page 119 |
| 21. | **John and Henry III** 1199AD to 1272AD | Page 125 |
| 22. | **Medieval Towns** 1100AD to 1500AD | Page 131 |
| 23. | **Newcastle Coal** 1100AD to 1500AD | Page 135 |
| 24. | **Bruce and Baliol** 1272AD to 1371AD | Page 139 |
| 25. | **Hotspur and the Percys** 1377AD to 1461AD | Page 145 |

| | | |
|---|---|---|
| 26. | **Wars of the Roses** 1455AD to 1508AD | Page 151 |
| 27. | **Reform and Rebellion** 1509AD to 1603AD | Page 157 |
| 28. | **The Border Reivers** 1400AD to 1611AD | Page 163 |
| 29. | **Elizabethans and Stuarts** 1560AD to 1714AD | Page 169 |
| 30. | **Cromwell to Queen Anne** 1560AD to 1714AD | Page 175 |
| 31. | **Coal and Industry** 1500AD to 1800AD | Page 181 |
| 32. | **The Georgian North** 1714AD to 1800AD | Page 187 |
| 33. | **Farming** 100AD to 1900AD | Page 193 |
| 34. | **The Locomotive Age** 1800AD to 1828AD | Page 197 |
| 35. | **A Town is born** 1828AD to 1839AD | Page 203 |
| 36. | **The Northern Coalfield** 1800AD to 1900AD | Page 209 |
| 37. | **Lead Mining** 1750AD to 1850AD | Page 215 |
| 38. | **The Age of Iron** 1839AD to 1879AD | Page 221 |
| 39. | **Shipbuilding** 1790AD to 1899AD | Page 227 |
| 40. | **Chemicals and Glass** | Page 233 |
| 41. | **The Electric Light Years** 1878AD to 1899AD | Page 239 |
| 42. | **The Victorian Age** 1837AD to 1901AD | Page 245 |
| 43. | **A New Century and World War One** 1901AD to 1919AD | Page 253 |
| 44. | **The 20s and 30s** 1920AD to 1939AD | Page 259 |
| 45. | **World War Two and the late 40s** 1939AD to 1949AD | Page 265 |
| 46. | **The 50s and 60s** 1950AD to 1969AD | Page 271 |
| 47. | **Pits and Politics** 1970AD to 1989AD | Page 279 |
| 48. | **Sport** 1700AD to 1999AD | Page 287 |
| 49. | **The 1990s - Towards a New Millennium** | Page 293 |
| 50. | **The North East of England** 1900AD to 1999AD | Page 299 |

# Acknowledgments

My sincere thanks are due to everyone who has supported this project. Those deserving special mention include Chris Lloyd, for all his comments and corrections; Andrew Smith for setting the project in motion; Peter Barron for his support; Petra Stanton and Chris Moran for their background work; Sue Kendrew for allowing me the work time. I would also like to thank all The Northern Echo photographers, past and present, whose work has been included in this book. Thanks should also go to all the local reference libraries and second-hand book dealers who I have pestered to death over the years. Thanks to Abigail Hagger for all her love and support and for putting up with me. Finally special thanks to Andrea Murphy of leighton for co-ordinating the project and to Tim Murphy for all the time and effort he has put into designing this book.

Angel of the North photographs by Mike Smith Photography.

# Foreword

I can still recall the smell of steam and coal at the railway celebrations of 1975. I was eight years old and remember the excitement of seeing all those wonderful locomotives in the railway cavalcade. This was a world event - the 150th anniversary of the Stockton and Darlington Railway. Returning home, and armed with felt pen, I re-created the action in a sketch of Locomotion Number One. I seem to remember winning some kind of prize for my effort, but whatever the result, my passion for local history was born.

But it was not just steam trains. Vikings, Saxons, Romans, Kings, Queens and peculiar place names all served to fire my love for history and it has stayed with me ever since. As I grew older, my interest in history would also grow, but I was frustrated that many people knew about the events of the Nation's history, but not those of their region. This frustration set me off writing books back in 1991 and also drove me to collect details of recorded historical events. Over the next two years, I would scribble down details for hundreds of events and hoped one day to publish them.

The opportunity arose in 1994 when I started work as a researcher with The Northern Echo newspaper. The following year Durham celebrated its Millennium and we published a book celebrating a thousand years of the city. A major feature of the book was a chronicle of events adapted from my research. Later, in 1998, The Northern Echo editor suggested we produce a history of the region. I was appointed to the task and my first job was to find fifty historical themes stretching from Roman times to the year 2000AD. These would be covered every Monday in the Northern Echo over fifty weeks and would eventually form the basis of the book.

This book covers two thousand years of history, a vast period of time in which many changes have occurred. Of course, not every event, occurrence or personality can be included and each chapter could be the subject of a book in its own right. Finally I should explain that for the purposes of this book, the North East of England includes Northumberland, Durham, North Yorkshire, the rivers Tyne, Wear and Tees and the historic City of York.

David Simpson

# The Roman Conquest

43AD to 122AD

Bust of Claudius

**THE ROMAN CONQUEST 43AD TO 122AD** Man's presence in the North dates from around 5,000BC. When the Romans arrived, they found Britain was a land of tribes and hill forts. The North-East was part of the territory of the Brigantes, a tribe led by a woman called Cartimandua.

**May 43AD - ROMANS INVADE (England)** An enormous army of 40,000 Roman troops led by Claudius has landed at Richborough in Kent. British resistance has been heavily crushed and Caractacus, a British resistance leader, has fled north.

**46AD - NORTHERN TRIBE IS ROMAN CLIENT (North)** The Brigantes, a huge tribe whose territory stretches from the Pennines of southern Yorkshire to north of the Tyne, are recognised as a client kingdom of the Romans - they have not been conquered by the Romans but, hoping to be left in peace, accept the invaders as their rulers. The Brigantes' queen is Cartimandua. Female leaders are quite acceptable to these war-like Britons. Their language resembles Welsh and is yet to be influenced by the Latin speech of the Romans.

**50AD - STANWICK A STRONGHOLD (Stanwick near Darlington)** The principal fort of the Brigantes is Stanwick St John, a few miles south of the River Tees. Other Brigantian forts are found throughout the North, particularly in the Pennines and include Ingleborough Hill and Almondbury near Huddersfield.

**51AD - QUEEN BETRAYS CARACTACUS (North Yorks)** Tribal support for Venutius, the husband of the Brigantian queen Cartimandua, is growing after the queen betrayed the popular British rebel Caractacus and revealed his whereabouts to the Romans.

**51AD - REBEL SET FREE IN ROME (Rome)** Caractacus, the leader of British resisitance, has been paraded in chains through Rome where his tough-minded defiance impressed the Roman Emperor. The emperor has released Caractacus from captivity and allowed him to live freely in Rome.

**51AD - QUEEN DIVORCES (North Yorks)** Cartimandua has divorced Venutius and is planning to marry her new lover Vellocatus who had been the armour-bearer of her husband. Civil war has broken out between the supporters of Cartimandua - who are backed by the Romans - and Venutius.

003

**56AD - ROMANS END NORTHERN WAR (North Yorkshire)** The Romans have sent a legion into the North to successfully end the rebellion of Venutius, husband of Cartimandua.

**61AD - BOUDICEA ATTACKS ROMANS AT LONDON (England)** In East Anglia, the Iceni tribe under Queen Boudicea have sacked the Roman towns of London, Colchester and St Albans. London is left burning.

**69AD - QUEEN FORCED OUT (Stanwick)** Venutius causes the Brigantes to rise up against his former wife who has been unpopular since the capture of British hero Caractacus. She is forced to flee the North, although the Romans rescue her from her angry tribesmen, and King Venutius becomes the new leader of the Brigantes.

**71AD - BATTLE OF SCOTCH CORNER (North Yorkshire)** After a whole series of great battles across the North, Venutius' Brigantes have been finally defeated by the Romans in battle at Scotch Corner. The Roman leader Petillius Cerealis has started building a series of forts across Brigantia to prevent further encounters and a legion has been stationed at York in a fortress of earth and timber.

**71AD - FORT BUILT ON TEES (Piercebridge)** The Romans are building a fort and bridge on the River Tees at Piercebridge. It will be of strategic importance in the subjugation of the Brigantes tribe, whose fort at Stanwick is nearby.

**73AD - BRIGANTES ABANDON STANWICK (North Yorkshire)** The Brigantes are forced to abandon their great tribal stronghold at Stanwick St John following Roman pressure.

**79AD - ROMANS MARCH TO TYNE (North-East)** The Romans have reached the River Tyne on the northern fringe of the Brigantes' land. Beyond the Tyne the major tribe are the Votadini who are based in the Bamburgh area of Northumberland with their territory extending north to Edinburgh. The people of Caledonia are now under threat from the Romans.

Tribal harness decoration from the Brigantes' fort at Stanwick, North Yorkshire

**80AD - GREAT NORTH ROADS ARE BUILT (North)** Julius Agricola, the Roman governor of Britain, has commenced his military campaign in Caledonia from his supply base at Corbridge. The Stanegate Roman road is being built through the Tyne Gap, from Corbridge-on-Tyne to Carlisle. Dere Street, a main route running from York to Caledonia in the north, is also being constructed. These roads will be complete by 85AD.

**81AD - AGRICOLA IMPROVES YORK (York)** Julius Agricola carries out improvements to the defences at the York legionary fortress.

**83AD - HIGHLANDERS DEFEATED IN GREAT BATTLE (Scotland)** Julius Agricola's army has been campaigning on the western coast of Caledonia. Agricola's campaign culminated in the heavy defeat of the Highland tribes, called the Caledonii, at the battle of Mons Grapius somewhere in the Caledonian mountains. The Roman subjugation of Britain is now complete. A fortress has been built at Inchtuthill in Tayside which will be the headquarters of the Roman 20th Legion.

**90AD - ROMANS LEAVE CALEDONIA (Scotland)** Difficult terrain and unpredictable tribes in Caledonia have made Roman administration of the land beyond the Rivers Forth and Clyde impossible. All Roman positions in Caledonia have now been abandoned.

**105AD - FORTS DESTROYED (Northumberland)** Permanent forts in southern Caledonia have been abandoned and the Roman frontier looks as if it is set to move south once again. Roman forts at Newstead, High Rochester and Glenlochar have been destroyed by the native Britons.

**117AD - HADRIAN BECOMES NEW EMPEROR (Rome)** Publius Aelius Hadrianus (Hadrian) has become the new Emperor of Rome.

Roman coin depicting Hadrian

Building the Roman Wall
A nineteenth century painting by William Bell Scott

# Hadrian's Wall

122AD to 303AD

**HADRIAN'S WALL 122AD TO 303AD** Hadrian's Wall was constructed in 122 AD to 'Separate the Romans from the Barbarians'. It was eighty miles long, six metres high, three metres wide and built of stone. Its defences were supplemented by turrets, ditches, milecastles and sixteen forts, each holding between five hundred and one thousand men. The men who occupied the Wall were sometimes recruited locally, but came from all parts of the Roman Empire including Spain, Switzerland, Germania, and even North Africa. They formed a Multi-Cultural Military Zone with their many different customs, languages and religions.

**122AD - HADRIAN VISITS THE NORTH (North)** Hadrian, Emperor of Rome, has visited northern Britain after increasing concern over tribal revolts in the region. The emperor has recognised an urgent need for improved defences and has ordered the construction of a great defensive wall.

**122AD - LEGION REPLACED (York)** The ninth legion has been replaced by the sixth legion at York.

**126AD - HADRIAN'S WALL COMPLETE (Northumberland)** Most of Hadrian's Wall, begun in 122, has been constructed. It will serve as a defensive zone and limit tribal movement between the north and south. Many of the early forts along the wall face south into the heart of the Brigantian territory, a recognition of the great threat that still exists from this large northern tribe.

**128AD - ROMANS BUILD SUPPLY PORT AT SOUTH SHIELDS (Tyneside)** Arbeia, a Roman fort has been built at South Shields. It will serve the role of a sea port and supply base for Hadrian's Wall.

**138AD - NEW EMPEROR ORDERS NORTHERN ADVANCE (Northumberland)** Romans are advancing into Caledonia again along the course of Dere Street. Antonius Pius, the new Emperor of Rome, has ordered the Roman advance and hopes to succeed where others have failed.

**142AD - NEW WALL BUILT IN FAR NORTH (Scotland)** Antonius Pius has ordered the construction of a new defensive wall in North Britain. Known as the Antonine Wall, it stretches from the Forth to the River Clyde. Hadrian's Wall still remains in use but has become more open.

**154AD - ANTONINE WALL ABANDONED AFTER NORTHERN UPRISING (North)** A major uprising by the Pennine based Brigantes against the Romans has forced the Romans to abandon the Antonine Wall in Caledonia, only twelve years after it first came into use. The Brigantian rebellion is centred on their new tribal capital at Aldborough near Boroughbridge.

**160AD - ROMANS RETAKE ANTONINE WALL (Scotland)** Romans have once again advanced north and re-established control of the Antonine Wall. A new Roman fort is being built at Chester-le-Street, where a Roman road runs north to the bridge over the River Tyne at Pons Aelius (Newcastle).

**163AD - HADRIAN'S WALL RESTORED (Northumberland)** Hadrian's Wall has been extensively restored following recent tribal unrest in north Britain.

**165AD - ANTONINE WALL ABANDONED (Scotland)** The Antonine Wall in Caledonia has been abandoned once again following tribal unrest and the death of the Emperor Antonius who instigated the wall. Recent restoration of Hadrian's Wall seems to have been a wise decision.

**180AD - ROMAN GENERAL KILLED IN NORTHERN REVOLT (Hadrian's Wall)** A Roman General has been killed after tribes crossed the wall in yet another northern revolt against the Romans.

**180AD - CIVILIAN GROWTH AT YORK (York)** The civilian settlement at York is undergoing rapid growth. It lies just to the south west of the River Ouse.

**193AD - CLODIUS TAKES WALL TROOPS INTO EUROPE (York)** Clodius Albinus, the Roman Governor of Britain and Deputy Emperor of the whole empire, has proclaimed himself Emperor of Rome at York. He is taking most of the British Roman army into Europe in a bid for the empire. It is hoped that an alliance of native tribes living in the land between the two Roman Walls will maintain peace during the absence of the Roman frontier troops.

**197AD - VIOLENCE AND REVOLT ON ROMAN WALL (Hadrian's Wall)** There have been further outbreaks of revolt and frontier disturbances in the vicinity of Hadrian's Wall.

The Maetae, an alliance of tribes situated between Hadrian's Wall and the Antonine Wall, have crossed to the south of Hadrian's Wall to cause major problems for the Roman military force. Meanwhile the former Roman governor Clodius Albinus, who left the North defenceless to campaign in Europe, has committed suicide after defeat by the Roman Emperor Septimius Severus on the continent.

**200AD - TEMPLES TO MITHRAS (Hadrian's Wall)** Four temples to Mithras exist on Hadrian's Wall. Mithraic worship is the most popular religion in the Hadrian's Wall area.

**205AD - HADRIAN'S WALL REPAIRS (Northumberland and Cumbria)** Roman Governor Alfenus Senicio has ordered extensive rebuilding and repair work on Hadrian's Wall following the heavy damage suffered during the disturbances of recent years. The next few years will see extensive fort building in the north.

**208AD - CALEDONIANS DEFEATED (Scotland)** After years of revolt the Roman Emperor Severus has heavily defeated the Caledonians and re-established military order in Britain. Corbridge on Tyne has formed an important supply base for the Roman campaign.

**208AD - YORK BECOMES CAPITAL OF INFERIOR NORTH (Yorkshire)** Septimius Severus, the Emperor of Rome, has divided Britain into two Roman provinces. York, where the Emperor has set up court, will become the capital of the northern province called Britannia Inferior, while London has been made capital of Britannia Superior, the southern province. York has gained the high status of a Roman Colonia.

**211AD - ROMAN EMPEROR DIES AT YORK (York)** Septimius Severus, Emperor of Rome, has died at York.

**212AD - BRITONS BECOME ROMANS (Rome)** It has been declared that all inhabitants of the Roman Empire are to gain Roman citizenship. This means that all inhabitants of Roman occupied Britain are now technically Romans.

The Corbridge Lion, probably originally designed for a tomb

**220AD - VILLAGES NEAR FORTS (Hadrian's Wall)** Civilian settlements called vici have been evolving around Roman forts in the Hadrian's Wall area, such as Corbridge. Vici are a kind of village settlement in which craftsmen, merchants and women live.

**240 - LANCHESTER REBUILT (County Durham)** Lanchester, a Roman fort south of the Tyne, has been rebuilt and regarrisoned by Roman troops. The fort is situated on the Roman road called Dere Street, an important military route into Caledonia. The Romans know Lanchester as Longovicium and there is a large civilian settlement near the fort. Lanchester supersedes the nearby forts at Binchester and Ebchester which are also on Dere Street.

**270AD - VILLAGE AT VINDOLANDA (Northumberland)** A Roman vicus or civilian setttlement has developed at Vindolanda on the Stanegate road near Hadrian's Wall.

**287AD - GERMAN INVADERS THREATEN OUR SHORES (England)** Germanic raids from the continent are becoming a problem throughout Britain. Raiders called Saxons could become a major threat to the stability which the Romans have brought to our island. Stone forts have been built along the coast of south-east England as a defence against the raiders.

**290AD - ROMANS USE NORTH RIVERS (North)** Ports on river estuaries such as the Tyne, Humber and possibly the Tees are used by Roman fleets.

**296AD - TRIBES OVERRUN WALL (Hadrian's Wall)** Many tribes have overrun Hadrian's Wall in a revolt against the Romans. York (Eboracum) has been heavily destroyed, along with Chester (Deva) on the River Dee. Hadrian's Wall had been left defenceless after a large portion of its garrison was removed to assist the usurping Roman governor Allectus in a military confrontation with Constantius, the deputy Governor of Rome.

**296AD - MORE PROVINCES FOR BRITAIN (Britain)** Britain has been broken into four new provinces by the Romans. Their names and respective capitals are; Britannia Secunda (York), Flavia Caesariensis (Lincoln), Britannia Prima (Cirencester) and Maxima Caeseriensis (London).

Our northern province called Britannia Secunda stretches from the Mersey and Humber to Hadrians Wall. Britannia Prima includes all of Wales and the South West.

**297AD - FORTS REBUILT (Hadrian's Wall)** Forts have been rebuilt on both sides of Hadrian's Wall following recent destruction by unruly tribes.

**300AD - TEES FORT (Piercebridge)** The Romans have rebuilt a fort and bridge on the River Tees at Piercebridge. Strengthening of the Legionary fortress at York is also being carried out.

**303AD - DEFENCES STRENGTHENED IN THE NORTH (Northumberland)** Many of the north's Roman defences are being strengthened following tribal revolts in recent years. The defences will play a part in Roman campaigns against the Picts. Repair work and improvements are being carried out at York, High Rochester, Risingham, Bewcastle, Birdoswald and Houseteads on the Roman Wall. Improvements to Roman roads in the northern region will also be made.

Hadrian's Wall

# Roman Sites in the North East

**ROMAN FORTS, TOWNS AND ROADS IN THE NORTH EAST : English Name - Roman Name**

**County Durham and Cleveland**

**Binchester - Vinovia or Vinovium**  Roman fort on Dere Street (Bishop Auckland)
Built by Julius Agricola in the 1st century for cavalry. The fort has Britain's best example of a Roman hypocaust or central heating system. In Anglo-Saxon times stones were plundered from Binchester for the construction of the church at Escomb.Stones from the fort were used in the construction of an Elizabethan hall, but this was destroyed in the nineteenth century by Bishop William Van Mildert whose palace at Auckland was nearby. Stones from the old fort were once used as supports in a nearby coal pit.

**Bowes - Lavatris**  Roman Fort (Bowes, west of Barnard Castle)
Built by Julius Agricola in 78 AD of turf and rebuilt in stone in the second century. Most of the fort is now occupied by the later Norman castle and St Giles churchyard. Finds from the fort are displayed at the Bowes Museum in Barnard Castle.

**Cade's Road - Roman name not known**  Roman road (County Durham and Yorkshire)
A road built around 138-161 AD at a later date to Dere Street. It runs from Newcastle to Brough on Humber. The only fort discovered on the road is Chester-le-Street (Concangium). The road follows the High Street in Gateshead and is the 'street' referred to in the names of Chester-le-Street, Stainton-le-Street near Sedgefield and Thornton-le-Street near Thirsk. It crossed the Tees near Middleton St George, where Pounteys Lane is named after the Roman Pons Tees - Bridge of Tees.

**Chester-le-Street - Concangis**  Roman fort on Cade's Road (County Durham)
Nothing can be seen of the Roman fort although its outline has been plotted. The ancient church of St Mary and St Cuthbert stands roughly at its centre. Pottery and altars have been found. The fort dates from the Antonine Period (138AD-161AD). It is the only fort on the hundred mile long Cade's Road. It was known to the Anglo-Saxons as Conecaster and the local stream is called the Cong Burn.

**Dere Street - Roman name not known** Roman road (Northumberland, Durham and Yorkshire)

The most important Roman road in the North running from York to the Scottish borders, built around 80 AD. The forts on the road include York, Aldborough, Catterick, Piercebridge, Binchester, Lanchester, Ebchester and Corbridge. The road stretches as far north as Newsteads (Trimontium) near the three distinctive peaks of the Eildon Hills, near Melrose.

**Ebchester - Vindomara** Roman fort (County Durham)

Roman fort guarding the Derwent. It is a pre-Hadrianic fort, occupied by the site of the parish church.

**Greta Bridge - Roman name not known** Roman fort (South East of Barnard Castle)

Roman fort located to the east of Bowes.

**Huntcliff - Roman name not known** Roman watchtower (Saltburn)

One of a series of Roman watchtowers built along the Yorkshire coast in the late fourth century.

**Lanchester - Longovicium** Roman fort on Dere Street (North West Durham)

Built around 140 AD to replace the forts at Binchester and Ebchester and save on manpower. It fell out of use in the late 3rd century but was back in use in the 4th. Two aqueducts brought water from four miles away. Many stones from the fort, including an altar to the British god Garmangabis, were incorporated into Lanchester church.

**Old Durham - Roman name not known** Roman farmstead (Near Durham City)

The northernmost Romanised villa-farmstead in the Roman Empire is located across the river from Shincliffe. The next nearest Romanised famstead is at Middleham in Wensleydale. The remains of a bathhouse were excavated at Old Durham in the 1940s. It is overlooked by Maiden Castle, a native fort, and there may have been links between the two. The peninsula where Durham Cathedral now stands is thought to have been the site of a Romanised native farm.

**Piercebridge - Morbium** Roman fort and bridge (4 miles west of Darlington)

Piercebridge was built to protect Dere Street crossing the River Tees. The main road through the village

A representation of the Roman god Harpocrates found at Piercebridge

follows the course of the fort's main street or Via Principalis. Much of Piercebridge's village green lies over the fort but there are extensive remains to be seen. A large Roman village settlement or vicus lay outside the fort and the remains of a Roman bridge can still be seen.

**Rey Cross - Roman name not known** Roman marching camp (Stainmore, Teesdale)
Has been described as the best preserved Roman marching camp in Britain. It has nine gates and nearby signal stations to communicate with neighbouring forts. It is thought to have been built around 72 AD.

**River Wear - Vedra** River (County Durham)
The Roman name for the River Wear was Vedra.

**Tees Mouth - Dunum Sinus** River estuary (Teesside)
The Roman name for the Tees bay (sinus). Dunum meaning place/hill is possibly the Hartlepool headland.

**TYNESIDE**

**Benwell - Condercum** Fort on Hadrian's Wall (West End of Newcastle)
Best known for the remains of a temple just outside the fort dedicated to a native god called Antenocticus. The temple is thought to have been destroyed in the second century. The fort was built in Hadrian's time and was occupied by a cavalry. For most of the third and fourth century it was occupied by soldiers from northern Spain.

**Newcastle upon Tyne - Pons Aelius or Pons Aelii** Roman fort and bridge (Beneath the castle)
Site of a small Roman fort on Hadrian's Wall built to guard a bridge over the River Tyne. Pons Aelius means Bridge of Hadrian's family (his full name was Publius Aelius Hadrianus). Altars have been found here dedicated to the Roman gods Neptune and Oceanus. They were probably erected on the Roman bridge and can now be seen in Newcastle castle which occupies the site of the fort. Pons Aelius was known to the later Anglo-Saxons as Monkchester. Many Roman finds and a reconstruction of the Carrawbrugh Mithras Temple can be seen in Newcastle's Museum of Antiquities.

**South Shields - Arbeia**  Roman Fort and supply port (Tyneside)

A seaport and civilian settlement with extensively excavated remains and an impressive reconstruction of a gateway. Arbeia played an important part in supplying Hadrian's Wall. Built around 128 AD it became a supply base around 208 AD. In the third century it was occupied by a cohort of Gauls (from France) and in the fourth century there was a unit of bargemen from the Tigris valley (now Iraq). The joint Roman emperors Caracalla and Geta are thought to have sailed from here to Rome after the death of their father Severus at York in 211 AD.

**Tyne - Tinea**  River (Tyneside)

The Roman name for the River Tyne.

**Wallsend - Segedunum**  Roman fort on Hadrian's Wall (Tyneside)

The eastern terminus of Hadrian's Wall, although for a time Hadrian's Wall terminated at Newcastle. It was strategically placed on a bend of the River Tyne so that the river provided a continuation of the wall's defences to the east. A Roman harbour will have existed here, presumably with a ferry to the port at South Shields. The wall from the fort actually extended into the Tyne ensuring every last inch of ground was covered by Hadrian's Wall.

**Washing Well Fort, Whickham - Roman name not known**  Roman fort (Tyneside)

Site of an early fort of the second century which predated Hadrian's Wall.

**Wrekendyke - Roman name not known**  Roman road (Tyneside)

A short eastern offshoot of Cade's Road at Wrekenton which terminates at South Shields Roman fort.

## HADRIAN'S WALL AND NORTHUMBERLAND

**Sites on Hadrian's Wall**

Some of the best views and sections of the wall are between Hexham and Haltwhistle including Steel Rigg, Cuddy's Crag, Walltown Crags and Sewingshields Crag. A well preserved Milecastle can be seen at Cawfields near Haltwhistle and a notable turret can be seen at Walltown Crags near Greenhead.

**Birdoswald - Banna**  Fort on Hadrian's Wall (Near Haltwhistle)
Roman fort on Hadrian's Wall near the River Irthing. Notable features include the nearby Roman Bridge at Willowford.

**Carrawburgh - Brocolitia**  Roman fort on Hadrian's Wall (Near Hexham)
The most famous finds here are Coventina's Well, a shrine dedicated to a Celtic water goddess, and just to the east, a temple dedicated to the Persian God, Mithras.

**Carvoran - Magnis**  Roman fort on the Stanegate road (Near Haltwhistle)
A Roman fort probably built by Julius Agricola in the 1st century. It is situated at the junction of the Roman roads called the Stanegate and the Maiden Way.

**Castlesteads - Camboglanna**  Roman fort on Hadrian's Wall (Near Birdoswald)
Castlesteads fort just to the west of Birdoswald was known to the Romans as Camboglanna, which is based on a Welsh name meaning 'crooked glen'. It is thought by scholars to be the most likely setting for King Arthur's last battle which was at 'Campglan' on the Roman wall.

**Chesters - Cilurnum**  Roman fort on Hadrian's Wall (Near Haltwhistle)
Roman fort where Hadrian's Wall crosses the North Tyne. The remains of a bath house have been found here. The nineteenth century Roman archaeologist and Newcastle town clerk John Clayton lived at the nearby mansion of Chesters House.

**Chesterholm - Vindolanda**  Roman fort on the Stanegate (Near Hexham)
Located on the Stanegate, not Hadrian's Wall, but one of the best known forts in the area and better known by its Roman rather than its English name. It was built around 95 AD. The headquarters building or Principia can be clearly seen, along with the remains of a 2nd century inn, in the vicus or civilian settlement outside the fort.

**Corbridge-on-Tyne - Corstopitum or Coriosopitum**  Roman town and fort on the Stanegate
A garrison town and supply base for troops on the frontier. It is the most important Roman site in the

north east, north of the Tees. Located on the Stanegate, it was built by Julius Agricola in the first century AD. The most famous find is a stone sculpture called the Corbridge Lion which was used to adorn a fountain.

**Devil's Causeway - Roman name not known**  Roman road (Northumberland)
An offshoot of Dere Street running across Northumberland from Corbridge to the mouth of the River Tweed.

**Great Chesters - Aesica**  Roman fort on Hadrian's Wall (Near Haltwhistle)
A large fort which was supplied with water by a six mile long Roman aqueduct which ran through the hills to the north.

**Housesteads - Vercovicium**  Roman fort on Hadrian's Wall (Near Hexham)
Large impressive Roman fort on Hadrian's Wall with remains of a large Roman civilian settlement outside. The civilian settlement includes 'Murder House' where the remains of a man and wife stabbed to death were found. The fort housed around 1,000 infantry including, in the fourth century, Anglo-Saxons from Northern Europe. The Anglo-Saxons were not native to Britain at that time.

**Maiden Way - Roman name not known**  Roman road (Northumberland and Cumbria)
Roman road running through the Pennines southward from Hadrian's Wall.

**Risingham - Habitancum**  Roman fort (North Tynedale)
One of a small number of outpost forts on Dere street, beyond Hadrian's Wall.

**Stanegate - Roman name not known**  Roman road (Tyne valley)
The Roman road from Corbridge to Carlisle which predates the Roman wall. The Stanegate was the northern frontier of the Roman Empire before Hadrian's wall was built. Famous Roman sites on the Stanegate include Corbridge and Vindolanda.

# The Anglian Invasions

## 306AD to 593AD

An early Anglian helmet with bronze panelling from Sutton Hoo, East Anglia

**THE ANGLIAN INVASION 306AD TO 593AD** The fifty years which followed the departure of the Romans from Britain is the most mysterious period of the last two thousand years. The most important figure of the age was Arthur, a Celtic leader, who may be just a legend. Arthur is said to have died near Hadrian's Wall fighting the Anglo-Saxons. If Arthur was a legend, the Anglo-Saxons he was fighting were a genuine threat. The Saxons from north Germany settled in the south of England, while the Angles from land between Germany and Denmark settled the North where their territory would eventually become the Kingdom of Northumbria.

**July 25 306AD - CONSTANTINE THE GREAT BECOMES EMPEROR AT YORK (York)** Constantius Chlorus, the Roman Emperor, has died at York. He has been succeeded by his son Constantine the Great who has been proclaimed Emperor at York. One of Constantine's first actions was to drive back an attack from the Picts in Caledonia.

**314AD - YORK IS HQ FOR BRITISH GENERAL (York)** The Dux, or commander of the Roman army in Britain, is now based at York.

**314AD - YORK HAS A BISHOP (York)** Christianity is now widely practised and accepted in Roman Britain along with many other religions. Christian Bishops from Britain have represented the province at a council at Arles, including a Bishop of York and a Bishop of London.

**320AD - IRAQ BOATMEN WORK ON TYNE (South Shields)** A unit of Tigris bargemen from Iraq are employed by the Romans at South Shields fort, Arbeia, on the Tyne.

**343AD - MORE TROUBLE ON THE WALL (Hadrian's Wall)** There has been much trouble on the Roman wall this year involving Roman scouts. The forts at Risingham and Rochester in North Tynedale have been burnt down.

**360AD - FRONTIER BATTLES STILL A PROBLEM FOR ROMANS (Hadrian's Wall)** Battles on the Northern frontier involving Picts and Scots are becoming a great problem for the Romans.

**367AD - BARBARIANS ATTACK WALL IN GREAT CONSPIRACY (Hadrian's Wall)** Tribes have overrun the Roman wall once again in what has become known as the Barbarian Conspiracy. Picts, Irish and Scots, assisted by Germanic Saxon Pirates from northern Europe, seem to have colluded to cause trouble for the Romans on the Northern frontier. This is certainly the biggest revolt against the Romans to date.

**369AD - DEFENCES AT SALTBURN AND SCARBOROUGH (Yorkshire Coast)** A series of fortified watch towers are being constructed along the North East coast to protect the Roman north from Barbarian invaders who are attacking from Germany and Denmark. Watch towers are located at Filey, Scarborough, Goldsborough and Huntcliff, near Saltburn. Other towers may have been placed along the coast, north of the Tees as far as South Shields. The towers can communicate to each other and to Roman soldiers stationed at York and Malton, using beacons of flame.

**369AD - WALL UNDER REPAIR (Hadrian's Wall)** Hadrian's Wall has been extensively restored following the great damage it suffered in the Barbarian Conspiracy two years ago. It is not the first time the Romans have had to carry out wide ranging re-construction following northern revolts.

**383AD - MAXIMUS CLAIMS TO BE EMPEROR (Britain)** While the Goths are attacking Rome, Magnus Maximus, a Roman governor, has taken advantage of the general turmoil and made himself an Emperor. It is a false claim but he is unlikely to be challenged during this difficult period. Magnus has taken many Roman troops from Britain in an attempt to seize Gaul and Spain. The Northern frontier has been left exposed and Hadrian's Wall is being heavily overrun with native tribes.

**388AD - ROMANS HEAVILY DEFEATED AFTER WALL OVERRUN (Hadrian's Wall)** Hadrian's Wall is undergoing heavy onslaught from the native tribes and the Romans have suffered great defeats in battle. Romans have become increasingly vulnerable to attacks in recent years, and are weakened by the Gothic invasions in the eastern parts of their empire.

**397AD - ST NINNIAN MONASTERY (Whithorn, Dumfries)** St Ninnian has established a monastery at Whithorn. Ninnian is a British saint trained in Rome.

**399AD - ROMANS EVACUATE TROOPS FROM BRITAIN (Britain)** The Romans have started to evacuate troops from Britain. Reinforcements are desperately needed on the continent to protect Rome and the eastern parts of the empire.

**408AD - NORTH REVOLTS AS ROMAN OCCUPATION NEARS A CLOSE (Scotland)** The depletion of the Roman army in Britain has left the Northern frontier exposed. Revolts against the Romans in North Britain are gaining momentum.

**410AD - ROMANS LEAVE BRITAIN DEFENCELESS (Britain)** Virtually all Roman troops have left Britain to assist the Roman army against the invasion of the Visigoths who are sacking Rome. Britain has to all intents and purposes ceased to be a part of the Roman Empire. Our island is left virtually defenceless and at the mercy of the Germanic Anglian and Saxon raiders.

**430AD - GERMANIC WARRIORS HIRED FOR PROTECTION (England)** Many of Britain's Roman towns have fallen into disrepair and disorder following the departure of Roman troops. Many native Britons have abandoned the towns altogether, but some are beginning to employ Germanic warriors called Angles (Anglians) and Saxons as mercenaries who will help to defend Britain in return for land. Angles from south Denmark have begun to settle in what will become East Anglia. They will eventually give their name to a whole nation, England (the Angleland).

**440AD - ANGLES MOVE INTO LINCOLN (Lincolnshire)** Angles from Denmark have penetrated into Lincolnshire following their recent arrival in East Anglia. The Kingdom of Lindsey (Lincolnshire) will gradually develop from this Anglian settlement and Lincoln, a former Roman site, will be their capital.

A German Renaissance statue of King Arthur

**445AD - NEWCASTLE STILL KNOWN AS HADRIAN'S BRIDGE (Newcastle)** Despite the recent departure of the Romans, Newcastle upon Tyne is still known by its Roman name Pons Aelius. This is the name of the fort overlooking the Roman Tyne Bridge. Its name consists of two elements, Pons meaning bridge, and Aelius, the family name of the Emperor Hadrian who built the Roman Wall.

**445AD - SAXON MERCENARIES TURN ON KENTISH LEADER (England)** The employment of Germanic troops as mercenaries by Vortigern, the Romano-British leader of Kent, has backfired with a revolt by the mercenaries who see an opportunity for seizing land in Kent.

**450AD - ANGLES INVADE NORTH (North East and Yorkshire)** Angles and Saxons are invading and settling Britain. Angles from southern Denmark are colonising land in the Yorkshire Wolds, north of the Humber (the north Humber land) and are also settling in the vicinity of the Rivers Tyne, Wear and Tees. In southern England settlement of Jutes and Saxons (from northern Germany) is taking place. Their settlements will form the kingdoms of Kent, Wessex, Essex and Sussex.

**455AD - JUTES ESTABLISH KINGDOM OF KENT (England)** The Jutes, a Germanic tribe recently settled in Britain, have established a Kingdom called Kent. Its name derives from the Romano-Celtic Canti tribe who occupy the area. Canterbury is the Kentish capital.

**477AD - KINGDOM OF SUSSEX ESTABLISHED BY SAXONS (England)** Sussex, the Kingdom of the South Saxons, has been established in the south of England to the west of Kent.

**500AD - BRITISH DEFEATED AT MONS BADONICUS (Britain)** Britons have been heavily defeated by Anglo-Saxon invaders at the Battle of Mons Badonicus despite the efforts of a legendary hero called King Arthur, a Romano British leader. Arthur has fought many battles across the country including possible battles in Durham, Northumberland and Scotland.

**537AD - DEATH OF KING ARTHUR OF THE BRITONS (Hadrian's Wall)** King Arthur is said to have died in this year while fighting for the Britons against the Anglo-Saxons. He is thought to have died somewhere near Hadrian's Wall, possibly Birdoswald in Cumbria.

**538AD - EDINBURGH BRITONS DEFEATED BY CALEDONIANS (Scotland)** Caledonians from northern Scotland have heavily defeated the ancient British tribe called the Goddodin in the Lothians whose tribal fort and capital is at at Din Eidyn (Edinburgh). The Goddodin are probably the descendants of the Votadini tribe which inhabited this territory in early Roman times.

**547AD - KING SEIZES JOYOUS GUARD (Bamburgh)** The Ancient British coastal stronghold of Din Guyardi (Bamburgh) on the North Eastern coast has been captured by an Angle chief called King Ida the Flamebearer. He is reputedly a descendant of the god Woden. Din Guyardi, situated on a promontory formed by the Great Whin Sill, is a magnificently defended site. Native British lands in the vicinity of Din Guyardi have been taken by Ida and added to his expanding Kingdom of Bernicia. Din Guyardi, romantically linked with the legendary 'Joyous Guard' fortress of Sir Lancelot, is to be the capital of Ida's kingdom in the North East.

**550AD - IDA BECOMES OVERKING OF THE NORTH (North East and North Yorkshire)** King Ida the Flamebearer who recently added Bamburgh to his kingdom has become an overking of the North following a conquest of neighbouring territories including land south of the Tees.

**560AD - THEODORIC SUCCEEDS IDA AS KING IN THE NORTH (North East)** Ida the Flamebearer, Angle King of the North has died. He has been succeeded by his son Theodoric whose name means 'King-King'. Theodoric's domain will be confined to Bernicia, the Anglian lands north of the River Tees. Some Celtic kingdoms in the neighbourhood will not accept his rule.

**560AD - AELLE ATTACKS BRITONS IN YORKSHIRE (Yorkshire)** Aelle, an Angle chief, is conducting his people against the native Britons in his newly established kingdom of Deira (The Yorkshire wolds) which he has seized following the death of the Bernician king, Ida the Flamebearer. Aelle is the first king of Deira. Meanwhile in the south Athelbert has become the new King of Kent.

**563AD - MONASTERY FOUNDED ON IONA (Scotland)** A monastery has been established by St Columba, on the island of Iona off the Caledonian coast. It will become one of the most important centres of Christianity in northern Britain.

**575AD - CUMBRIANS BESEIGE NORTHERN KING ON LINDISFARNE (Holy Island)** Urien, the leader of the British kingdom of Rheged (Cumbria), has besieged King Theodoric of Bernicia on the island of Lindisfarne. The siege lasted three days.

**577AD - WEST SAXONS CAPTURE FORMER ROMAN SITES (England)** The West Saxons have captured the strongholds of Gloucester and Bath, former Roman sites now occupied by the Ancient Britons.

**588AD - KING OF DEIRA DIES (Yorkshire)** Aelle, the first King of Deira (Yorkshire), has died. His successor is not known.

**590AD - KING OF NORTH BRITONS MURDERED ON LINDISFARNE (Holy Island)** Urien of Rheged, the leader of the native British of northern England, has been murdered on Lindisfarne during his campaign against the Anglo-Saxons. He is thought to have been betrayed by Morgan, a leader of the Goddodin tribe from north of the Tweed.

**593AD - AETHELFRITH IS NEW KING IN THE NORTH (North East)** Aethelfrith, a grandson of Ida the Flamebearer, has become King of Bernicia in the north east of England.

**597AD - SAINT COLUMBA DIES (Iona)** Caledonia is mourning the loss of its great saint, Columba, who died on the island of Iona where he had successfully introduced Christianity to northern Britain.

**597AD - KING OF KENT BECOMES A CHRISTIAN (England)** St Augustine's mission recently arrived in Kent from Rome with the intention of converting the Anglo-Saxons to Christianity. The mission has been a great success in the south and the Kentish King Athelbert has become a Christian. The king has appointed Augustine as the first Archbishop of Canterbury.

# The Rise of Northumbria

## 598AD to 633AD

Reconstruction of King Edwin's palace of Ad Gefrin near Yeavering Bell, Wooler, Northumberland

**THE RISE OF NORTHUMBRIA 598AD TO 633AD** Northumbria, 'North of the Humber' was an Anglo-Saxon kingdom formed by the merging of Bernicia, to the north of the Tees with Deira to the south. Northumbria's first two kings were a Bernician called Aethelfrith and a Deiran called Edwin. Aethelfrith was a Pagan, but Edwin became the North's first Christian King after baptism at York in 627 AD. During Edwin's reign the west of the region remained Celtic where a language similar to Welsh was spoken in Celtic Kingdoms like Leeds, Elmet and Craven. In time the Celtic kingdoms would be subdued by the outward expansion of Northumbria.

**598AD - BATTLE OF CATTERICK (North Yorkshire)** Anglo-Saxons have heavily defeated the native Britons at Catterick. The ancient British tribal kingdom of Catraeth centred near the valleys of the Tees and Swale has been subdued by the Germanic Angles. The Catterick area was the scene of fierce resistance against the Romans in earlier centuries. Britons at Catterick were supported by a huge army of Britons from a tribe called the Goddodin (formerly Votadini) who assembled at Edinburgh (Din Eidyn) before marching south. Britons from North Wales and Cumbria also gave their support.

**603AD - NORTHERN KING DEFEATS THE SCOTS (Scotland)** Aethelfrith, King of the North-Eastern kingdom of Bernicia has defeated Aidan MacGabrain, King of the Dalriada Scots, at the Battle of Degastan in Liddesdale. The Dalriada Scots who live in western Caledonia originate from Hibernia (Ireland) and were assisted by a large force of Ulstermen in the battle. Aethelfrith's victories in battle have forced the Kingdoms of Strathclyde in the west, Rheged in Cumbria and Gododdin in the Lothians to recognise Bernician superiority.

**604AD - AETHELFRITH TAKES NORTHUMBRIAN CROWN (North East)** Aethelfrith has usurped the crown of Deira in the Yorkshire wolds. He has become the King of both Deira and Bernicia uniting all the Anglo-Saxon territory north of the River Humber into one kingdom which will be called Northumbria. Bernicia and Deira have been reduced to the status of sub kingdoms.

**604AD - NORTHUMBRIAN KING MARRIES YORKSHIRE PRINCESS (North East and Yorkshire)** Aethelfrith, King of Northumbria, gains support from the recently captured Yorkshire province of Deira by marrying Acha, of the Deiran royal family. The marriage is unlikely to stop Acha's brother Edwin from claiming the Deiran throne.

**610AD - MIDLAND KING SHELTERS NORTHERN CLAIMANT (England)** King Cearl of Mercia (The Midlands) has taken Prince Edwin of Deira under his protection. Edwin's presence in the Mercian court will be a great threat to Aethelfrith, the King of Northumbria.

**615AD - JOYOUS GUARD RENAMED BAMBURGH (Northumberland Coast)** The Bernician fortress capital of Din Guyardi has been renamed Bebbanburgh (Bamburgh). It has been named after Queen Bebba, the new wife of King Aethelfrith of Northumbria. Bamburgh has continued to be known by its old Celtic name despite its capture by the Anglo-Saxon chief Ida in 547. Since that time it has been the chief fort and capital of northern Northumbria. The site's new name means Bebba's fort.

**615AD - NORTHUMBRIANS FORCE EDWIN INTO EXILE (England)** King Aethelfrith has ousted King Cearl from the Kingdom of Mercia and employed another Mercian to take care of his Northumbrian interests in the midland kingdom. Aethelfrith is now a virtual ruler of Mercia. Edwin, Prince of Deira, who had been under the protection of King Cearl, has taken refuge with the Royal family of East Anglia.

**615AD - NORTHUMBRIANS SLAUGHTER MONKS AT CHESTER (North West)** King Aethelfrith of Northumbria has defeated the Welsh in battle at Chester. Many Welsh monks were slaughtered in the battle.

**615AD - NORTHUMBRIANS CAPTURE CUMBRIA (North)** Cumbria has been seized by King Aethelfrith and added to the Kingdom of Northumbria. The seizure of Cumbria has isolated the Britons of North Wales from those of Strathclyde and the Lothians.

**616AD - NORTHUMBRIAN KING KILLED IN SOUTH YORKSHIRE (South Yorkshire)** Aethelfrith, King of Northumbria, has been killed in battle against Raedwald of East Anglia at Bawtry on the River Idle. Oswald, Aethelfrith's son, has fled Northumbria and taken refuge on the Scottish island monastery of Iona.

**616AD - EDWIN TAKES NORTHUMBRIAN THRONE (North)** Edwin, prince of Deira becomes King of Northumbria, although he has to fight rivals in the North to get the approval of the Bernician province.

**624AD - KING OF THE SOUTH DIES (England)** Raedwald, King of the East Anglians, who was also the ruler of all the Saxons in southern England, has died. For many years Raedwald sheltered Prince Edwin, who is now the King of Northumbria. Sutton Hoo, the great burial ship in Suffolk, is thought to have been built for Raedwald. Meanwhile, Cuichelm, the King of the West Saxons (Wessex) has defeated the East Saxons of Essex in a great battle.

**625AD - EDWIN MARRIES A CHRISTIAN (North)** King Edwin of Northumbria has married a Christian Princess called Ethelberga of Kent. The decision is thought to reflect Edwin's desire to form an alliance with King Eadbald of Kent, who is at present the only Christian king in England.

**626AD - EDWIN EXPELS LEEDS KING (West Yorkshire)** Edwin, King of Northumbria, has expelled a client king called Ceretic from the ancient British kingdom of Elmet near Leeds.

**626AD - EDWIN TAKES HATFIELD AND LINCOLNSHIRE KINGDOMS (South Yorkshire)** The native Celtic kingdom of Meicen (Hatfield) near Doncaster and the Anglian Kingdom of Lindsey (Lincolnshire) have been captured by Edwin for his Northumbrian kingdom. Edwin's power in the North is unequalled by any Anglian predecessor.

**626AD - ASSASSINATION ATTEMPT ON NORTHUMBRIAN KING (East Yorkshire)** Eumer, an agent of Cuichelm King of the West Saxons, has attempted to assassinate King Edwin while he was celebrating the Pagan festival of Easter at his royal palace by the River Derwent in the Yorkshire wolds. The assassin entered the King's court and asked to speak with the king on the pretence of having an important message from the West Saxon King. On seeing the king, Eumer produced a poisoned dagger from beneath his cloak with which he attempted to stab Edwin. Fortunately one of Edwin's men, Lillam jumped in the way and suffered a blow from which he was killed. A fight followed in which Edwin was injured but Eumer was eventually put to death. On the same night of the assassination attempt King Edwin's queen, Ethelburga gave birth.

**626A - NORTHUMBRIANS DEFEAT KINGDOM OF WESSEX (England)** Angered by the recent assassination attempt by the West Saxons on his life, King Edwin of Northumbria has defeated the West Saxons in a great battle in Wessex and proclaimed himself overking of all England.

**April 11  627AD - KING BECOMES CHRISTIAN AT YORK (York)** King Edwin of Northumbria has been converted to Christianity by a missionary called St Paulinus. Edwin promised to become a Christian after defeating the West Saxons. He underwent the baptism at York in the new wooden church of St Peter (a predecessor of York Minster). Coifi, a Pagan high priest under Edwin, has followed Edwin's example and has also converted to Christianity. To demonstrate his new faith Coifi destroyed the great heathen temple of Goodmanham near the River Derwent in East Yorkshire.

**627AD - PAULINUS BAPTISES NORTHUMBRIANS (Coquetdale, Northumberland)** St Paulinus has been appointed Bishop of York where he has established a song school dedicated to the new Christian faith. Paulinus is keen to encourage followers of the new faith in the North and has baptised thousands of Northumbrians at Holystone in Coquetdale, Northumberland. Paulinus has been using the Northumbrian palace at Yeavering near Wooler as the base for his mission of conversion in northern Northumbria.

**628AD - EDWIN REBUILDS EARLY MINSTER (York)** King Edwin has begun rebuilding the wooden church of St Peter's in stone. The church is a predecessor of York Minster.

**October 12  633AD - NORTHUMBRIA MOURNS DEATH OF GREATEST KING (South Yorkshire)** King Edwin of Northumbria has been killed in Battle at Heathfield (Hatfield near Doncaster) by Penda, a Mercian chief. Penda was assisted in the battle by the Welsh under the leadership of the fierce Caedwalla. Osric, a possible successor to Edwin, has also been killed in the battle. Edwin's son Edfrith has surrendered to Penda.

# Oswald and Aidan

633AD to 655AD

Statue of St. Aidan unveiled in 1958 on Lindisfarne

**KING OSWALD AND SAINT AIDAN 633 AD TO 655 AD** Oswald, King of Northumbria, was from a rival dynasty to King Edwin, who died in 633 AD. During Edwin's reign, Oswald sought exile on the Christian island of Iona, where he learned about the new religion. Oswald remained a pagan, but his defeat of the Welsh at Hexham in 634 AD persuaded him to convert. Before the battle, he prayed to the Christian God for victory. His prayers were seemingly answered. Oswald employed a monk from Iona called Aidan to become Bishop of his people. Aidan chose Lindisfarne as the centre of his see.

**633AD - ENEMY TAKES MIDLAND CROWN (England)** Penda celebrates his victory over King Edwin of Northumbria and becomes King of Mercia (The Midlands). Penda is one of the most powerful kings in the country along with his Welsh ally Caedwalla who claims the throne of Deira.

**633AD - NORTH RETURNS TO PAGANISM (York)** Eanfrith, pagan son of Aethelfrith, is the new King of Northumbria. Northumbria reverts to paganism. St Paulinus, the Christian Bishop of York, returns to Kent.

**634AD - KING OSWALD (North)** King Eanfrith, eldest son of Aethelfrith, is killed by his younger brother Oswald who has returned from exile on Iona. Oswald becomes King.

**635AD - BATTLE OF HEAVENFIELD (Hexham)** King Oswald heavily defeats Penda of Mercia and the Welsh under Caedwalla at the battle of Heavenfield near Hexham. The Welsh leader is killed during the battle.

**635AD - OSWALD IS OVERKING OF ENGLAND (North East)** Oswald's victory over Penda at the Battle of Heavenfield has made him undisputed overking (Bretwalda) of all England. The title was also held by King Edwin.

**635AD - OSWALD SUPPORTS CHRISTIAN CAUSE (North East)** Oswald attributes his victory at Heavenfield to the work of God. He asked his men to pray to God prior to the battle and is convinced that the Christian faith helped to bring victory. Oswald is determined to reintroduce Christianity to the North East.

**635AD - AIDAN TO CONVERT NORTHUMBRIANS (North)** King Oswald is to employ St Aidan, an Irish monk from the Scottish island of Iona, to convert Northumbria to Celtic Christianity. The Celtic Christianity is different to the Roman style of Christianity introduced by Paulinus.

**635AD - AIDAN MAKES LINDISFARNE A HOLY ISLAND (Northumberland Coast)** St Aidan, employed by King Oswald to convert the Northumbrians to Christianity, has chosen Lindisfarne as the centre for a bishopric. Aidan establishes a monastery on the island and becomes the first Bishop of Lindisfarne.

**638AD - NORTHUMBRIANS ATTACK LOTHIANS (Scotland)** The Lothians and Edinburgh are besieged and captured by Oswald who adds them to Northumbria. Edinburgh was the chief fortress of an ancient British tribe called the Gododdin.

**640AD - MONASTERY AT HARTLEPOOL (North East Coast)** A monastery has been established on the coastal headland at Hartlepool by Hieu an Irish princess who becomes the first abbess there.

**642AD - OSWALD COMPLETES FIRST MINSTER (York)** King Oswald completes the work begun by King Edwin on St Peter's Church in York.

**August 5  642AD - OSWALD KILLED AT MASSERFELTH (South Lancashire)** Oswald, King of Northumbria, is killed in battle at Maserfelth (Makerfield) fighting against Penda of Mercia. Oswald's body is hung from a tree at Oswestry.

**642AD - NORTHUMBRIA SPLITS (North)** Oswald is succeeded by his brother Oswy in Bernicia (North East) and by the rival Oswine in Deira (Yorkshire), splitting Northumbria into two parts.

**643AD - MIDLANDS TAKE NORTHUMBRIAN LAND (Yorkshire)** Penda of Mercia seizes Northumbrian land in Deira, Lincolnshire and Elmet near Leeds. He places these under the rule of Osric, a grandson of Edwin.

**649AD - HILDA OF HARTLEPOOL (Hartlepool)** Hieu, the founder and abbess of the monastery at Hartlepool, has been succeeded by St Hilda.

**651AD - AIDAN DIES AT BAMBURGH (Bamburgh)** St Aidan dies in the church at Bamburgh. He is succeeded by Bishop Finan. Meanwhile, a shepherd boy called Cuthbert sees the death of Aidan in a vision while shepherding on the moors near the Tweed. Cuthbert decides to become a monk and joins the monastery of Melrose.

**651AD - YORKSHIRE KING MURDERED (Catterick)** Oswine, King of Deira, is murdered after backing down from military confrontation with Oswy of Bernicia at Wilfar's Hill near Catterick. Oswine's hiding place at Gilling is discovered by one of Oswy's men and he is killed. Oswine is buried at Tynemouth. Oswy claims Deira on the strength of his marriage to Eanfled, daughter of the late King Edwin.

**651AD - YORKSHIRE UNDER NORTH-EAST CONTROL (North)** Oswy, King of Bernicia, appoints Ethelwald, son of Oswald, as King of Deira but Deira (Yorkshire) is subordinated to Bernicia (The North East).

**652AD - PAGAN ATTACKS NORTHUMBRIA (North East)** Penda, the pagan king of Mercia, attacks Northumbria as far as Bamburgh in an alliance with Ethelwald, King of Deira.

**653AD - PICTISH KING IS OSWY'S NEPHEW (Scotland)** The Picts elect Talorgen, nephew of the Northumbrian King Oswy, as their king.

**653 - GOAT'S HEAD ON TYNE (Gateshead)** Uttan is the abbot at the monastery of Ad Caprae Caput on the south bank of the River Tyne. Ad Caprae Caput means Goat's Head (Gateshead). It may refer to some kind of totem signifying a meeting place.

**654AD - LASTINGHAM PRIORY FOUNDED (North Yorkshire)** Lastingham Priory has been founded by St Cedd in North Yorkshire.

**November 15  655AD - WELSH AND MIDLANDERS LOSE BATTLE NEAR LEEDS (West Yorkshire)** The Mercians and Welsh are defeated in battle near Leeds. Penda, King of Mercia and thirty enemy chieftains are killed. Many Mercians are drowned in a nearby river as they try to escape.

**655AD - OSWY CAPTURES NORTH MIDLANDS (England)** Oswy, King of Northumbria, is proclaimed Bretwalda or 'overking' of all England. He appoints Penda's son Peada as King of Mercia, south of the Trent. Oswy takes north Mercia for himself.

# Wilfrid and Cuthbert

## 657AD to 688AD

**WILFRID AND CUTHBERT 657AD TO 688AD** St Cuthbert was a quiet, but athletic man, who loved nature and seclsuion but who still had great compassion for his fellow men. St Wilfrid by contrast was a restless controversial man who desired change. Wilfrid distanced himself from the austere Celtic Christianity and favoured the grandeur of Roman practices. At the Synod of Whitby in 664 AD, Wilfrid got his way and the North converted to Roman Christianity.

**657AD - MONASTERIES AT RIPON AND WHITBY (Ripon)** A monastery has been founded at Ripon by Irish monks from Melrose. Meanwhile St Hilda, abbess of Hartlepool, has established a monastery at Streanashalch (Whitby).

**664AD - WILFRID MAKES BIG CHANGES AT WHITBY SYNOD (Yorkshire Coast)** A great synod was held at Whitby to discuss the controversy regarding the timing of the Easter festival. Much dispute has arisen between the practices of the Celtic church in Northumbria and the beliefs of the Roman church which have a stronghold in the south of the country. The main supporters of the Celtic Christianity at Whitby are Colman of Lindisfarne, Hilda of Whitby and Cedd, Bishop of Essex. St Wilfrid, a well travelled man, champions the Roman Christian cause and persuades the Northumbrians to reject old ways. Colman, Bishop of Lindisfarne, resigns and returns to Iona. He is replaced by Bishop Tuda.

**664AD - WILFRID BISHOP OF YORK (York)** Tuda, Bishop of Lindisfarne, dies of plague and is succeeded by St Wilfrid who transfers the bishopric to York. Wilfrid claims no person in England can consecrate him and goes to France to be ordained. King Oswy replaces the absent Wilfrid with St Chad of Lastingham.

**669AD - KING ECGFRITH (York)** Oswy, King of Northumbria, dies and is succeeded by his son Ecgfrith.

**669AD - WILFRID'S SCHOOL (York)** St. Wilfrid returns to England as Bishop of York. He establishes a grammar school at St Peter's in York and starts buidling a new minster in the city. He also establishes a new monastery at Ripon.

**672AD - NORTHUMBRIAN EXPANSION CONTINUES (North)** The Celts of Cumbria and Dumfries are conquered by Northumbria. The Picts of Caledonia are defeated in battle.

**673AD - KING DIVORCES VIRGIN (North)** King Ecgfrith divorces his virgin queen Ethelreda of Ely to marry his new love Ermenburga. Ethelreda becomes a nun and is given land at Hexham by the King.

**673AD - WILFRID TO BUILD HEXHAM MONASTERY (Hexham)** Former queen, Ethelreda gives the land at Hexham to St Wilfrid to build a monastery. Ethelreda establishes a monastery at Coldingham near St Abbs Head, north of Berwick.

**673AD - NORTH DEFEATS MIDLANDS (England)** Ecgfrith of Northumbria defeats the Mercians (Midlanders) in battle.

**674AD - MONASTERY AT WEARMOUTH (Sunderland)** The Monastery of St Peter's, Monkwearmouth is founded by a noble called Benedict Biscop on land granted by King Ecgfrith. A great library will develop here with books from France and Rome and the first coloured glass in England will be introduced into the monastery by continental glaziers. Gregorian chanting is also introduced.

**676AD - ST CUTHBERT RETREATS TO REMOTE ISLAND (Northumberland)** Cuthbert, a popular young man noted for his power to work miracles and his gift for athletics, has retreated to the island of Inner Farne to live as a hermit.

**678AD - ST WILFRID BANISHED (North)** King Ecgfrith has banished Wilfrid from Northumbria. Ecgfrith may be jealous of Wilfrid's long standing friendship with his former wife.

**678AD - BISHOPRICS BROKEN (North)** The bishopric of York is broken into two parts based at York and Hexham. The bishopric of Hexham extends from the Tweed to the Tees, York extends from the Tees to the Humber.

**678AD - WILFRID PREACHES TO FRISIANS (Europe)** St. Wilfrid is preaching to the Frisians of Holland during his banishment.

Cuthbert's pectoral cross, made from gold and inlaid with garnets

Detail from St. Cuthbert's 1300 year old coffin

**680AD - WILFRID ARRESTED (Dunbar)** St Wilfrid is arrested and imprisoned at Dunbar after returning to Northumbria with papal documents overthrowing the division of the Northumbrian bishoprics. Wilfrid is released but flees to Sussex to help convert this last pagan kingdom in England to Christianity.

**November 17  680AD - SAINT HILDA DIES (Whitby)** St Hilda, Abbess of Whitby, dies. She is succeeded by Aelfled, daughter of the late King Oswy. Meanwhile Caedmon of Whitby is becoming famous for poetic compositions based on religous themes and is arguably England's first known poet.

**681AD - HEXHAM DIOCESE DIVIDED (North East)** The Bishopric of Hexham has been divided into two with the re-establishment of a separate bishopric at Lindisfarne. Hexham's diocese now extends from the River Aln to the River Tees.

**684AD - NORTHUMBRIANS INVADE ULSTER (Ireland)** King Ecgfrith of Northumbria has sent an army into Meath in Northern Ireland in the hope of expanding his Kingdom. St Cuthbert strongly advised him against the attack.

**685AD - CUTHBERT BISHOP OF LINDISFARNE (York)** St Cuthbert is elected Bishop of Hexham at a synod near Alnmouth but he requests a transfer to Lindisfarne. He is consecrated Bishop of Lindisfarne at York on April 7th in the presence of King Ecgfrith.

**May 20  685AD - PICTS KILL NORTHERN KING (Caledonia)** King Ecgfrith of Northumbria is killed fighting Brude, King of Caledonia. It symbolises the end to a period of Northumbrian expansion. The Northumbrian bishopric of Abercorn near Edinburgh is abandoned.

**685AD - NEW KING ENCOURAGES CELTIC ART (North)** Aldfrith is the new King of Northumbria. He is the illegitimate son of the late King Oswy and an Irish princess. Art and learning will flourish and great works of Celtic art will be encouraged by the new King who was educated in Ireland.

**685AD - JARROW ESTABLISHED (Jarrow and Wearmouth)** Benedict Biscop has completed the monastery of St Paul's Jarrow as a twin monastery to Monkwearmouth. Bede, a young boy of nine, is transferred from Wearmouth to the new site.

**686AD - PLAGUE HITS WEARMOUTH AND JARROW (Jarrow)** Plague has hit the twin monasteries of Wearmouth and Jarrow while their founder Benedict Biscop is in Rome. Bede and the Abbot Ceolfrith of Jarrow are among the few survivors of the plague.

**March 30  686AD - ST CUTHBERT BECOMES A HERMIT (Lindisfarne)** St Cuthbert has resigned as the Bishop of Lindisfarne and returned to the island of Inner Farne as a hermit. St Wilfrid returns to Northumbria to become Bishop of Lindisfarne.

**686AD - ST CUTHBERT DIES ON INNER FARNE (Lindisfarne)** St Cuthbert has died on Inner Farne Island with only sea birds and seals for company. Northumbria is mourning the loss of one of its best loved saints.

**688AD - WILFRID BECOMES BISHOP OF HEXHAM (Hexham)** Wilfrid has become the Bishop of Hexham after the bishopric was ceded to him by John of Beverley who has retired to become a hermit. Eadbert succeeds Wilfrid at Lindisfarne.

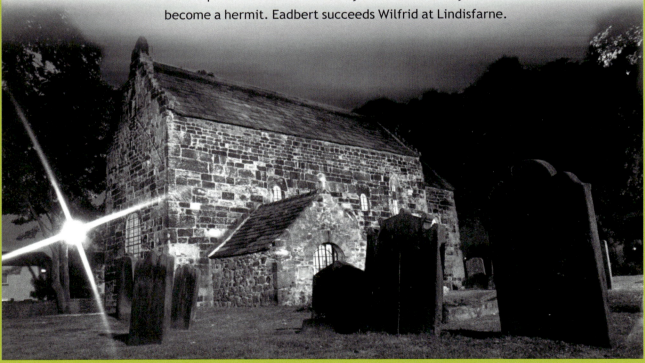

The Anglo-Saxon Church at Escomb in County Durham is thought to be the oldest in England and dates from 670AD

# The Age of Bede

690AD to 735AD

**THE AGE OF BEDE 690AD TO 735AD** Bede was the greatest man of learning of the Anglo-Saxon age. His works were known throughout Europe and his monastery at Jarrow was the brightest light of learning in 'Dark Age' Europe. Bede's importance to history cannot be understated. He was the first man to write a history of the English and his chronological works were an important factor in encouraging Europe to adopt the numbering of years from Christ's birth. Anno Domini (AD) - 'The Year of Our Lord', was a phrase used by Bede in his chronogical works. Our celebration of the two-thousand years is in part a celebration of a system of dating popularised by Bede twelve hundred years ago.

**January 12  690AD - BENEDICT BISCOP DIES (Sunderland)** Benedict Biscop, the founder of Monkwearmouth and Jarrow, has died of palsy. He has been succeeded by Ceolfrith who becomes abbot of both Monkwearmouth and Jarrow.

**692AD - BEDE A DEACON (Jarrow)** Bede, a scholar at Jarrow monastery, has been ordained a deacon at the age of nineteen.

**692AD - WILFRID BANISHED (Hexham)** St Wilfrid has been banished from Northumbria once again following his refusal to allow the creation of a new bishopric based at Ripon. John of Beverley has replaced him as Bishop of Hexham.

**November 21  695AD - NORTHUMBRIAN IS DUTCH BISHOP (Europe)** A Northumbrian monk called Willibrord was consecrated Bishop of the Frisians (Holland). Willibrord was trained by St Wilfrid during his time as a monk at Ripon.

**March 20  698AD - ST CUTHBERT'S MIRACLE COFFIN (Lindisfarne)** On the anniversary of his death, St Cuthbert's tomb is opened at Lindisfarne and his body has been found incorrupt. The body is transferred from the stone coffin into a wooden chest.

The oldest stained glass in Europe, made in AD681 for St. Paul's Monastery, Jarrow

**698AD - LINDISFARNE GOSPELS (Holy Island)** Eadfrith has become the new Bishop of Lindisfarne where the Lindisfarne Gospels are now being written.

**701AD - JARROW MONKS VISIT ROME (Europe)** Monks from Jarrow have visited Rome at the invitation of Pope Sergius.

**703AD - BEDE BECOMES A PRIEST (Jarrow)** Bede has been ordained a priest by Bishop John of Hexham at the age of thirty.

**705AD - WILFRID RETURNS (Hexham)** St Wilfrid, founder of Ripon, has been reinstated as Bishop of Hexham after a synod was held near the River Nidd in North Yorkshire.

**December 4 705AD - BOY KING ATTACKED (Bamburgh)** Aldfrith King of Northumbria has died at Driffield in the Yorkshire Wolds and has been succeeded by his son Osred who is only a boy. Osred is besieged at Bamburgh but his attacker Eardulph has been captured and beheaded.

**709AD - ST WILFRID DIES AT OUNDLE (Northamptonshire)** St Wilfrid aged 75, has died while visiting his monastery at Oundle in Northamptonshire. He is succeeded by Acca as the new Bishop of Hexham. Wilfrid has been buried at Ripon. Acca, the new Bishop of Hexham is an associate of Bede.

**711AD - PICTISH EXPANSION CURBED (Scotland)** The Northumbrians have defeated the Picts in battle and prevented the expansion of their kingdom.

**716AD - IONA ABANDONS OLD FAITH (Scotland)** The island monastery of Iona in Caledonia has abandoned Celtic Christian beliefs in favour of Roman Christian ways following the advice of Ceolfrith, the Abbot of Jarrow and Monkwearmouth.

**July 4  716AD - WEARMOUTH ABBOT DIES ABROAD (Monkwearmouth and Jarrow)** Abbot Ceolfrith, retiring from Monkwearmouth, has died at Langres en route for a papal visit. Meanwhile an illuminated bible called the Codex Amiatinus has been produced at Jarrow.

Bede's Tomb at Durham Cathedral

**716AD - BOY KING ASSASSINATED (North)** Osred, the nineteen year old King of Northumbria, has been assassinated near the southern borders of his kingdom by his kinsmen Cenred and Osric. Cenred has become the new King of Northumbria.

**717AD - JARROW ABBOT CONVERTS PICTS (Jarrow)** The abbot of Jarrow has persuaded Nechtan, King of the Picts to convert to Roman Christianity. Nechtan expels Celtic-Christian monks from his kingdom.

**718AD - NEW BISHOP AT YORK (York)** Following the resignation of St John of Beverley, Wilfrid II has become Bishop of York. He is the second bishop of York to bear the name Wilfrid.

**October 718AD - OSRIC BECOMES NEW KING IN THE NORTH (North)** Cenred, King of Northumbria has died and has been succeeded by Osric who helped murder the boy King of Northumbria two years ago.

**May 7 721AD - JOHN OF BEVERLEY DIES (East Yorkshire)** St John of Beverley, formerly Bishop of York and Hexham, has died at Beverley.

**721AD - GREAT WORKS COMPLETED AT LINDISFARNE AND JARROW (North East)** The Lindisfarne Gospels have been completed on Lindisfarne. At Jarrow, Bede has completed his Life of St Cuthbert. The work has been specially written for the monks of Lindisfarne.

**725AD - BEDE SETS THE DATES - ANNO DOMINI (Jarrow)** A chronological work by Bede has introduced dating from Christ's birth - Anno Domini.

**729AD - CEOLWULF BECOMES NEW KING (North)** Osric, King of Northumbria has died and has been succeeded by the monk-like King Ceolwulf, brother of the late King Cenred.

**731AD - FIRST HISTORY OF ENGLAND COMPLETED BY BEDE AT JARROW (Tyneside)** Bede has completed his greatest work, the History of the English Church and People, at Jarrow. He has dedicated his work to King Ceolwulf of Northumbria.

**732 AD- REBELS CUT OFF KING'S HAIR (North)** King Ceolwulf of Northumbria has been captured and forcibly tonsured. The action is thought to be an attempt to ridicule him for his interests in the way of life followed by monks .

**734AD - FIRST ARCHBISHOP OF YORK (York)** Egbert, Bishop of York, has been successful in his application to the Pope to make York an archbishopric, following the advice of Bede. As an archbishopric York will now be independent of Canterbury. Egbert was a former pupil of Bede.

**May 25 735AD - BEDE DIES AT JARROW (Tyneside)** The Venerable Bede has died at Jarrow. Northumbria mourns the loss of its greatest scholar and historian. His name will be remembered in history for centuries.

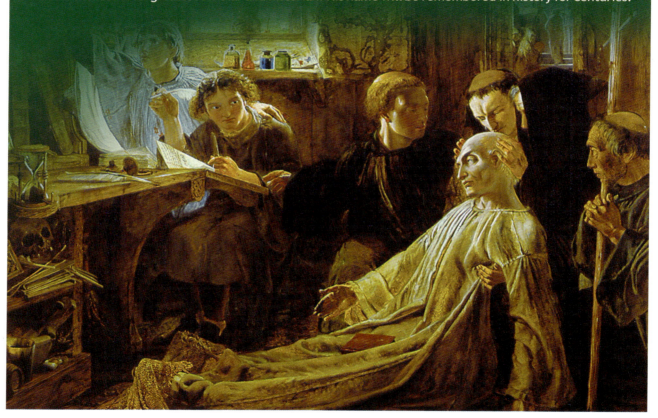

The Death of the Venerable Bede in Jarrow Priory
A nineteenth century painting by William Bell Scott

# Kingdom at War

736AD to 854AD

An Anglian helmet found at York (c.750-755AD)

**A KINGDOM AT WAR 736AD TO 854AD** In the late eighth century Northumbria was plagued with weak leadership and collapsed into a state of anarchy caused by rivalry between the royal houses of Deira and Bernicia. From 737AD to 806AD Northumbria had ten kings, of which three were murdered, five were expelled and two retired to become monks. It brought an instability to the Kingdom which may well have encouraged the first Viking raiders to attack the Northumbrian coast from 793AD.

**737AD - NORTHUMBRIAN KING BECOMES A MONK (Lindisfarne)** King Ceolwulf of Northumbria becomes a monk on Lindisfarne. He is succeeded by Eadbert.

**April 24  741AD - MINSTER HIT BY FIRE (York)** York Minster is damaged by fire.It will be rebuilt in 770.

**746AD - ROME WRITES TO JARROW (Rome)** Bishop Boniface of Rome has written to Northumbria for editions of the works of Bede - the most popular titles in Europe.

**750AD - BISHOP PLOTS AGAINST KING (Bamburgh)** Cynewulf, Bishop of Lindisfarne is imprisoned for plotting against King Eadbert.

**758AD - KING BECOMES A MONK (York)** Eadbert of Northumbria has retired from his kingdom to become a monk at York. He is succeeded by his son Oswulf.

**August 5  759AD - KING MURDERED (Great Whittington  near Corbridge)** Oswulf, King of Northumbria is assassinated near Corbridge and succeeded by a Deiran, called Athelwald Moll of Catterick, who may be responsible.

**761AD - CHIEFTAIN KILLED AT CONISCLIFFE (High Coniscliffe)** A Bernician noble called Oswin is murdered at Coniscliffe by Athelwald Moll.

**762AD - CONSECRATION AT ELVET (Durham City)** Peothwine is consecrated Bishop of Whithorn at Aelfet Ee (Elvet). It is the first mention of Christian activity in the Durham City area.

**October 30 765AD - MOLL FORCED OUT (Finchale)** Following a meeting at Finchale, King Athelwald Moll is forced out and succeeded by Alhred.

**774AD - KING DRIVEN OUT (York)** Alhred is driven out of Northumbria by Athelred, son of Athelwald Moll.

**779AD - CONISCLIFFE MURDERS (High Coniscliffe)** Athelred has been ousted by a Bernician called Alfwold. A number of royal nobles are murdered at Coniscliffe during the coup.

**780AD - FRISIANS AT YORK (York)** A community of Frisian merchants is trading at York.

**781AD - CONSECRATION ON TEES (Sockburn on Tees near Darlington)** Higbald has been consecrated Bishop of Lindisfarne at Sockburn.

**782AD - SCHOLAR LEAVES THE COUNTRY (York)** Alcuin of York, who has built up a huge library at his school in the city, has left the country to study at the court of Charlemagne in France.

**788AD - BOY KING FLEES (Chesters near Hadrian's Wall)** King Alfwold is murdered by his uncle Sicga and buried at Hexham. He is succeeded by his boy nephew Osred II who flees to the Isle of Man. Athelred begins a second period as King.

**789AD - AYCLIFFE MEETINGS (County Durham)** A Synod has been held at Aycliffe regarding religious matters and discipline. It follows a similar meeting at Aycliffe in 782.

**792AD - ATHELRED KILLS RIVALS (Cumbria)** King Athelred drowns a rival prince in Windermere and beheads Osred II at Maryport.

**September 26 792AD - ROYAL MARRIAGE AT CATTERICK (North Yorkshire)** Athelred of Northumbria marries the daughter of King Offa of Mercia at Catterick.

Viking Bronze ring-brooch, used to fasten a man's cloak at the shoulder

**June 8th  793AD - VIKINGS RAID ISLAND (Lindisfarne)** In an unprecedented attack which shocks Europe, a raiding party of Vikings from Norway attacked Lindisfarne today. Monks fled in fear and many were slaughtered. Bishop Higbald sought refuge on the mainland. A Chronicler records- "On the 8th June, the harrying of the heathen miserably destroyed God's church by rapine and slaughter."

**793AD - SCHOLAR SAYS RAIDS ARE PUNISHMENT FROM GOD (Europe)** In a letter from Charlemagne's court in France, Alcuin, former head of York School, blamed the recent Viking attack on a fall in moral standards in Northumbria. He sees the raid as punishment from God.

**794AD - MORE VIKING RAIDS (Tyneside)** In 794 Vikings attacked the famous monastery at Jarrow but the Northumbrians were prepared for this attack and managed to surprise and utterly destroy the Viking attackers. Further Viking raids on Lindisfarne and Jarrow occurred this year.

**April 18th - May 26  796AD - SHORT REIGN FOR MURDEROUS KING (Corbridge)** King Athelred of Northumbria is murdered at Corbridge and succeeded by Osbald who plotted the murder. Osbald is eventually forced out by Eardwulf.

**800AD - MORE VIKING RAIDS (Hartlepool, Whitby, Tynemouth)** Vikings are raiding the monasteries at Whitby, Hartlepool and Tynemouth.

**801AD - CHURCH AT GAINFORD (Gainford on Tees)** A Church is established at Gainford where a chieftain called Ida is said to be buried.

**804AD - ALCUIN DIES (France)** Alcuin of York has died at Charlemagne's court in France. He was one of the most highly respected men of learning in Europe.

**808AD - EARDWULF RESTORED (North)** In 806 King Eardwulf was driven out and succeeded by Alfwold II but Eardwulf is restored following Alfwold's death.

**810AD - SYNODS AT FINCHALE (Finchale)** A synod has been held at Finchale on the River Wear to discuss Northumbrian church matters and discipline. Similar meetings took place at Finchale in 792 and 798.

**811AD - EARDWULF OUSTED AGAIN (North)** Eardwulf has been deposed as King of Northumbria. He is succeeded by King Eanred.

**821AD - BISHOPRICS MERGE (Tweed to Tees)** The Bishopric of Hexham has been absorbed by Lindisfarne. The new bishopric extends from Tweed to Tees.

**829AD - POWERS MEET AT NORTHUMBRIA'S 'DOOR' (Dore near Sheffield)** Egbert King of Wessex and Mercia and Eanred of Northumbria meet at Dore. Their aim is to ensure peace. Eanred accepts Wessex supremacy and recognises Egbert as 'overking' of England. Dore is the 'doorway' between Northumbria and the South.

**830AD - MONKS FLEE LINDISFARNE (Holy Island)** The monks of Lindisfarne leave the island with St Cuthbert's body to escape further raids. They settle inland at Norham on Tweed where a church is built for the saint's shrine.

**840AD - KING EANRED DIES (North)** Eanred, King of Northumbria dies. He is succeeded by his son Athelred II.

**841AD - DUBLIN VIKINGS (Ireland)** Vikings from Norway establish Dublin as their chief coastal stronghold in the British Isles.

**844AD - KING KILLED BY VIKINGS (North)** King Athelred II is temporarily expelled and succeeded by King Raedwulf who is killed by Vikings in a coastal attack. Athelred II is restored.

**848AD - KING OSBERT (North)** Athelred II, King of Northumbria, is killed and succeeded by King Osbert.

**854AD - LAST LINDISFARNE BISHOP (York and Lindisfarne)** Eardwulf has been appointed Bishop of Lindisfarne. He is the last person to hold the post.

# Jorvik

866AD to 900AD

**JORVIK 866 AD TO 900 AD** Most people have heard of the Norman Conquest of 1066, but the Danish conquest of 866 made just as great an impact on the North. The Danes brought cultural, linguistic and political changes to the North and made southern Northumbria the Danish Kingdom of York which they divided into three 'ridings'. It was in Yorkshire that most Danish settlement fell, while the land north of the Tees remained largely Anglo-Saxon. Many Danish place names survive in Yorkshire today like Thornaby, Wetherby and Danby, but the most important Viking settlement in England was, of course, the city of York.

**866AD - OSBERT OVERTHROWN BY NORTHUMBRIANS (North)** Osbert, King of Northumbria, is overthrown by his people and replaced by his brother Aelle II.

**866AD - IVAR THE BONELESS INVADES EAST ANGLIA (England)** A Danish army of around ten thousand men invade East Anglia where they encamp the whole winter. The Danes are led by Ivar the Boneless along with his brothers, Halfdene and Hubba.

**866AD - DANES CROSS HUMBER TO INVADE THE NORTH (Yorkshire)** The Danes take advantage of turmoil in Northumbria and cross the Humber into the Deiran province of Northumbria (Yorkshire).

**November 1 866AD - DANES SACK YORK (York)** York is sacked by the Danes under Ivar, Halfdene and Hubba. Aelle of Deira and Osbert of Bernicia unite against the Danes.

**March 23  86AD7 - DANES MURDER KING IN BLOOD EAGLE ORDEAL (York)** Aelle, King of Northumbria, is captured attempting to retake York from the Danes. Earl Osbert of Bernicia is killed during the battle. Aelle is subjected to the horrific Blood Eagle ordeal by the Vikings. His ribs are torn out and folded back to form the shape of an eagle's wings. It is reputedly punishment for his alledged murder of Ragnor Lodbrook, a great Danish leader who was the father of Ivar, Halfdene and Hubba.

**867AD - DANES EMPLOY A CLIENT (North East)** The Danes employ an Anglo-Saxon called Egbert as temporary King of Northumbria.

**869AD - DANES RETURN NORTH AFTER NOTTINGHAM SEIZED (York)** The Danish army return to York following an excursion into the Midlands where they seized Nottingham.

**871AD - ALFRED THE GREAT (England)** Alfred the Great is King of Wessex. Earlier this year he defeated the Danes at Ashdown in Berkshire.

**872AD - BERNICIANS EJECT KING (North East)** The Bernicians of North Northumbria reject the appointment of King Egbert of Northumbria and hope to replace him with a nobleman called Ricsige.

**873AD - IVAR THE BONELESS DIES (Ireland)** Viking leader Ivar the Boneless dies in Ireland. He is succeeded by his brother Halfdene at York.

**875AD - CUTHBERT PEOPLE FLEE VIKINGS (Lindisfarne)** Eardwulf, Bishop of Lindisfarne, leaves Norham on Tweed with the Community of St Cuthbert carrying St Cuthbert's coffin to escape anticipated Danish attacks. The community settle in Cumbria where Eadred, the abbot of Carlisle, becomes their new leader.

**875AD - HALFDENE KING OF YORK (Yorkshire)** Halfdene becomes King of York (Yorkshire) on return from a victory over the Mercians. The old Anglo-Saxon estates in Yorkshire are to be shared out among his army and followers. Yorkshire will be divided into the three Ridings (thirds) which are 'shifts' of the Danish Army.

**875AD - DANES ATTACK TYNE (Tynemouth and Gateshead)** The Danes, under the leadership of Halfdene, enter the Tyne and destroy Tynemouth Priory before wintering at the mouth of the River Team near Gateshead. Once the winter is over the Danes begin their battle campaign in Bernicia and Scotland. Hexham is ransacked.

**875AD - NORTHUMBERLAND AND DURHAM ESCAPE DANISH SETTLEMENT (North East)** Bernicia north of the Tees (Northumberland and Durham) is defeated by the Danes but generally escapes Danish settlement. There will be pockets of Danish settlement here and there, particularly in southern Durham around Sadberge and Gainford, but most of the region remains Anglo-Saxon and will continue to speak the Anglian language with some Viking influence. Descendants of the old Kings of Bamburgh continue to rule the North East region but as clients of the Danish Kings of York.

The Alfred Jewel, made for Alfred the Great as a handle to a pointer to aid reading

**875AD - ARMY SHARES MIDLANDS AND YORKSHIRE (England)** One half of the huge Danish army under Halfdene is settling in Yorkshire while the other half is taking control of the East Midland shires of Derby, Nottingham, Leicester, Lincoln and Stamford. The East Midlands is known as the Danish Five Boroughs. The West Midlands remain Anglo-Saxon.

**877AD - DANISH KING OF YORK DIES (Ireland)** Halfdene, the Danish King of York, has been killed in battle in Northern Ireland fighting a rival faction of Irish Norsemen from Dublin.

**878AD - ALFRED DEFEATS THE DANES (England)** Alfred the Great of Wessex defeats a Danish army under the leadership of Guthred.

**882AD - CUTHBERT PEOPLE SUPPORT DANES (Cumbria)** Abbot Eadred of Carlisle, the leader of the Communuity of St Cuthbert, has supported the claims of Guthred the King of York to the Northumbrian throne.

**883AD - THE BEGINNINGS OF COUNTY DURHAM (Chester-le-Street)** Guthred the new Danish King of York, has granted an area of land between the Tyne and Tees to the Community of St Cuthbert, which recently fled to Cumbria. The grant of this land signifies the beginning of what will later become County Durham. The Community of St Cuthbert has settled within this territory at Chester-le-Street (Conecaster). Their territory will be called the Land of the 'Haliwerfolk' - meaning the holy man people.

**883AD - ST CUTHBERT REBURIED (Chester-le-Street)** St Cuthbert's body is interred in a new church at Chester-le-Street. Eardwulf the former Bishop of Lindisfarne becomes the first Bishop of Chester-le-Street.

**899AD - DANISH KING OF YORK DIES (York)** Guthred, the Danish King of York has died.

**899AD - DEATH OF KING ALFRED THE GREAT (England)** Alfred the Great, King of Wessex has died. He is succeeded by Edward the Elder. Alfred was recognised as King of all England, although the Danish Kings of York are virtual rulers of the North.

# The Irish-Norwegians

900AD to 945AD

The Cuerdale Hoard, the largest Viking Age hoard ever found in Britain

**924AD - EDWARD THE ELDER DIES (England)** Edward the Elder, King of Wessex has died. He has been succeeded by King Athelstan who also becomes the 'over-king' of England. Sihtric, King of York acknowledges Athelstan's superiority.

**927AD - KING GUTHFRITH (York)** Sihtric, King of York dies and is succeeded by Guthfrith, a Dublin Norseman.

**July 12  927AD - ATHELSTAN MEETS NORTHERN KINGS IN CUMBRIA (Eamont Bridge, Cumbria)** King Athelstan meets the Kings of Strathclyde and Scotland at Eamont Bridge in Cumbria. The kings acknowledge Athelstan's superiority. Ealdred, Earl of Bamburgh who rules the Anglo-Saxon territory of the North East also gave his support. No Viking kings were present.

**927AD - KING OF YORK EXPELLED (York)** King Athelstan captures York and Guthfrith, the new Viking king of York, is expelled.

**934AD - KING OF ENGLAND VISITS CHESTER LE STREET (Chester-le-Street)** Athelstan, King of the English has visited the shrine of St Cuthbert at Chester-le-Street and bestowed many great gifts. The gifts include a work by Bede entitled the Life of St Cuthbert which depicts Athelstan on the cover.

**934AD - SUNDERLAND GIVEN TO BISHOP (Chester le Street)** During his visit to Chester-le-Street, Athelstan gives Bishopwearmouth (Sunderland) to the Bishop of Chester-le-Street. It was part of the land taken by the Irish Vikings in 918.

**934AD - ATHELSTAN ATTACKS SCOTLAND (Scotland)** King Athelstan has severely ravaged Scotland to enforce his superiority in the North.

**934AD - KING GRANTS RIPON SANCTUARY (Ripon)** King Athelstan has granted rights of sanctuary to the monastery at Ripon.

Silver coin of Eric Bloodaxe minted at York. The sword symbolises his heathen rule.

**ERIC BLOODAXE AND THE FALL OF NORTHUMBRIA 946AD TO 989AD** When Eric Bloodaxe was murdered on Stainmore in 954 AD the three hundred and fifty year old history of Northumbria came to an end. Eric, King of Norway, had been appointed King of York in 948 AD and claimed all Northumbria as his own. Further north, in the Anglo-Saxon territory north of the Tees, an earl called Oswulf of Bamburgh was plotting against Eric. Supported by the King of Wessex, Oswulf employed an agent to murder Bloodaxe and on Eric's death, the King of Wessex became King of all England. The North had lost its independence for good.

**May 26  946AD - ENGLISH KING ASSASINATED (England)** Edmund King of England has been assassinated. He is succeeded by his son Eadred.

**946AD - ARCHBISHOP SUBMITS BUT PLANS TO GIVE NORTH TO BLOODAXE (West Yorkshire)** Wulfstan, the Archbishop of York, has submitted to Eadred, the new King of Wessex and England, at Tanshelf. Eadred is unaware that Wulfstan plans to offer the Kingdom of York to Eric Bloodaxe, the King of Norway.

**948AD - ERIC BLOODAXE BECOMES KING OF YORK (York)** Eric Bloodaxe, part Norse, part Danish, has been elected King of York and lays claim to the whole of Northumbria.

**948AD - BLOODAXE OUSTED BY NEW WESSEX KING (Ripon)** Yorkshire support for Eric Bloodaxe has been subdued following an attack from Eadred, the King of England. Bloodaxe has been ousted by Eadred in favour of a new candidate. Ripon minster was severely destroyed during the confrontation.

**948AD - ST WILFRID'S RELICS MOVED TO CANTERBURY (Ripon)** Odo, Archbishop of Canterbury, has removed the relics of St Wilfrid from Ripon and reburied them at Canterbury.

**948AD - SCOTTISH RAIDING (North East)** King Malcolm of Scotland has raided Northumbria as far south as the River Tees.

**949AD - OLAF SIHTRICSON BECOMES KING OF YORK (York)** Olaf Sihtricson, a Viking from Dublin, has become the King of York. He is thought to have gained the support of Eadred, King of England, who would rather see Olaf in power than the powerful Eric Bloodaxe who is somewhere in exile. Wulfstan I, Archbishop of York, has been imprisoned by King Eadred for supporting Eric Bloodaxe.

**952AD - BLOODAXE REINSTATED AT YORK (York)** Olaf Sihtricson has failed to gain support for the kingship of York and Eric Bloodaxe has been reinstated by the men of Yorkshire.

**952AD - ERIC BLOODAXE VISITS CHESTER-LE-STREET (County Durham)** Eric Bloodaxe, the Viking King of York, has visited the shrine of St Cuthbert at Chester-le-Street. His action of pilgrimage has become something of a tradition among powerful kings. In previous years English kings who have visited St Cuthbert's shrine at Chester le Street have included King Athelstan, King Edmund and King Eadred.

**954AD - BLOODAXE MURDERED ON BLEAK STAINMORE (Stainmore, Teesdale)** Eric Bloodaxe, King of Yorkshire, has been murdered on the bleak moors of Stainmore in Teesdale by Maccus, an agent of Oswulf Ealdulfing, the High Reeve or Earl of Bamburgh, who rules Northumbria north of the Tees. Oswulf is a supporter of Eadred, the King of Wessex and England, who may have encouraged the murder. Eric's death signifies the end of northern independence and from now on Yorkshire and the North East will be ruled as part of England by Kings in the South.

**954AD - SCOTS TAKE EDINBURGH (Lothian)** The Scots under King Indulf have taken Edinburgh from the Northumbrians.

**955AD - EADWIG KING OF ENGLAND (England)** King Eadred has died and has been succeeded by his nephew Eadwig.

**957AD - NORTHUMBRIANS REBEL AGAINST EADWIG (North)** Mercia and Northumbria have rebelled against Eadwig in favour of his brother Edgar who they wish to appoint king.

**October 1  959AD - EDGAR IS KING OF ENGLAND (England)** Edgar is the new King of England.

**966AD - OUTSIDER BECOMES YORK CITY LEADER (York)** The newly appointed Earl of York (Yorkshire) is Oslac, a nobleman from the fenlands of Mercia. His appointment is made by Edgar, the King of England, and Oslac is expected to keep the North at peace for his sovereign.

**966AD - NORWEGIANS ESTABLISH SCARBOROUGH (Scarborough)** Viking brothers called Thorgils and Kormak, in the service of King Harald Grafeld, King of Norway have established a stronghold at Scarborough while harrying in Ireland, England and Wales. Thorgils was known to his brother by the nickname 'Hare Lip', or in the Viking language 'Skarthi' . It is probable that 'Hare-Lip' gave his name to Scarborough. There may already have been an Anglo-Saxon settlement on the site and there was certainly a Roman signal station here.

**971AD - SCOTS RAID AS FAR AS TEESDALE (North East)** Kenneth, King of Scotland, has raided the North East as far as Stainmore, Teesdale.

**972AD - St OSWALD BECOMES ARCHBISHOP OF YORK (York)** St Oswald, the Bishop of Worcester, has been appointed the Bishop of York. He is a Midlander by birth but is of Danish descent. St Oswald replaces St Ethelwold who only became Archbishop of York last year. He is sometimes confused with the earlier St. Oswald who was a king of Northumbria.

**974AD - KING DISCUSSES THE NORTH EAST'S FUTURE (Cheshire)** King Edgar has held a meeting with Kenneth, King of the Scots, and the Kings of Cumbria, the Islands and five other kings at Chester. The meeting is thought to have been a discussion regarding the Scottish claim to North Eastern England, north of the Tees. Edgar, who impressed the northern kings with his great army, is likely to have told them to keep their hands off the region which has been a great supporter of kings in the south.

**975AD - EDWARD THE MARTYR BECOMES KING (England)** King Edgar dies and is succeeded by King Edward 'the Martyr'.

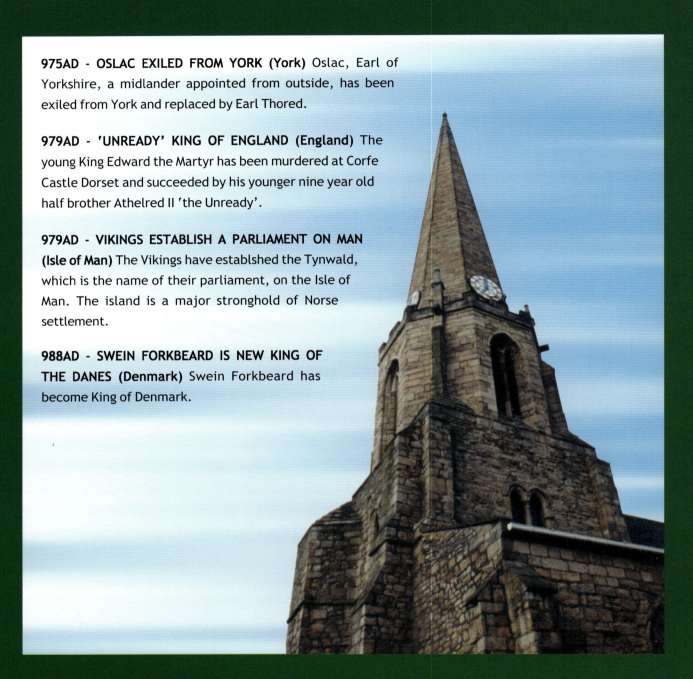

**975AD - OSLAC EXILED FROM YORK (York)** Oslac, Earl of Yorkshire, a midlander appointed from outside, has been exiled from York and replaced by Earl Thored.

**979AD - 'UNREADY' KING OF ENGLAND (England)** The young King Edward the Martyr has been murdered at Corfe Castle Dorset and succeeded by his younger nine year old half brother Athelred II 'the Unready'.

**979AD - VIKINGS ESTABLISH A PARLIAMENT ON MAN (Isle of Man)** The Vikings have establshed the Tynwald, which is the name of their parliament, on the Isle of Man. The island is a major stronghold of Norse settlement.

**988AD - SWEIN FORKBEARD IS NEW KING OF THE DANES (Denmark)** Swein Forkbeard has become King of Denmark.

Chester-le-Street Church stands on the site of an Anglo-Saxon Minster visited by Eric Bloodaxe in 952AD

# The Birth of Durham

990AD to 1031AD

King Canute

**THE BIRTH OF DURHAM 990 AD TO 1031AD** The rising power of Wessex weakened the North of England in the last decade of the first millennium and left the region vulnerable to the attacks of Danes and Scots. The Community of St.Cuthbert at Chester-le-Street, a remnant of Northumbria's greater days, fled to Ripon in 995 to escape one such raid. They returned north in the same year, but chose Durham as their new home where their visitors would include King Canute.

**990AD - ALDHUN IS LAST BISHOP AT CHESTER-LE-STREET (County Durham)** Aldhun has become the Bishop of Chester-le-Street.

**993AD - NEW VIKINGS ATTACK BAMBURGH (Northumberland Coast)** A new force of Vikings under Olaf and Swein Forkbeard have attacked Bamburgh, the coastal stronghold of the Eadulfsons, who are the virtual rulers of Bernicia. This is a completely fresh raid of Danes with no British links. The Danes who invaded Yorkshire in 866 have now integrated and intermarried with the English.

**995AD - SCOTS ATTEMPT TO SEIZE NORTH EAST (North East)** Kenneth of Scotland is defeated in an invasion of the North East. His attack was fought off by Uhtred Eadulfson, son of the Earl of Bamburgh.

**995AD - CUTHBERT FOLK FLEE (Chester-le-Street)** The Monkish Community of St Cuthbert has fled Chester-le-Street with St Cuthbert's body, to escape Scottish raids. Accompanied by Bishop Aldhun, they settle for a short time at Ripon.

**995AD - CITY OF DURHAM FOUNDED BY MONKS OF ST CUTHBERT (Durham City)** St Cuthbert's community have returned north to settle at Dunholm (Durham). The site is naturally defended like an island, formed by the horse-shoe gorge of the River Wear. They are said to have been guided by a vision, but it is likely to have been a deliberate political decision.

**995AD - DURHAM MINSTER BUILT (Durham City)** A minster called the 'White Church' has been constructed of wood for St Cuthbert's remains at Durham. Uhtred Eadulfson of Bamburgh employed labour from the Coquet to the Tees to fortify the site. Aldhun is the first Bishop of Durham.

**999AD - STONE MINSTER AT DURHAM  (Durham City)** A new 'White Church' minster is built at Durham, but this time of stone, for the shrine of Cuthbert.

**1000 AD - A NEW MILLENNIUM (The Christian World)** The Christian world enters a new millennium. It is thought to be 1000 years since the birth of Jesus Christ.

**1000AD - DANES ATTACK (England)** England is being subjected to continuous raiding by the Danes.

**1003AD - DARLINGTON GIVEN TO BISHOP OF DURHAM (York)** Darlington receives its first mention in history. It has been given to the Bishop of Durham by Styr, son of Ulphus, at a ceremony in York. Archbishop Wulfstan and King Athelred were present. Darlington may be part of the territory seized by Vikings in 918.

**1005AD - PLAGUE CHASES DANES (England)** A major outbreak of Plague has spread across England, killing many. The Danish fleet has temporarily returned to Denmark to escape the plague.

**1006AD - SCOTS MASSACRED AT DURHAM (Durham City)** The Scots, under King Malcolm, are heavily defeated during an attack on Durham. Malcolm was attempting to seize the North East. Heads of the best looking Scottish soldiers were displayed around the city walls. Durham women were presented with the gift of a cow for washing the heads and combing the hair. The Northumbrians who defeated the Scots were led by Earl Uhtred Eadulfson of Bamburgh. Uhtred is the son-in-law of the Bishop of Durham.

**1006AD - ATHELRED APPOINTS NORTHERN EARL (North East and Yorkshire)** Athelred, King of England, has appointed Uhtred of Bamburgh as Earl of York. Uhtred is now Earl of all Northumbria.

**July to December 1013AD - FORKBEARD SEIZES NORTH (North)** Swein Forkbeard, King of Denmark, returns to England with an army, to become King of England. Entering the Humber, he encamps at Gainsborough and forces Uhtred, the Earl of Northumbria, to submit. He captures London and seizes the throne.

**February  1014AD - CANUTE THE DANE TAKES KINGDOM (York)** Swein Forkbeard has died at York. His son Canute is elected King by the Danish army.

**1016AD - CANUTE OUTMANOEUVRES EARL (York)** Uhtred, the Earl of Northumbria, has led an army into the West Midlands to trouble Canute, but Canute moves up the eastern flank of the country into Lincolnshire and crosses to York.

**1016AD - EARL OF NORTH ASSASSINATED (York)** Uhtred, the Earl of Bamburgh, has been assasinated at Canute's court at Wighill, near York. The Earl was visiting Canute in the hope of making peace. He never got to see the King.

**November 30  1016AD - KING CANUTE APPOINTS NORTHERN EARLS (North East and North Yorkshire)** King Canute has appointed a Norwegian called Eric Hlathir as Earl of York, and Eadulf Cudel, of the house of Bamburgh, as the Earl of Northumbria, north of the Tees. Canute is dividing England into Earldoms.

**1018AD - DURHAM TERRITORY GROWS (Bishop Auckland and Stockton)** The territory of the Bishops of Durham, which will develop into County Durham, is expanding. Lands acquired by Bishop Aldhun since 995 include territory in the Tees and Wear valleys, some of which belonged to the Vikings. Sockburn on Tees and land near Sedgefield have been acquired from Snaculf, while Norton and Stockton were acquired from Ulfcytel. Escomb and Aucklandshire in the Wear Valley, which belonged to an earl called Northman, have also been acquired.

**1019AD - SCOTS PUSH BORDER TO TWEED (Carham on Tweed)** The Scots, under Malcolm II, have defeated the Northumbrians, under Eadulf Cudel, in battle at Carham on Tweed. Northumbrian territory from Edinburgh to the Tweed is seized by the Scots. Canute is in Denmark.

**1019AD - BISHOP DIES AFTER BATTLE (Durham City)** Aldhun, Bishop of Durham, has died, heartbroken by the defeat at Carham.

**1022AD - BEDE'S BONES PINCHED (Jarrow)** The relics of Bede have been brought to Durham from Jarrow by Aelfred, the Durham sacrist and relic collector. Aelfred is a notorious collector of saints' relics.

**1023AD - YORK ARCHBISHOP DIES (York)** Archbishop Wulfstan has died, a man of great learning and wisdom.

**1027AD - CANUTE MEETS THE SCOTS (North)** Canute has gained tribute from Malcolm, King of the Scots.

**1027AD - CANUTE VISITS DURHAM (Durham City)** Canute has made a visit to Durham, where he walked bare foot from Garmondsway, six miles to the south of the city, to visit St Cuthbert's shrine.

**1031AD - CANUTE INVADES NORTH EAST (North East)** King Canute the Dane has invaded the North East to quell all rebellion.

**1031AD - CANUTE GIVES STAINDROP TO DURHAM (Staindrop)** Canute gives land around Staindrop to the Bishops of Durham. Canute is known to own a mansion in the district, probably located at Raby.

Raby Castle is thought to occupy the site of a mansion belonging to Canute

# The Norman Conquest

## 1031AD to 1066AD

**THE NORMAN CONQUEST 1031AD TO 1066AD** In the years before the Conquest the North was administered by Earl Siward who died in 1055. Siward was succeeded by Tostig, brother of Harold who became King of England in January 1066. The unpopular Tostig was exiled from the North but joined a Norwegian invasion of Yorkshire in September 1066. King Harold defeated the Norwegians and his brother at Stamford Bridge, near York, but had to immediately return south to deal with yet another invasion, this time from the Normans in Sussex. On October 14 1066 Harold was killed at the Battle of Hastings and William the Conqueror became king.

**1031AD - SIWARD BECOMES EARL OF YORK (York)** Siward has become the Earl of York. He is encouraged to settle disputes between his deputies, Carl the Hold of York and Ealdred the Earl of Bamburgh. Ealdred has been earl since the death of Eadulf Cudel, sometime after 1019.

**November 12  1035AD - CANUTE DIES (Shaftesbury)** King Canute dies at Shaftesbury and is buried at Winchester.

**1038AD - EARL OF NORTH EAST KILLED IN DISPUTE (North)** Ealdred of Bamburgh, the Earl of the North East, is killed by Carl the Hold of York following a long standing dispute. He is succeeded by Eadulf, the second earl of this name.

**1038AD - SCOTS REPELLED FROM DURHAM (Durham City)** King Duncan of Scotland besieges Durham City but is repelled.

**1041AD - ANOTHER EARL KILLED (North East)** Eadulf of Bamburgh, the Earl of the North East, is killed. The assailant was probably Siward, who becomes Earl of all Northumbria.

**1042AD - CONFESSOR IS KING (England)** Edward the Confessor has become King of England. For the last twenty five years Edward has lived in Normandy.

**1050AD - DARLINGTON IS DEARTHINGTON (Darlington)** At this time Darlington was known as Dearthington.

**1051AD - WESSEX EARL (England)** Harold Godwinson becomes Earl of Wessex but Edward the Confessor is still King of England

**1054AD - SIWARD DEFEATS MACBETH (Battle of Dunsinane, near Scone, Perthshire)** Siward, Earl of Northumbria, defeats the Scots under King Macbeth and installs his nephew, Malcolm Canmore, as Lord of Strathclyde and the Lothian.

**1055AD - SIWARD DIES (York)** Siward dies at York and is buried at St Olaf's church. The Earldom is given to Tostig Godwinson, brother of Harold, the Earl of Wessex.

**1056AD - NEW BISHOP AT DURHAM (Durham City)** Aegelwine becomes the last Anglo-Saxon Bishop of Durham.

**1056AD - CHESTER-LE-STREET CHURCH REBUILT (County Durham)** Chester-le-Street church, a former minster, is rebuilt in stone.

**1058AD - KING MALCOLM CANMORE (North)** Malcolm Canmore, a nephew of the late Northumbrian Earl Siward, becomes King Malcolm III of Scotland after King Macbeth is killed in battle. Malcolm gives allegiance to Edward the Confessor at York.

**1061AD - SCOTS ATTACK LINDISFARNE AND CUMBERLAND (Lindisfarne)** King Malcolm of Scotland ravages Lindisfarne and north Northumbria and captures Cumberland. It is a major defeat for Tostig, Earl of Northumbria.

**1064AD - BAMBURGH NOBLE MURDERED (Wessex)** Cospatric, a respected noble of Bamburgh, is murdered in Wessex by Tostig, the unpopular Earl of Northumbria.

A penny with the head of William the Conqueror

Harold Hardrada of Norway fights the Northern Earls at Gate Fulford near York in 1066

**1065AD - THE NORTH REBELS (North East and York)** Rebellion breaks out against Earl Tostig in the North, following the murder of Cospatric, but Tostig is safe in Wiltshire.

**1065AD - MORCAR REPLACES EXILED TOSTIG (Northampton)** Edwin, Earl of Mercia, joins Northern rebels against Tostig and King Edward is forced to exile Tostig to keep the peace. Morcar, a Mercian, is appointed Earl of York and is served by Osulf of Bamburgh, the Earl north of the Tees.

**January 6   1066AD - KING HAROLD (London)** Edward the Confessor dies and Harold Godwinson is crowned King of England. William of Normandy protests that he is heir to the English throne.

**Easter   1066AD - HAROLD KEEPS BROTHER EXILED (York)** King Harold visits York and promises to keep his brother Tostig in exile.

**August   1066AD - NORWEGIAN KING ATTACKS CLEVELAND (North East coast)** Harald Hardrada, King of Norway, attacks the coasts of Northumberland and Cleveland and prepares to invade Yorkshire from the Humber. Tostig, the exiled Earl of Northumbria, also plans an invasion.

**September   1066AD - TOSTIG JOINS NORWEGIANS (York)** Tostig's invasion of Yorkshire is repelled but during his retreat from Northumbria he is forced to join the army of the invading Norwegians. The Norwegians land at Riccall, ten miles from York.

**September 20   1066 - THE BATTLE OF GATE FULFORD (York)** The Norwegians under Hardrada defeat Morcar and his brother Edwin in a great battle at Gate Fulford, near York. The citizens of York give their support to the Norwegian King.

**September 25   1066AD - THE BATTLE OF STAMFORD BRIDGE (York)** Norwegian King Harald Hardrada encamps at Stamford Bridge, near York, but is defeated in battle by Harold, King of England, who has marched from the south. The King of Norway is shot dead by an arrow through the throat. Tostig is also killed.

**September 28  1066AD - NORMANS INVADE (Pevensey, Sussex)** A huge force of Normans, under Duke William, landed in Sussex this morning. They set up a base at Hastings.

**October 1 1066AD - HAROLD RECEIVES INVASION NEWS AT YORK (York)** Harold, celebrating his victory over the Norwegians at York, receives news of the Norman invasion. He takes his tired army south to fight the Normans.

**October 14  1066AD - HAROLD KILLED AT BATTLE OF HASTINGS (Battle, near Hastings Sussex)** William of Normandy has been victorious at the Battle of Hastings. King Harold was shot dead with an arrow in the eye. William will be crowned King on Christmas Day.

# Conquest of the North

## 1067AD to 1080AD

The first castle at Newcastle was built in 1080 by Robert Curthose.
Above is a Victorian view of the Keep which dates from the 12th Century

088

**CONQUEST OF THE NORTH 1067AD TO 1080AD** William the Conqueror's conquest of the North was not immediate. The Northerners massacred his troops at Durham and York and murdered his appointed earls. It was only after William's 'Harrying of the North' in the winter of 1069 that the conquest of the North began. It was completed by the construction of Norman castles at York, Richmond, Durham and 'New Castle', which became the strongholds of Norman control and authority in the North.

**1067AD - EARL MURDERED (NEWBURN ON TYNE)** King William appoints Copsig, a former lieutenant of Tostig, as Earl of Northumbria but Copsig is captured and beheaded at Newburn. Osulf of Bamburgh claims the Earldom but is killed by an outlaw. William appoints a noble called Gospatric.

**1068AD - NORTH REBELS AGAINST WILLIAM (North)** Gospatric supports the Midland based rebellion of Edwin and Morcar against the king but the rebellion fails and the rebels flee to Scotland.

**1068AD - NORMAN TROOPS AT YORK (York)** King William enters York and builds a castle. William grants Yorskhire to William Malet and Robert Fitz Richard. The troops are based at York Castle.

**January 30  1069AD - NORMANS SEIZE DURHAM (Durham City)** Robert Comines, a Norman knight is appointed Earl of Northumbria by the King. Comines' 700 strong army seizes Durham City and the Normans murder many people. Aegelwine, Bishop of Durham, warns Robert he will be defeated.

**January 31  1069AD - MASSACRE IN DURHAM (Durham City)** Early this morning a mob of Northumbrians break the gates of Durham and storm through the streets killing the Normans. Earl Comines flees for safety in the bishop's palace but is killed when it is set alight. The blaze threatens the tower of Durham Minster but the locals pray and the wind diverts the flames. Only two Normans survive and flee.

**February  1069AD - SIEGE AT YORK (York)** The natives of York besiege their castle. Robert Fitz Richard, a Norman commander, is killed.

**March  1069AD - WILLIAM SACKS YORK (York)** York is sacked by the Normans under King William. Churches, including the Minster, are plundered by the Normans and the rebels flee. King William builds an additional castle and the garrison is placed under William FitzOsbern.

**September 8 1069AD - DANES AND REBELS ENTER THE HUMBER (East Yorkshire)** The Danes, under King Sweyn, enter the Humber with a fleet of ships accompanied by Edgar of Wessex, who claims England's throne. They march for York.

**September 1069AD - NORMANS RETREAT AFTER ST CUTHBERT MIRACLE (Northallerton)** Norman soldiers retreat at Northallerton during a march north to attack Durham. Durham folk claim the Normans were frightened by a miracle fog created by St. Cuthbert. The real reason is the Danish invasion in Yorkshire.

**September 1069AD - NORMANS PERISH IN YORK BLAZE (York)** The Normans foil hopes of the Danes making York their headquarters by burning the city. Blazes go out of contol and many Normans are killed. The Anglo-Saxon Minster is destroyed.

**December 1069AD - AXHOLME DANES DRIVEN OUT BY CONQUEROR (Axholme and York)** Danes fortify the Isle of Axholme, near Doncaster, but King William's army attack them and they flee. William spends the winter at York.

**1069AD - CUTHBERT FOLK TAKE FLIGHT (Durham City and Lindisfarne)** St Cuthbert's Community flee from Durham with St.Cuthbert's coffin to escape the Norman army. They seek refuge on Lindisfarne and are surprised by the receding tide allowing them to cross to the island. They proclaim it a miracle of St Cuthbert.

**December 1069AD to January 1070 - HARRYING OF THE NORTH (North East and North Yorkshire)** King William lays waste to the North in a campaign which will be remembered as the 'Harrying of the North'. He destroys all farmland and property between Durham and York. The area is reduced to a desert by fire and sword. Many Northerners flee to the hills.

**December 1069AD - BISHOP PLUNDERS DURHAM MINSTER (Durham City)** St Cuthbert's Community return to Durham from Lindisfarne with their saint's body to find the environs destroyed. The worst discovery is that Bishop Aegelwine has robbed Durham of its richest treasures and fled.

**1070AD - SCOTS ATTACK NORTH (The North East)** Scots, under King Malcolm, invade the North from Cumbria. They are victorious at Hunderthwaite in Teesdale before plundering Cleveland, Hartlepool and Monkwearmouth. Gospatric, the reappointed Earl of Northumbria, attacks Malcolm's territory in Cumbria.

**1070AD - YORK MINSTER (York)** Thomas of Bayeux becomes the first Norman Archbishop of York. He starts building a new Norman Minster.

**1070AD - NORMANS IN THE DALES (Swaledale and Wensleydale)** King William bestows Richmond (Hindrelac) to Alan the Red, Count of Brittany, for building a castle. Alan also constructs a castle at Middleham for his brother Ribald.

**April 1072AD - YORK MUST ANSWER TO CANTERBURY (York)** King William issues orders that the Archbishop of York must answer to Canterbury in terms of seniority. It is a demoralising decision for the North.

**August 1072AD - WALTHEOF AND WALCHER (North)** King William replaces Gospatric, Earl of Northumbria, with Waltheof, an Anglo-Saxon of Northampton. Waltheof's powers extend from the Tees to the Tweed. Waltheof builds a castle at Durham for protection against the Scots. Frenchman William Walcher of Lorraine becomes Bishop of Durham.

**1074AD - MONASTERIES REFOUNDED (Sunderland and Jarrow)** Jarrow and Monkwearmouth monasteries are refounded by three Mercian monks.

**May 1075AD - EARL-BISHOP OF DURHAM (Durham City)** Waltheof, Earl of Northumbria, has been executed at Winchester for plotting against the King. Walcher, the Bishop of Durham, is given the earl's powers and becomes an Earl-Bishop.

**1079AD - SCOTS RAID NORTHUMBERLAND (Northumberland)** Scots under King Malcolm III ravage the North East.

**THE PRINCE BISHOPS 1081AD TO 1135AD** The powers of the Prince Bishops of Durham, in the land between Tyne and Tees, were the last vestiges of powers once held by the Kings and Earls of Northumbria. Ultimately the Bishops answered to the Kings of England, but their powers in Durham were very similar to those held by the King of England in other parts of the country.

**January 1081AD - BISHOP OF DURHAM APPOINTED (Gloucester)** William St Carileph becomes Bishop of Durham. Carileph has not inherited the political powers held by his predecessor, which are now held by the Earl of Northumberland. William removes non-celibate monks from Durham and replaces them with celibate monks from Jarrow and Wearmouth. The non-celibate monks are moved to sites at Darlington, Norton-on-Tees and St Helen Auckland.

Framwelgate Bridge in Durham, built by Prince Bishop Ranulf Flambard in 1128

**1086AD - NORTH EAST ESCAPES DOMESDAY (North East)** England north of the Tees is left out of the Domesday Book, a survey of the King's territory, which is an indication of desolation in the region. Yorkshire is included.

**1087AD - BISHOP FLEES TO NORMANDY (Durham)** King William dies in Normandy. William Rufus becomes King and rebuilds the New Castle on Tyne. Bishop William of Durham and Robert Mowbray of Northumberland support the claims of the Duke of Normandy, Robert Curthose, to the throne. They join a long list of plotters. Durham castle is besieged by Rufus and Bishop William flees to Normandy.

**May 1091AD - SCOTS ATTACK NORTH (North)** Scots under King Malcolm Canmore invade as far as Chester-le-Street. A Norman fleet of ships is wrecked off Tynemouth during a counter attack.

**September 14 1091AD - FIRST PRINCE BISHOP (County Durham)** William St Carileph is restored as Bishop of Durham after a three year exile. The King allows Carileph to buy political rights held by Mowbray, the Earl of Northumberland, between the Tyne and Tees. Only the south Durham district called Sadberge remains in Mowbray's Northumberland. As 'Prince Bishop', Carileph can raise armies, appoint sheriffs, administer laws, levy taxes and customs, create fairs and markets, issue charters, salvage shipwrecks, collect revenue from mines, administer forests and mint coins.

**1092AD - CARLISLE PROTECTS NEWCASTLE (Carlisle)** King Rufus builds a castle at Carlisle. It restricts Scottish invasions along the Tyne Gap and will enable commercial development at Newcastle.

**August 11 1093AD - DURHAM CATHEDRAL (Durham City)** Durham Cathedral is started by Bishop William. The old Durham minster is demolished. William is inspired by churches seen in Normandy during exile. The first stones are laid by the Bishop and King Malcolm of Scotland.

**November 13 1093AD - MALCOLM KILLED AT ALNWICK (Alnwick)** Malcolm Canmore, King of the Scots, is slain during a raid on Alnwick. He was tricked by Arkil Morel, nephew of Robert Mowbray. Malcolm is buried at Tynemouth and Mowbray forms an alliance with Donald, the new Scottish king.

**1095AD - NORTHUMBERLAND UNDER KING'S RULE (Bamburgh)** Bamburgh Castle is besieged by King William against Robert Mowbray, who has rebelled against him. William builds an 'evil neighbour' fort on the walls of Bamburgh and captures Mowbray. Mowbray's castles at Newcastle, Tynemouth and Morpeth are seized. Northumberland is taken under direct rule of the King. It stretches from Tyne to Tweed but includes land in south Durham.

**January 6 1096AD - CARILEPH DIES (Windsor)** Carileph, Bishop of Durham, dies at Windsor where he was summoned to meet the King on suspicion of revolt. A new appointment is postponed until 1099 when Ranulf Flambard, chief adviser to Rufus, becomes Bishop. Flambard has acquired wealth for the King by collecting revenue from postponed appointments and through his tough approach to taxing the barons.

**1100AD - BISHOP OF DURHAM IN TOWER (London)** Selby-born Henry I becomes King. Bishop Flambard is imprisoned in the Tower of London by Henry after advice from council. Flambard, who has many enemies, is the first man to be imprisoned here. He later escapes using a rope smuggled in by a butler in a cask of wine. Flambard seeks refuge in Normandy.

**July 1101AD - BISHOP SUPPORTS INVASION (Hampshire)** Flambard persuades Robert Curthose, Duke of Normandy, to invade England. King Henry backs down and pardons the Duke's allies. Flambard is restored as Bishop of Durham.

**September 1104AD - SAINT BURIED IN CATHEDRAL (Durham City)** St Cuthbert's body is buried in Durham Cathedral. It rested in a nearby chapel while the cathedral was built. Ten monks inspect the corpse finding it incorrupt with a fragrant smell. It may be embalmed.

**1107AD - TEESDALE CASTLE (Barnard Castle)** A Teesdale castle is built which will later be called Barnard Castle. The forests of Teesdale have belonged to Guy Baliol since 1093.

Seal of Prince Bishop Thomas Hatfield who became bishop in 1345

**May 1108AD - ARCHBISHOP OF YORK DABBLES IN OCCULT (York)** Archbishop Gerard dies in mysterious circumstances. He is thought to have been involved with the occult and is refused burial in the minster.

**1115AD - GODRIC OF FINCHALE (Finchale)** St Godric is granted land for a hermitage at Finchale, near Durham, by Bishop Flambard.

**1119AD - YORK FREE OF CANTERBURY (York)** Thurstan, Archbishop of York, is consecrated by the Pope who releases him from obedience to Canterbury.

**1120AD - CHAPEL AT MIDDLESBROUGH (Middlesbrough)** Robert Brus presents a chapel at Middlesbrough to Whitby Abbey.

**1121AD - BISHOP'S BORDER FORT (Norham on Tweed)** Norham Castle is built on the Tweed by Bishop Flambard. Norhamshire is a part of Durham which neighbours Scotland. Flambard attacks Scotland from this base. Meanwhile Berwick is established as Scotland's first Royal burgh by King Alexander.

**1121AD - BISHOP RETIRES TO WEARMOUTH (Sunderland)** Turgot, Bishop of St Andrews, retires to Wearmouth after a dispute with the Scottish King Alexander over obedience to the Archbishop of York.

**1124AD - DAVID IS SCOTS KING (Scotland)** David, Earl of Huntingdon, becomes the King of Scotland. He is the son of Malcolm Canmore but was brought up as a Norman in England.

**1125AD - ROBERT BRUCE OF CLEVELAND (Scotland)** Robert De Brus, a Norman landowner at Skelton in Cleveland, is granted land in Scotland by King David.

**1126AD - WARK TAKEN BY SCOTS (River Tweed)** King David of Scotland seizes the English castle at Wark on Tweed.

**1126AD - YORK AND CANTERBURY EQUAL (Rome)** The Pope declares York and Canterbury equal but Canterbury's Archbishop is papal legate.

**1128AD - BISHOP FLAMBARD DIES (Durham)** Flambard dies after twenty nine years as bishop. He recently built Durham's Framwelgate Bridge.

**1131AD - CASTLES AND MANORS (Alnwick, Scarborough and Raby)** Ivo de Vesci, a Norman baron, builds a castle at Alnwick. A castle was also recently built at Scarborough by William le Gros. Meanwhile the Manor of Raby recently passed to an Anglo Saxon called Dolphin.

**1132AD - NEW CATHEDRALS (Durham City and Carlisle)** Durham Cathedral is virtually complete. Meanwhile Carlisle's Augustinian church becomes a cathedral.

**1135AD - MINT ESTABLISHED (Durham City)** A mint is established at Durham where unique Durham coins are produced.

Durham Cathedral

# Two Great Cathedrals - Durham and York

York Minster: A Gothic Cathedral

**TWO GREAT CATHEDRALS - DURHAM AND YORK** York Minster and Durham Cathedral are historically and architecturally two of the most important cathedrals in Europe. They were the only cathedrals in the region until Ripon's Minster and Newcastle's church of St Nicholas became cathedrals in 1836 and 1882. York Cathedral, although known as a minster, is officially the 'Cathedral and Metropolitical Church of St Peter in York'. By definition a cathedral is the site of a bishop's throne (a 'Cathedra') but the word Cathedral did not come into use until after the Norman conquest. In Anglo-Saxon times important churches were minsters, but not all were bishops' seats.

**YORK'S ANGLO-SAXON MINSTER** York Minster's history began in 627 AD when King Edwin of Northumbria was baptised in a simple wooden church at York, within the site of the old Roman fort. The church was approved by the Pope and its dedication to St Peter reflected its links with Rome. The wooden church was rebuilt in stone and completed by King Oswald but the bishop's seat was transferred for a time to Lindisfarne. The minster was rebuilt again in 664 AD and again after a fire in 741 AD. It was eventually destroyed during the Norman siege of the city in 1069.

**THE DURHAM MINSTER** The predecessors of the Bishops of Durham were the Bishops of Lindisfarne who transferred their diocese to Chester-le-Street in 883AD. A Saxon Minster was built and a succession of 9 bishops reigned until moving to Durham in 995AD. A wooden minster was built at Durham in 995 and rebuilt in stone in 999AD. It stood for 94 years until 1093 when it was replaced by the Norman Cathedral.

**YORK'S LOST NORMAN CATHEDRAL** York Minster is built in the Gothic style of architecture but what is not widely known is that York was once, like Durham, a Norman Cathedral. The Norman Cathedral at York was started before Durham in 1070 by the Archbishop of York, Thomas of Bayeux, and a Norman choir was added towards the end of the following century (after Durham) by Archbishop Roger of Pont L'Eveque. Roger's work seems to have been influenced by Durham Cathedral, but the only remains of the Norman Cathedral at York are below ground level in the Minster crypt.

**DURHAM'S NORMAN CATHEDRAL** Durham Cathedral is widely regarded as Europe's finest Norman (or Romanesque) Cathedral. It is almost entirely Norman in style and the work of Bishop William of St Carileph. It was completed in 39 years from 1093-1132 but some of the old priory buildings around the cloisters are earlier. One notable feature of the cathedral is the rounded pillars (or piers) with their zig zags, spirals and other patterned decorations.

**DURHAM'S ARCHITECTURAL ACHIEVEMENTS** The innovative ribbed vaulting at Durham was the first of its type in the world and enabled much higher vaulting through the use of pointed, ribbed arches. The pointed arches in the Norman nave at Durham were the embryonic stages of the style of architecture which would come to be known as Gothic. Another architectural feature developed at Durham were Flying Buttresses which gave extra support to the vaulting. They are high in the roof of the Triforium and not on view to the public.

**YORK'S CONVERSION FROM NORMAN TO GOTHIC** York Minster represents almost every stage of the Gothic style of architecture from 1230 to 1475. The Gothic style is most notable for its distinctive pointed arches and its rich decoration. The present York Minster was built from 1220 and the old Norman Cathedral was dismantled in stages as Gothic additions were made. The Gothic style was adopted at York to keep up with the new fashion and allow considerable enlargement to the cathedral in keeping with its status as the centre of an Archbishopric.

**YORK'S GOTHIC MINSTER** York's Gothic Minster was started around 1220 by Archbishop Walter de Grey (1216-1255). Grey replaced the Norman transepts with 'Early English' Gothic transepts in the period 1227 to 1260. The new transepts dwarfed the Norman nave of the cathedral so one of Walter's successors, Archbishop John Romanus, replaced the nave with a new Gothic structure from 1291. The Norman choir was replaced by Archbishop Thoresby from 1361 and by 1400 the Minster was entirely Gothic. The central tower was added in 1405-1415, using money donated by Walter Skirlaw, the Bishop of Durham, and the two western towers added from 1433 to 1475. The Minster was finally completed and consecrated on July 3rd 1472.

**DURHAM'S LADY CHAPEL** Although most of Durham Cathedral was built in the period 1093-1132, there were three major additions;- the Galilee Chapel, the Chapel of the Nine Altars and the Great Central Tower. The Galilee chapel (or Lady Chapel) is situated at the west end of the cathedral beneath the twin towers and is most famous as the site of Bede's tomb. It was built by Bishop Hugh Pudsey in 1174 and is late Norman in style. The building has the appearance of a Moorish palace.

**DURHAM'S GOTHIC ADDITION** Durham's Chapel of the Nine Altars (a transept) lies at the east end of Durham Cathedral and is Early English Gothic in style dating from the time of Bishop Richard Poore (1228-1237). Poore later became Bishop of Salisbury and built the cathedral there. The Nine Altars was built to accommodate vast numbers of pilgrims visiting St Cuthbert's shrine. Its measurements and structure were based on a transept at Fountains Abbey, but the mason miscalculated dimensions. Examination of the chapel roof reveals the mistake. The main feature of the chapel is the great Rose Window.

**SAINTLY SHRINES** Pilgrims were a rich source of revenue for medieval cathedrals and before the murder of Thomas Beckett at Canterbury Cathedral in 1170 St Cuthbert's shrine at Durham was the most visited. The shrine was one of the most richly decorated monuments in England. The remains of Bede were an added attraction at Durham but York lacked a saint's shrine. In the 13th century William Fitzherbert, a popular Archbishop of York, was posthumously canonized and became St William of York. This encouraged pilgrims to visit York and helped York to compete with other shrines such as St John Lee's at Beverley Minster.

**THE BUILDING MATERIALS** Durham Cathedral is built of sandstone mined from quarries like Kepier, a mile or so along the Wear, east of Durham. Black Frosterley marble from Weardale, to the west of Durham, is extensively used for decoration in the cathedral. It is embedded with fossilized sea shells. York Minster is built of Oolitic limestone from the Tadcaster area and gives the minster its white appearance.

**STAINED GLASS** Fine examples of stained glass can be found in both Durham and York, but York has the highest proportion of medieval stained glass of any European cathedral. Both cathedrals have magnificent

The great west window at York

Rose Windows, the one at York known as the Heart of Yorkshire. One of the more unusual windows at Durham is the Last Supper, a beautiful twentieth century window installed in 1984.

**ARCHBISHOPS AND PRINCE BISHOPS** In terms of the church the Archbishops of York were always of senior rank to the Bishops of Durham but in medieval times the Bishops of Durham held political powers (as Prince Bishops) which gave them additional status. It is worth noting that the Bishop of Durham's throne at Durham is the highest in Christendom and higher than that of the Archbishop of York.

**WICKWANE AND BEK** An interesting incident occurred in 1283 when the Archbishop of York, William Wickwane, visited Durham Cathedral to inspect the wealthy monastery there, before the appointment of a new bishop at Durham. The Durham monks locked him out, clipped the tail of his horse and chased him out of the market place. The following year Anthony Bek was appointed Bishop of Durham and Wickwane ordered Bek to excommunicate the monks. Bek refused so Wickwane excommunicated the bishop. Bishop Bek complained to the king that the Arhbishop had no right to excommunicate a Prince Bishop and the decision was overthrown.

**DURHAM MONASTERY** One of the key differences between Durham Cathedral and York Minster is that Durham had a monastery attached to it and York did not. The buildings of Durham monastery (dissolved in 1540) were those clustered around the cloister on the south side of the cathedral and were administered by a Prior.

**OTHER CATHEDRALS** Ripon Cathedral dates from between 1080 and 1500 but it did not become a cathedral until 1836. Its diocese stretches from the outskirts of Leeds to the south side of Teesdale. Beverley Minster and Hexham Abbey, although not cathedrals, are historic churches with architectural features to rival many smaller cathedrals. Newcastle's cathedral of St Nicholas was the most important medieval parish church in Newcastle until it became a cathedral in 1892. The church dates from around 1350. The diocese of Newcastle covers the whole of Newcastle and Northumberland, which formerly belonged to Durham.

# The Monastic Revival

1080AD to 1536AD

**THE MONASTIC REVIVAL 1080AD TO 1536AD** From around 1074 the monasteries, which made the region famous in Anglo-Saxon times, were revived. Many of these great institutions had been destroyed by Vikings, abandoned or had fallen into disrepair, except in certain centres like Durham and York. In 1083 the Normans erected a Priory at Durham which dominated the county to the exclusion of all but affiliated cells. Extensive monastery building began in Yorkshire and the Borders from around 1108 with new monasteries at Melrose, Hexham, Rievaulx, Guisborough and Fountains, encouraged by Thurstan, the Archbishop of York, and his friend David the King of Scotland. The monasteries would own and dominate vast areas of the Northern landscape until their ruthless destruction by Henry VIII in the 1530s.

## THE YORKSHIRE MONASTERIES

**BYLAND ABBEY, COXWOLD - (Cistercian Monks)** Originally established at Byland, not far from a rival Cistercian Abbey at Rievaulx, in 1143. This proved to be too close to Rievaulx and the monks were confused by which monastery bell was ringing when they were called to order. In 1147 the Abbey moved to Stocking, near Coxwold, and the old site came to be known as Old Byland. The Byland monks were affiliated to the Monastery of Savigny in France.

**EGGLESTONE ABBEY, TEESDALE - (Premonstratensian Canons)** Built in 1195 near Barnard Castle but on the Yorkshire side of the Tees. The abbey was attacked by Scots in 1315.

**FOUNTAINS ABBEY, NEAR RIPON - (Cistercian monks)** Fountains was founded on December 27, 1132 by 13 monks from St Mary's Benedictine Abbey in York. They included the Prior, Richard, who wished to obey a stricter order of life. Archbishop Thurstan of York granted land near the River Skell and the monks set up Fountains Abbey against the wishes of Geoffrey, the abbot of St Mary's. Like Rievaulx, Fountains was a daughter of Clairvaux Abbey in Burgundy. Geoffrey D'Ainai, an experienced monk, came from France to teach the Cistercian way and in 1135 the Dean of York retired to Fountains Abbey. His wealth helped the abbey to grow.

**GISBOROUGH PRIORY, CLEVELAND - (Augustinian Canons)** Established around 1128 by Robert Bruce of Skelton. The abbey is spelled Gisborough but the town is spelled Guisborough.

**HOLY TRINITY PRIORY, YORK- (Benedictine monks)** Founded by Robert Pagnell in 1089 and attached to the abbey of Marmoutier, near Tours. The present church of Holy Trinity in York's Micklegate was part of the priory.

**JERVAULX ABBEY, WENSLEYDALE - (Cistercian monks)** Originally established at Fors near Aysgarth in Wensleydale in 1145 by Akar Fitzbardolph. While here, the French monks are thought to have perfected the making of Wensleydale cheese. In 1156 they moved further down the valley to a new site which they called Jervaulx. Jervaulx means Ure Valley as the Ure is the river of Wensleydale. Unlike Rievaulx and Fountains, this abbey was affiliated to the French monastery of Savigny rather than Clairvaux. When the monastery was dissolved in 1536, the last abbot of Jervaulx was executed for his part in the Pilgrimage of Grace.

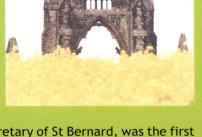

**MOUNT GRACE PRIORY, OSMOTHERLEY - (Charterhouse of Carthusian monks)** Founded in 1398 Mount Grace Priory was the north's first Carthusian monastery or 'Charterhouse'. It was established by Thomas of Holland, Duke of Surrey.

**RIEVAULX ABBEY, NEAR HELMSLEY - (Cistercian Monks)** Rievaulx Abbey was founded in 1131 with the support of St Bernard of Clairvaux. It was Britain's first Cistercian monastery and was built by monks from Clairvaux Abbey in France. William of Clairvaux, a secretary of St Bernard, was the first abbot of the monastery.

**ST MARY'S ABBEY AT YORK - (Benedictine monks)** Founded by King William Rufus in 1089 and probably located on the site of an Anglo-Saxon monastery. Most of the present building dates from the thirteenth century and lies just outside York city walls, although it is enclosed by walls of its own. The nearby King's Manor was once the abbot's house.

**WHITBY ABBEY - (Benedictine monks)** Re-established by Reinfrid in 1078 on the site of St Hilda's Anglo-Saxon monastery. Robert De Brus presented a small chapel at Middlesbrough to the abbey around 1120 to

Gisborough Priory dominates the town of Guisborough

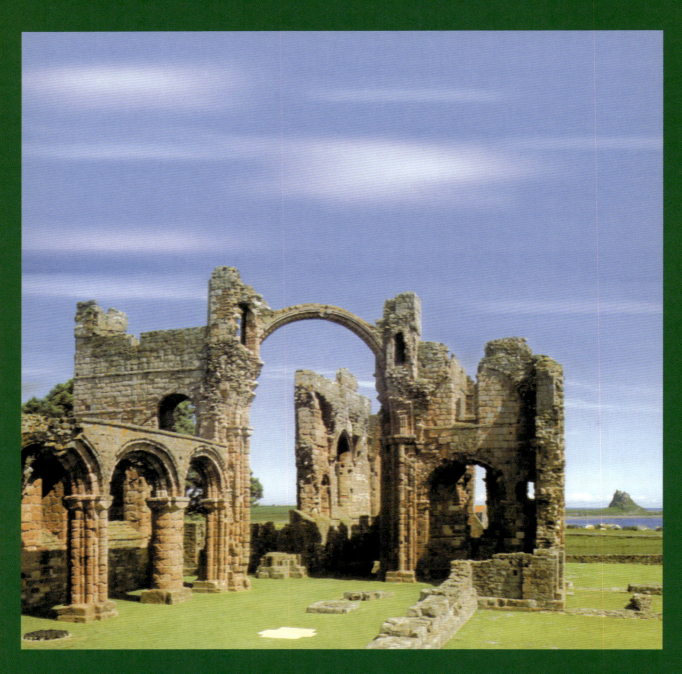

Lindisfarne Priory

be staffed by its monks and in 1215 the hermitage at Saltburn was granted to the Whitby Abbey by Roger de Argentum.

## OTHER YORKSHIRE MONASTERIES

**BAYSDALE NUNNERY** Cistercian nuns moved here from Nunthorpe in 1163.
**BRIDLINGTON PRIORY** Augustinian canons established 1120.
**COVERHAM ABBEY** Premonstratensian canons established in Coverdale 1212.
**ELLERTON ABBEY** 12th Century Gilbertine Abbey in Swaledale.
**KIRKHAM PRIORY** Augustinian canons established near Malton 1125.
**KIRKSTALL ABBEY** Cistercian monks established near Leeds 1152.
**NEWBURGH PRIORY** Augustinian canons established near Coxwold 1150.

## THE NORTHUMBERLAND MONASTERIES

**BLANCHLAND ABBEY (Premonstratensian Canons)** Founded by a Norman Baron called Walter de Bolbec on the Northumberland side of the Derwent valley in 1165. Stones from the Abbey were later used in building Blanchland village.

**HEXHAM ABBEY (Augustinian Canons)** Established by Thomas II, the Archbishop of York, on the site of St Wilfrid's Saxon monastery in 1113. It has an Anglo-Saxon crypt.

**LINDISFARNE PRIORY (Benedictine Monks)** Established by the Bishop of Durham, William St Carileph, on the site of the Anglo-Saxon monastery. It was probably founded around 1093, the same time as Durham Cathedral. Its architecture is strikingly similar to Durham Cathedral.

**TYNEMOUTH PRIORY (Benedictine Monks)** Founded around 1090 as a cell of Durham. Robert Mowbray, Earl of Northumberland, transfered its jurisdiction to St.Albans in 1093. Whitley Bay was conferred to the Priory of Tynemouth by Henry I in 1100. The priory developed a coal port at North Shields in the thirteenth century which would rival the port at Newcastle.

## OTHER NORTHUMBERLAND MONASTERIES

**ALNWICK ABBEY (Premonstatensian Canons)** Founded by the De Vesci family in 1147.
**BRINKBURN PRIORY, COQUETDALE (Augustinian Canons)** established 1135.
**NEWMINSTER ABBEY** Near Morpeth, established as a daughter of Fountains in 1139.

## COUNTY DURHAM MONASTERIES (ALL BENEDICTINE AND AFFILIATED TO DURHAM PRIORY)

**DURHAM CATHEDRAL PRIORY (Benedictine Monks)** The Norman monastery was built here around 1080 by William Walcher, Bishop of Durham, and the monastic buildings are concentrated around the cathedral cloister. The monastery was dissolved by King Henry VIII on December 31 1540.

**FINCHALE PRIORY, NEAR DURHAM (Benedictine Monks)** St Godric was granted land at Finchale, near Durham, by the Bishop of Durham in 1115 for a hermitage. Godric died in 1180 and was buried on the site. The Priory was founded around 1196 for eight Durham monks and was a cell of Durham monastery. It was often used as a holiday retreat by the Durham monks.

**WEARMOUTH AND JARROW (Benedictine Monks)** The famous Anglo-Saxon monasteries at Wearmouth and Jarrow had fallen out of use but were revived, as small cells, around 1076 by Aldwin of Winchester during the time of Bishop William Walcher. They were both affiliated to the monastery at Durham. Turgot, the Bishop of St Andrews, retired to Wearmouth after a dispute with the Scottish King over his obedience to the Archbishop of York in 1121.

**NEASHAM ABBEY (Benedictine Nuns)** Neasham Abbey was located near Darlington and was the home to eight nuns. It was first mentioned in a papal bull in 1156. A nineteenth century house called 'Neasham Abbey' stands near to the site of the nunnery.

**FRIARIES - MONASTERIES IN THE TOWN** Newcastle never had a medieval cathedral or monastery like Durham or York but there was a nunnery and a number of Friaries. Friars were supported by charitable donations in populous towns and Newcastle's Friaries included the Dominican Blackfriars (1239), Carmelite White Friars (1262), Sack Friars (1266), Franciscan Grey Friars (1274) and Austin Friars (1286). Substantial remains of Blackfriars can still be seen. Other Friaries could be found in the North at Hartlepool, Richmond, Yarm, Scarborough, York, Hull, Beverley, Penrith, Appleby, Hexham and Alnwick (Hulne Priory)

## THE MONASTIC ORDERS

**Benedictines** The oldest monasteries in the region tended to be Benedictine and followed the rule of St Benedict of Nursia. The rules of the order were set out around 520 AD at the monastery of Monte Casino. The order later moved to Rome where, under the patronage of St Gregory, they sent monks to Canterbury under St Augustine and established the first Benedictine house outside Italy. The Benedictine order was more practical and less austere than some of the later monastic orders, but included some of Britain's most powerful monasteries, including the Priory of Durham.

**Cistercians** The Cistercian order was based on Benedictine monasticism and was founded in 1098 by St.Robert De Molesme at Citeaux in France. It undertook the literal observance of the rule of St. Benedict and was stricter than the Benedictine order, living by poverty, prayer, ardous labour, long fasts and little sleep. The monks cultivated vast tracts of land with the help of numerous lay brothers.

**Augustinians and Premonstratensians** The Augustinians followed the rule of St Augustine of Hippo (354AD-430AD) but the rules of the Augustinians were never written or detailed to the extent of the Benedictine order and there were many different types of Augustinian orders, including Premonstratensians and Gilbertines. The Premonstratensian order was founded in 1119 at Premontre in France by St.Norbert. Their life is devoted to penitence and preaching.

**Carthusians** The Carthusians were one of the strictest monastic orders, dedicating their life to solitude and silence. Each monk lived in a hermitage, or cell, with its own living room, workshop, garden and ambulatory. The monks occupied their time praying, studying or labouring. Once a week the monks would break their solitude and silence for three or four hours and get together with the other monks to walk and talk together. The order was established by St Bruno in 1084 in the Chatreuse mountains, north of Grenoble in France. Cathusian monasteries are called Charterhouses. The only North Eastern example is Mount Grace Priory near Osmotherley.

Mount Grace Priory, Osmotherley

# A part of Scotland

## 1135AD to 1157AD

An illuminated initial letter from the charter of Kelso Abbey depicting David I and his grandson Malcolm IV

**A PART OF SCOTLAND 1135AD TO 1157AD** When King Henry I died in 1135, he was succeeded by his nephew Stephen, instead of his daughter Matilda. David, the King of Scotland, attacked Northumberland in support of Matilda, but, as time passed, it was clear David wanted Northern England for himself. David was defeated in battle at Northallerton in 1138, but he was given Northumberland the following year. When the Scottish Chancellor, William Cumin, usurped the Bishop of Durham's throne in 1141, David's control of the North-East was complete.

**December 25  1135AD - STEPHEN IS CROWNED (London)** Stephen becomes King of England following the death of Henry I. The late King Henry hoped his daughter Matilda would succeed. King David of Scotland, a Norman, invades England in support of Matilda.

**February 5  1136 - PEACE TREATY SIGNED IN DURHAM (Durham City)** Stephen of England and David of Scotland sign a treaty at Durham to settle land disputes. David's son Henry is granted Huntingdon, but Stephen keeps Northumberland, which has been claimed by the Scots for many years.

**1138AD - DAVID INVADES (Northumberland)** David invades Northumberland four times this year in support of Matilda. His real aim may be the acquisition of Northern England, which has close religious, linguistic and cultural ties to lowland Scotland. David claims Northern England through his wife, who is the granddaughter of Earl Siward, the pre-conquest ruler of the North.

**August 22  1138AD - BATTLE OF THE STANDARD (Cowton Moor near Northallerton)** The Scots invade England under David and fight the men of Yorkshire at the Battle of the Standard, near Northallerton. The battle takes place despite the peace making efforts of the Bruces and Baliols, who are landowners in Scotland, Yorkshire and the Tees valley. The English, composed almost entirely of Yorkshire barons, are led by Thurstan, Archbishop of York, who was once a close friend of David. Before the battle Thurstan set up a mast with standards of Yorkshire saints tied to it for good luck. St Cuthbert's banner was not represented, suggesting a lack of support from Durham and Northumberland. Thurstan's supporters include the Mowbrays, Lacys and Percys. David's supporters are Norman barons from Scotland, but he has some Yorkshire support. David's army is heavily defeated in the battle and he is forced to retreat to his castle at Carlisle.

**September 26  1138AD - POPE'S MAN DRAWS UP PEACE TREATY AT CARLISLE (Carlisle)** Alberic, Bishop of Ostia, representing the pope, negotiates a peace treaty between Stephen of England and David of Scotland at Carlisle.

**April 9  1139AD - RIVER TEES BECOMES SCOTTISH BORDER (Durham City)** A peace treaty is signed at Durham, following constant Scottish raids. David's son Henry is given Northumberland, but not the castles of Bamburgh and Newcastle, which remain property of the English King. The Tees forms the border between England and Scotland, because Northumberland's territory extends to the district of Sadberge on the north side of the river. The district of Sadberge stretches from Hartlepool to Teesdale, but does not include Stockton and Darlington, which belong to the Prince Bishop of Durham. The Prince Bishop's territory remains outside Scottish control. The treaty is witnessed by the Archbishops of Canterbury, York, St Andrews and Glasgow.

**1141AD - USURPER SEIZES BISHOP'S CASTLE (County Durham)** A usurper called William Cumin claims to be Prince Bishop of Durham, following the untimely death of Bishop Geoffrey. Cumin, the Chancellor of Scotland, has no real claim to the bishop's throne, but has support from the royal claimant Matilda and from David, King of Scotland. Cumin gains the support of a number of local barons, including the Baliol family of Teesdale and the Bruces of Hartlepool, who also own land in Scotland.

**1143AD - DURHAM MONKS ELECT TRUE BISHOP (Rome and York)** William Cumin forges papal documents confirming him as the Bishop of Durham, but the monks of Durham cathedral monastery have refused to accept Cumin. A number of monks escape from Durham despite Cumin's attempts to surround the city with soldiers. They escape to Rome to clarify whether or not Cumin has a right to be bishop. The Pope instructs the monks that Cumin is not a bishop and orders that they elect a new bishop within forty days. William of St Barbara, Dean of York, is elected to the Prince Bishop's post.

King Stephen, who gave Northumberland to the Scots

**1143AD - BISHOPS BATTLE AT GILESGATE (Durham)** William St.Barbara tries to take the bishopric of Durham from William Cumin but Cumin's retainers defeat him in a battle at St Giles Church at Gilesgate, on the outskirts of Durham. Cumin has seized Durham Castle and denied St.Barbara access. St Barbara's supporters attack the church of Kirk Merrington, which has been fortified by Cumin's retainers and fortify the village of Thornley against him. Cumin's men have been terrorising the County of Durham.

**1144AD - USURPER SURRENDERS (Durham City)** After severe pressure from Durham barons, led by Roger Conyers, William Cumin, the usurper bishop of Durham finally surrenders Durham Castle to the true bishop who takes up his post as Bishop of Durham.

**1147AD - HENRY PROMISES SCOTS THE NORTH (Cumbria)** Henry Plantagenet (the future King Henry II), promises King David of Scotland that, when he is king, he will continue to recognise David's right to Cumberland and Northumberland.

**June 12  1152AD - EARL OF NORTHUMBERLAND IS BURIED AT KELSO (Kelso)** Henry, the son of King David, has died and is buried at Kelso Abbey, near the River Tweed. Meanwhile the Scots recently began the construction of Berwick upon Tweed castle.

**1153AD - DAVID, KING OF SCOTLAND DIES (Carlisle)** King David of Scotland has died at his castle at Carlisle. David is succeeded by his grandson Malcolm IV, (Malcolm the Maiden), who also inherits Northumberland. David was one of the most powerful Scottish kings and has increased the Norman influence in Scotland. He encouraged the building of great Scottish monasteries like Kelso and Melrose, many having strong ties to monasteries in Yorkshire and France. Ailred, Abbot of Rievaulx, an associate of David has written an epitaph to David which reads- 'O desolate Scotia who shall console thee now?. He is no more who made an untilled and barren land a land that is pleasant and plenteous.'

**1153AD - PIRATES ATTACK HARTLEPOOL (Hartlepool)** Norwegian pirates led by King Eystein have attacked and plundered Hartlepool after raiding several parts of the Scottish coast. This is the last recorded Viking raid on England.

**1154AD - BISHOP PUDSEY (Rome)** Hugh Pudsey is consecrated as the new Bishop of Durham. He will become one of the most powerful men in the North.

**1154AD - KING ABOLISHES EARLDOM OF YORK (England)** King Henry II, the new King of England, abolishes the Earldom of York (Yorkshire). William le Gros surrenders Scarborough castle to the king because it was built without Royal permission.

**1157AD - SCOTS LOSE NORTHUMBERLAND (Northumberland)** Despite his promises in 1147, King Henry reclaims Northumberland from the Scots. It had been part of Scotland since 1139. Henry does, however, let the Scots keep the valleys of Tynedale.

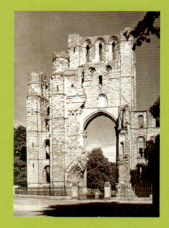

Kelso Abbey where Henry, the Earl of Northumberland, was buried

# Bishop Pudsey

1154AD to 1198AD

**1171AD - FLANDERS FLEET AT HARTLEPOOL HARBOUR (Hartlepool)** Pudsey's nephew Hugh, Earl of Bar, brings a fleet of ships from Flanders to Hartlepool to assist King William of Scotland in an invasion of England. Pudsey has probably encouraged his nephew.

**1172AD - NEW CASTLES (Newcastle and Wensleydale)** Maurice 'the engineer' is rebuilding Newcastle castle in stone for King Henry. A castle has also been built at Middleham in Wensleydale, replacing a nearby castle built by Count Alan in 1070.

**1173AD - SCOTS INVADE (Northumberland)** William, King of Scotland, invades the North East to support a rebellion by King Henry III's sons. Pudsey does not challenge William's movement through Durham. Bowes Castle in Yorkshire is attacked.

**July 1174AD - SCOTTISH KING CAPTURED (Alnwick and Richmond)** William of Scotland is captured at Alnwick and surrenders Berwick to the English. He is imprisoned in Richmond Castle before transportation to Normandy. The fleet of Hugh de Barr at Hartlepool returns to Flanders.

**1174AD - KING DESTROYS REBEL CASTLES (North Yorkshire)** King Henry destroys the castles of the Mowbrays at Thirsk and Kirkby Malzeard. The Mowbrays had rebelled against him.

**1174AD - LADY CHAPEL AT CATHEDRAL (Durham City)** Pudsey builds the Galilee Chapel or Lady Chapel at the western end of Durham for ladies who, according to Benedictine rules, are not allowed into the main cathedral.

**August 10 1175AD - SCOTS SUBMIT (York)** The barons of Scotland swear allegiance to King Henry at York.

**1175AD - BIGG MARKET AMONG NEWCASTLE STREETS (Newcastle)** Westgate and Bigg Market are among Newcastle's streets. Newcastle's growth was spurred by the establishment of a castle here ninety five years ago. Newcastle is well situated to prosper as a port and military garrison and has risen from obscurity. In pre-Norman times it was home to a religious community called Monkchester.

**Christmas Day 1179AD - HELL'S KETTLES (Croft on Tees, Darlington)** Pits called Hell's Kettles were said to be formed by an earthquake this year.

**1179AD - TOWN AND CITY CHARTERS (Durham, Sunderland and Gateshead)** Durham's City Charter from Bishop Pudsey is confirmed by the Pope and a market is established. The borough of Sunderland (Wearmouth) receives a charter from Bishop Pudsey, giving its merchants similar rights to those at Newcastle. Pudsey also establishes a borough at Gateshead.

**1180AD - MR WASHINGTON (Washington)** William De Hartburn (of Hartburn near Stockton) has bought the manor of Washington from the Bishop of Durham. Washington is then known as Wessington so William becomes William de Wessington. William is the first member of the Washington family (ancestors of American president George Washington who gave his name to Washington DC). The Washington coat of arms will later include stars and stripes.

**1183AD - DURHAM DOMESDAY (North East)** Hugh Pudsey carries out the Boldon Buke survey of his territory in Durham and Northumberland. It is Durham's equivalent of the Domesday Book.

**1185AD - ROBERT BRUCE BUILDS HARTLEPOOL CHURCH (Hartlepool)** Robert De Brus IV builds St Hilda's Church on the site of an Anglo-Saxon monastery.

**1189AD - HARTLEPOOL FLEET FOR CRUSADE (Hartlepool)** Richard 'The Lionheart' becomes king of England. Pudsey assembles a fleet at Hartlepool to join Richard in the Crusades but Richard persuades the bishop to stay and defend the north and gives the bishop new political powers. The king makes use of the fleet and provisions.

**1189AD - PUDSEY IS JUSTICIAR, REGENT AND EARL (Durham)** King Richard appoints Pudsey as Justiciar of England and Regent of the North, sharing responsibilities with Longchamp, Bishop of Ely. Pudsey is also made Earl of Northumberland and acquires the town of Newcastle. The Earldom of Sadberge, stretching from Teesdale to Hartlepool, is acquired by Pudsey and added to Durham. Sadberge formed an outlying part of Northumberland. Pudsey is still Prince Bishop of Durham.

**March 16 1190AD - JEWS MASSACRED IN YORK (Clifford's Tower, York)** Over a hundred Jews are massacred or commit suicide in anti-Jewish rioting at York. 150 Jews took refuge in the castle and were told to convert to Christianity or be killed. Many kill their own wives and children while others are butchered as they escape.

**1190AD - PUDSEY ARRESTED BY RIVAL BISHOP (London)** Pudsey is tricked, arrested and locked in the tower by Bishop Longchamp of Ely during King Richard's absence. Pudsey is released after agreeing to give Windsor, Northumberland and Newcastle to Longchamp. Pudsey's son Henry is taken hostage by Longchamp as a means of security but King Richard's brother Prince John exiles Longchamp.

**1195AD - PUDSEY DIES (Doncaster)** Pudsey dies aged seventy. He was heading south to answer to King Richard when he took ill at Doncaster. Pudsey had raised money for Richard's ransom while Richard was imprisoned in Austria but the bishop spent some of the money on projects like the new church of St Cuthberts, Darlington.

Seal depicting Bishop Hugh Pudsey

# John and He

1199AD to 1272AD

## Robobug

**O**ne day engineers may be bugging Mars or the Moon. Engineers at MIT's Insect Lab are designing and testing foot-long robots built to replicate the most basic behavior of a house-fly or bee—crawling, climbing, and avoiding danger.

Because the Robobugs are small and relatively inexpensive, they could be sent to distant planets to transmit data and images back to earth.

The mechanical bugs use sensors on their legs to gauge the terrain they walk on. Sensors enable them to "see" and metal whiskers guide them past obstacles. The computer critters may even pause to sun themselves in order to recharge their batteries.

So, the next time you try to swat that pesky housefly, better look closely. Be sure you're not aiming at Robobug.

**Discover the
World of
Engineering**

**National Engineers Week
February 16-22, 1992**

125

Newcastle's Blackgate was built by Henry III in 1247

**KING JOHN AND HENRY III 1199AD TO 1272AD** Tensions between the Scots and English were high during the reigns of King John and Henry III and there were many disagreements over the exact course of the Scottish border. Meanwhile, Newcastle's importance as a town and port was increasing and important new defences were added in 1247 and 1265.

**1199AD - JOHN CROWNED (England)** Prince John, brother of the late Richard I, becomes King of England

**1199AD - PILGRIM'S STREET (Newcastle)** Pilgrim Street is among Newcastle's streets. It is the site of inns and places of hospitality used by travellers and pilgrims.

**Circa 1200AD - FERRY KILLS WILD BOAR (Ferryhill, County Durham)** Roger De Ferry has killed the last of Durham's wild boars. These beasts have roamed the forests here since ancient times.

**November 22 1200AD - SCOTS CLAIM NORTH (Lincoln)** William of Scotland claims Northumberland is his in a meeting with John.

**1201AD - HARTLEPOOL BECOMES A BURGH (Hartlepool)** King John grants Hartlepool 'Royal Burgh' status, giving its merchants the same rights as Newcastle. The Bishop of Durham claims Hartlepool should be a bishop's burgh.

**1209AD - SCOTS KING SUBMITS TO JOHN (Norham on Tweed)** In 1203 John held a conference at Norham with King William of Scotland, to keep peace, but tensions continued to mount. This year, John marched to Norham to prepare for an invasion of Scotland and William submitted to John.

**1210AD - ALEXANDER GIVES ALLEGIANCE (Alnwick)** Alexander, son of William, King of Scotland, gives his allegiance to John at Alnwick. In 1214 Alexander becomes the new king of Scotland as Alexander II.

**1212AD - JOHN SEEKS CORBRIDGE TREASURE (Corbridge on Tyne)** King John visits Corbridge in the hope of finding Roman treasure, which is said to be buried there. It follows similar searches in 1202 and 1208, but he finds nothing. Meanwhile, John confirms certain privileges held by the leading merchants at Newcastle. John also strengthens Newcastle castle.

**June 15 1215AD - MAGNA CARTA SIGNED (Runnymede, Thames Valley)** The Magna Carta is signed by King John in the presence of the barons . It reduces the excesses and abuses of the monarch's power. The Northumberland barons are still not happy and transfer allegiance from King John to Alexander, King of Scotland. Alexander raids England as far as Newcastle.

**1216AD - JOHN ATTACKS (Northumberland)** John burns Morpeth, Alnwick and Berwick and drives out the Scots, then attacks the Scottish lowlands. Cumbria is harried by the Scots, as John returns to England, and Bowes Castle in Teesdale is attacked by John's enemies.

**October 1216AD - KING HENRY III (England)** John dies and is succeeded by the nine year old Henry III. The Scots raid the north throughout the following year.

**1221AD - ANGLO SCOTTISH MARRIAGE (York)** Alexander II of Scotland marries Henry III's sister, Joan, at York.

**Circa 1230AD - WEARDALE HUNTING PARK (Upper Weardale)** The Bishop of Durham sets aside an extensive area of Weardale as a hunting ground. Meanwhile the official residence of the Archbishop of York has been established at Bishopthorpe, just outside York.

**1230AD - ROBIN HOOD IS SOUTH YORKSHIRE REBEL (South Yorkshire)** Although normally associated with Sherwood Forest in Nottinghamshire and the reign of Richard I, most of Robin Hood's activities took place in the South Yorkshire forests during Henry III's reign. Robin may also have been involved with smuggling at Robin Hood's Bay on the North Yorkshire coast.

**1234AD - PLAGUE AT NEWCASTLE (Newcastle)** Plague breaks out in populous Newcastle, killing many over three years.

**September 1237AD - THE SCOTTISH BORDER (York and Northumberland)** The Treaty of York recognises the rights of Scottish kings in Tynedale and Cumberland but not sovereignty. Henry III and Alexander II, King of Scotland, agree the Scottish border should be fixed along the Tweed-Esk-Solway line.

The Magna Carta of 1215

**1237AD - TIGHTROPE WALKER FALLS TO DEATH (Durham City)** A man employed by the Prior of Durham to entertain the monks is said to have fallen to his death while walking on a tightrope stretched between the central tower and a western tower of Durham Cathedral. Henry III informs the prior that he has destroyed his chances of becoming the next Bishop of Durham.

**August 14 1244AD - BORDER TRUCE AT NEWCASTLE (Newcastle)** Disputes over the exact course of the Scottish border arise but Kings Henry and Alexander meet at Newcastle to declare a truce. Alexander's troops have been threatening the border all year and had besieged Prudhoe Castle.

**1247AD - NEWCASTLE BLACKGATE (Newcastle)** Henry III builds Newcastle Blackgate, an extension of the castle.

**1248AD - TYNE BRIDGE FIRE (Newcastle)** A fire in Newcastle upon Tyne destroys the old Tyne bridge. It may have incorporated part of the old bridge of Roman times

**1249AD - FIXING THE BOUNDARY (Northumberland)** An attempt is made to fix a proper Scottish border. Border laws are established including the rights of masters to reclaim servants who seek refuge across the border within forty days.

**1249AD - WEARMOUTH RECTOR ESTABLISHES OXFORD'S FIRST COLLEGE (Sunderland and Oxford)** William, Rector of Wearmouth, establishes the first College at Oxford University, bequeathing money for the maintenance of 10 theological students.

**1251AD - NEWCASTLE MINT AND MAYOR (Newcastle)** Newcastle's civic status is increasing. In 1249 Henry III established a mint here and this year the Chief Bailiff earned the title of Mayor.

**December 25 1251AD - ANGLO SCOTTISH MARRIAGE (York)** Alexander III of Scotland marries Henry III's daughter Margaret at York. The marriage took place in St Mary's Abbey for a dowry of £5000 marks. Alex is ten years old, Margaret is 11.

**1263AD - BALLIOL COLLEGE (Oxford)** Balliol College is established at Oxford after John Baliol insulted Walter Kirkham, the Bishop of Durham, in a land dispute. As a penance Baliol agrees to finance students at Oxford to form what becomes Balliol College.

**1265AD - NEWCASTLE TOWN WALLS (Newcastle)** Newcastle is granted a right to construct defensive walls.

**1266AD - SCOTLAND GAINS VIKING ISLANDS (Isle of Man)** The Isles of Man and Hebrides are sold by Norway to Alexander of Scotland. Held by Norway since Viking times, they still speak Norse.

**1270AD - NEVILLES INHERIT MIDDLEHAM (Middleham)** Middleham Castle in Wensleydale passes into the hands of the powerful Neville family of Raby Castle, by marriage.

**1272AD - GREATHAM HOSPITAL (Greatham near Hartlepool)** Bishop Stitchill of Durham establishes a hospital at Greatham.

**1272AD - EDWARD I ASCENDS TO THE THRONE (England)** Edward I becomes the new King of England.

# Medieval Towns

1100AD to 1500AD

**MEDIEVAL TOWNS 1100AD TO 1500AD** Throughout medieval times the north was ravaged by Scottish raids, but this did not deter the development of early towns and boroughs. For many centuries York had been the only real city in the region in terms of population, but towns and cities like Durham were steadily growing, along with important river and sea ports like Hartlepool and Yarm.

**BARNARD CASTLE AND BISHOP AUCKLAND** Bishop Auckland was a borough by 1242 and grew around the 12th century manor of Auckland Palace. Most of the palace has a 17th century facade built around genuine medieval buildings. Barnard Castle was founded around 1093 by Guy Baliol and the town grew around the castle. His successor, Bernard Baliol, named the castle and the town.

**BERWICK - A WEALTHY SCOTTISH TOWN** Berwick reached the height of prosperity as a Scottish town in 1286 when its customs contributed to the Scottish Exchequer the equivalent of about a quarter of that of all England. The remarkable thing is that trade ever developed at all in this troubled border town, which changed hands between England and Scotland no less than 13 times between 1018 and 1482. The most important medieval features at Berwick were its castle and defensive walls, replaced in Elizabethan times.

**BILLINGHAM - A MEDIEVAL MANOR** Billingham was an important medieval manor and from at least 1229 the Bishop of Durham took customs from ships landing on the Tees here. From as early as 1314 a bridge and causeway existed here, linking Billingham to Norton across a swampy beck. A Friday market was granted to Sedgefield, north of Billingham, in 1312 and although a market was held at Billingham before 1497 it was illegally held and banned by the Bishop of Durham.

**CHESTER-LE-STREET AND ITS ANCHORAGE** The parish church here was once collegiate - administered by a semi-monastic college of canons. The church has an anchorage or cell where a succession of anchorites lived from 1383 until the reign of Henry VIII. Anchorites lived their whole life in solitary confinement.

**DARLINGTON - TWO BOROUGHS IN ONE** Knowledge of medieval Darlington is frustratingly limited and no borough charter survives. It was two separate medieval boroughs called Darlington Borough, and Bondgate-in-Darlington, although the Boldon Buke of 1183 treats them as one. The borough inhabitants lived freehold and Bondgate's tenants held land in bond-tenure. Darlington's Market Place and central street lay-out is medieval in origin but the most important medieval feature of Darlington is St Cuthbert's, a Collegiate Church administered by a vicar and four Prebends. A wool trade existed in Darlington from at least the 14th century, when John and William Durham of Darlington exported Darlington wool for the King, through Hartlepool.

**DURHAM - THE PRINCE BISHOP CITY** A market place existed on Palace Green until the 12th century when it was moved to its present location by Bishop Flambard to reduce fire risk to the cathedral. The city received a retrospective Charter in 1179 confirmed by the Pope. Medieval Hospitals were established at Kepier and Sherburn in the 12th century and a medieval manor house built at Crook Hall in 1386. All can still be seen.

**GUISBOROUGH, COATHAM AND CARGO FLEET** Guisborough grew around a priory founded by Robert Brus in 1120 and the town developed further after a market was granted by Henry III in 1263. Coatham, near Redcar, was a medieval port, where a market and fair were granted in 1257. Redcar was described as 'a poore fishing toune' in 1510. A medieval fishing port also existed on the Tees at a place called Caldecoates, now known as Cargo Fleet.

**HARTLEPOOL - BRUCES VERSUS THE BISHOP** Hartlepool was the most important medieval port in Durham but there was some dispute over whether it belonged to tenants of the King or Bishop. King John granted a Wednesday market and royal status in 1201 but the status was disputed by the Bishops of Durham who issued a new charter in 1230. The De Brus or Bruce family owned Hartlepool in medieval times and often disobeyed the bishops, claiming to be Royal tenants. Hartlepool was confiscated from Robert Bruce when he became King of Scotland in 1306 but he came back later to sack the town in 1312 and 1322. Edward II fled here after fighting Bruce at Bannockburn in 1314. Franciscan Grey Friars existed at Hartlepool from 1258.

**HULL AND LEEDS** Cloth making was recorded in Leeds village in 1275, but was already an established trade. Hull started life as Wyke village on the little River Hull. Edward I established a port here in 1293 renaming it Kingston upon Hull.

**MORPETH, ALNWICK AND HEXHAM** Morpeth was granted a market by John in 1199 and Alnwick received a market in 1291. Hexham and its abbey belonged to the Archbishops of York who built a jail here in 1330. Hexham 'Moot Hall' dates from around 1400.

**NORTH YORKSHIRE TOWNS** Northallerton had a medieval castle and still has a 12th century church. Bedale was granted a market in 1251, still held today. Other towns which saw growth in medieval times were Knaresborough, Richmond and Middleham, which developed around their Norman castles.

**STOCKTON AND THE BISHOPS** Stockton was the site of a medieval hall belonging to the Bishops of Durham, described as a castle in 1376. A chapel was established at Stockton in 1234 and a market established here in 1310 by Bishop Bek. Shipbuilding was recorded at Stockton in 1470 when a great ship was constructed for the Bishop of Durham. Built of wood, it required the working of 32 stones of iron into nails at six and a half pence per stone.

**YARM - A MEDIEVAL PORT** In 1205 King John's custom's toll from Yarm returned £43 compared to 17 shillings from the port of Coatham near Redcar. Yarm was the site of a market and fair from 1207 when Peter De Brus granted licenses for both and a Dominican Friary was established here in 1260. Until 1400 Yarm was linked to Egglescliffe in Durham by a ford. In that year Bishop Skirlaw of Durham built a bridge across the Tees which still stands today.

**YORK - A MEDIEVAL METROPOLIS** York was by far the largest town in the North in medieval times with a population of over 10,000 throughout the period. Two Norman castles were built here and the English government often moved to York in the fourteenth century during English campaigns against the Scots. The Shambles is a fine example of a medieval street but other medieval buildings include the Guildhall, King's Manor, Merchant Adventurer's Hall, Merchant Taylors hall, St Mary's Abbey, nineteen medieval churches and, of course, the Minster.

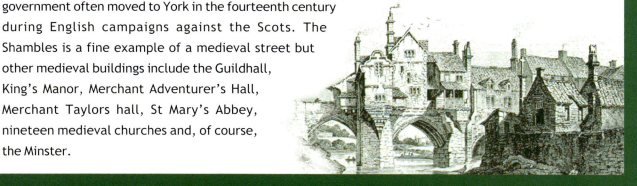

Medieval buildings on Elvet Bridge in Durham

# Newcastle Coal

## 1100AD to 1500AD

**NEWCASTLE COAL 1100AD TO 1500AD** Coal had been mined in the region since ancient times but became more widespread in the 13th and 14th centuries. Among those to profit from coal were the Bishops of Durham and merchants of Newcastle. As a sea port, Newcastle could benefit from the trade because shallow coal seams lay close to the Tyne. Ports like Hartlepool and Stockton lay outside the coalfield and Sunderland coal lay deep underground. Nevertheless Newcastle merchants still had to contend with the development of rival Tyneside ports.

**MINING MONKS AND BISHOPS** The earliest reference to Durham coal is in the Boldon Book of 1183 which records a coal miner at Escomb. Coal was often called 'Sea Coal' in medieval Durham because it was washed up on local beaches, but inland 'Sea coal' was mined at Hett near Spennymoor in 1298. The Prince Bishops owned rights to mining coal and lead in Durham but in 1303 the Bishop gave lesser landowners the right to mine their land. Durham monks exploited coal from at least the 14th century and in the 1350s owned or leased mines at Lumley, Rainton and Ferryhill. The first record of coal mining beneath the level of free drainage in Durham was at Moorhouse, near Rainton, where monks of Finchale provided a water pump for a mine.

**MEDIEVAL COAL MINES** Medieval mines were usually shallow bell pits, dug downwards from the surface and then outwards into the coal seam in the shape of a bell. Coal and miners were hoisted up and down in the manner of a bucket in a well. Mine roofs only collapsed if the 'colliers' burrowed too far outwards, which is presumably what caused deaths in coal mines at Whickham and Thrislington in 1329.

**NEWCASTLE'S COAL TRADES** In 1286 Newcastle was the leading English port for exporting leather from local livestock. The border wars that ravaged the countryside destroyed this trade, but coal was beginning to dominate. In 1291, 80 quarters of coal were sent to Corfe Castle in Dorset from Newcastle and coal

An illustration of a typical bell pit

was shipped to London from at least 1305. Newcastle's walls were falling into decay but still protected the town from the Scots and enabled trade to continue. Newcastle was the fourth wealthiest town in England by 1334, after London, Bristol and York, and the eleventh largest in 1372 with 2,637 tax payers.

**COALS TO NEWCASTLE** Recorded coal mines supplying coal to Newcastle existed at Elswick, Winlaton, Heworth and the Town Moor. By 1378 Newcastle shipped 15,000 tons of coal per year and exported coal to many parts of Europe, as well as importing iron ore from Sweden. In 1452 trades included the Keelmen who ferried the coal to collier ships in the centre of the Tyne. The phrase 'Coals to Newcastle', meaning unnecessary pursuit, was first recorded in 1538.

**NEWCASTLE'S CREEKS AND PORTS** Newcastle was the most important medieval port in the region, demonstrated no more so by the establishment of the Society of Masters and Mariners of Newcastle at Trinity House in 1492. Their jurisdiction covered every single port and creek from Whitby to Holy Island. Shipping and shipbuilding were important at Newcastle and the town was building ships from at least 1296 when a galley was completed for King Edward's fleet.

**GATESHEAD DISPUTES** Gateshead belonged to the Bishops of Durham but was often claimed by the Newcastle merchants as their own. In 1334 King Edward banned Newcastle's mayor and bailiffs from mooring ships here and in 1344 the Bishop of Durham prosecuted Newcastle merchants for wrecking his quays at Gateshead and Whickham. Disputes over the Tyne Bridge were another problem. In 1415 the Bishop obtained a suit from the King's Court recovering his third of the bridge taken from him by the Newcastle mayor. The problem was that the Bishops did not always maintain their side of the bridge and this was damaging Newcastle's trade. Newcastle would not succeed in annexing Gateshead until the sixteenth century.

**NORTH AND SOUTH SHIELDS - MONKS VERSUS MERCHANTS** Germanus of Tynemouth Priory created North Shields port in 1225. It traded peacefully until 1267 when Newcastle merchants attacked the inhabitants and seized a ship. Newcastle saw the port as a threat and in 1292 gained support from Edward I, who ordered the dismantling of the North Shields jetties. The king objected because part of

Newcastle's revenue belonged to him while the North Shields revenue belonged entirely to the Priors. In 1303 Edward III banned markets, fairs and the unloading and loading of ships by the Tynemouth Priors. In 1258 the Newcastle merchants persuaded the Priors of Durham not to develop port facilities at South Shields and in 1303 Edward III banned loading and unloading of ships here by the Durham Priors.

**NORTH SHIELDS FISHING AND COAL** North Shields fishing port facilities were banned in 1303 and re-established in 1390 but trading in coal and other commodities remained illegal. By 1429 there were 14 fish quays and 200 houses at North Shields where fishermen ventured as far as Iceland in boats and cobles. Coal trading was restored to North Shields in 1446 and Tynemouth Priory could ship coal without reference to Newcastle, but it was banned in 1530 and once again restricted to Newcastle.

**SUNDERLAND COAL** Sunderland, more usually known in medieval times as Wearmouth, received a charter from Bishop Pudsey in 1179 giving its merchants the same rights as Newcastle, but Sunderland never really developed as a medieval port. This was due to the difficulties of developing a port in the Wear gorge and the fact that the Wearside coal was deep and inaccessible. Nevertheless Sunderland was shipping cargoes of coal to Whitby Abbey in 1396 and ships were built here from 1346 by Thomas Menvill of Hendon.

**MEDIEVAL IRON AND COAL** Associated with coal mining was iron mining, an important medieval trade recorded at Muggleswick in Durham in 1298. Most iron was made by heating iron ore in simple blast furnaces called Bloomeries using charcoal made from the wood of the extensive medieval forests. Coal was not normally used because its sulphur content caused the iron to be brittle. In 1306 a petition was handed to parliament against the Bishop of Durham for his destruction of Weardale forests for charcoal for iron bloomeries.

**MEDIEVAL SALT AND COAL** In 1290 Robert de Brus granted permission to John Rumundebi to make salt at Hart near Hartlepool and in the following century large quantities of salt were traded at nearby Cowpen and Greatham. South Shields became the most important salt making centre in the region from around 1448. Salt making involved heating huge quantities of sea-water brine in large salt pans using coal.

# Bruce and Baliol

## 1272AD to 1371AD

Robert the Bruce

**BRUCE AND BALIOL 1272AD TO 1371AD** At the forefront of Scottish raids on Northern England in the thirteenth and fourteenth century was King Robert the Bruce, a member of a family of Norman origin which originally settled at Hartlepool and Skelton in Cleveland. Robert was succeeded by his son David Bruce in 1329 but both kings were challenged by their rivals John and Edward Baliol, Scottish kings who were the son and grandson of Hugh Baliol of Barnard Castle.

**November 1272AD - KING EDWARD I (England)** Edward I becomes King of England.

**1291AD - EDWARD SELECTS SCOTTISH KING (Berwick Castle)** A meeting at Berwick decides who is Scottish King. Twelve claimants attend including Robert Bruce and John Baliol. Edward I of England is host and appoints Baliol, son of Hugh Baliol of Barnard Castle, as King.

**1296AD - BISHOP ACQUIRES TEESDALE (Teesdale)** Scots invade Northumberland under the rebellious Baliol but are defeated at Dunbar in April. Edward carries off the Scottish coronation stone from Scone and Anthony Bek, Bishop of Durham, seizes Baliol's estates in Teesdale.

**1297AD - BRAVEHEART ATTACKS (Northumberland)** Scotsman William Wallace (Braveheart) takes up the Scottish cause against English domination in Scotland. He attacks Northumberland, burning Hexham, Corbridge and Ryton but is driven back from Newcastle.

**1298AD - EDWARD DEFEATS BRAVEHEART (Falkirk)** Government moves to York while Edward defeats the Scots under Wallace at Falkirk. He was assisted in battle by Bek, the Bishop of Durham.

**1307AD - BRUCE LOSES HARTLEPOOL (Hartlepool)** Last year Robert Bruce became King of Scotland. King Edward confiscates Hartlepool from Bruce and takes Teesdale from Bishop Bek, which he gives to Guy Beauchamp. The English invade Scotland to subdue Bruce but Edward dies at Burgh on Sands in Cumbria during the campaign. Edward II becomes king.

**1309AD - PERCYS BUY ALNWICK FROM BISHOP (Alnwick)** The Percy family purchase Alnwick from Bishop Bek of Durham. It may not have rightfully been his to sell.

**1312AD - KING'S LOVER CAPTURED (Scarborough)** King Edward gives Scarborough Castle to his male lover Piers Gaveston who is later captured by rebels and executed.

**1312AD - ROBERT BRUCE ATTACKS NORTH (Durham and Hartlepool)** Bruce burns and plunders Durham in a raid as far south as Hartlepool. The men of Northumberland pay him £2000 in a truce at Hexham.

**1312AD - GOVERNMENT AT YORK AGAIN (York)** Government is moved to York while Edward fights the rebellious Earl of Lancaster, who builds a stronghold at Dunstanburgh in Northumberland. On December 12 Robert Bruce fails to take Berwick from the English after a dog barked and alerted the town guards.

**June 24 1314AD - BANNOCKBURN (Bannockburn, Scotland)** Bruce invades England and regains Tynedale, which declares him king. On June 24, the English are routed at Bannockburn. Edward flees to Berwick by boat and then to Hartlepool and York. Scottish raids reach as far as Swaledale.

**1319AD - ENGLISH DEFEATED IN NORTH YORKSHIRE (Myton on Swale)** Edward's army of 8000 fail to capture Berwick. The English take flight and Scots raid as far as York. An army headed by Nicholas Flemming, Mayor of York, is defeated at Myton on Swale by the Scots under the Earl of Moray.

**March 1322AD - EDWARD IN BATTLE (Boroughbridge and Byland, North Yorks)** Edward's forces under Andrew Harclay defeat the Earl of Lancaster at Boroughbridge in March. Lancaster has supported Robert Bruce. The Scots plunder Stockton and Hartlepool and on October 14 Edward II is almost captured during a raid at Byland.

**1323AD - LIMBS DISPLAYED AT NEWCASTLE AND YORK (Newcastle)** Andrew Harclay is executed for visiting Robert Bruce in Scotland to make peace without Edward's consent. Harclay's limbs are displayed on York bridge, at Carlisle and Newcastle Castle

**1324AD - PEACE TREATY FAILS (Bishopthorpe, York)** A peace treaty drawn up at York last year between England and Scotland loses the support of Bruce.

**1325AD - DURHAM DEFENCES (Dalden near Seaham)** Jordan Dalden is granted a licence to build a tower at Dalden for protection against the Scots. Meanwhile Durham's defensive walls are restored.

**1327AD - TEN THOUSAND SCOTTISH SHOES (Weardale)** Edward III becomes King of England. Bruce invades Northumberland and Durham and evades Edward in Weardale where a Scottish camp leaves behind 10,000 pairs of shoes and many other items. Edward encamps in Weardale for a month hoping to encounter the elusive Scots.

**7 June 1329AD - BRUCE DEAD (Cardross, Strathclyde)** Robert Bruce of Scotland dies and is succeeded by his son David II.

**1331AD - WARKWORTH PERCYS (Warkworth)** Edward III sells Warkworth to the Percys.

**24 September 1332AD - EDWARD BALIOL OF SCOTLAND (Scone, Scotland)** Edward Baliol becomes King of Scotland. He will be deposed and restored a number of times during his reign.

**July 19 1333AD - HALLIDON HILL (Halidon Hill, Berwick)** Baliol, the deposed King of Scotland, besieges Berwick with the support of Edward of England. The English capture Berwick and the Lothians.

**August 18 1335AD - SCOTS ATTACK HARTLEPOOL (Hartlepool)** Scots invade the Tees valley via Cumberland as far as Hartlepool. Hartlepudlians take refuge at sea. Scots resent the rule of Edward Baliol, an English puppet.

**1338AD - ANGLO-SCOTTISH JOUSTING (Berwick)** A jousting match is held between Scotland and England at Berwick in the presence of King Edward. The English kill two Scots, the Scots one Englishman.

**August 15 1339AD - NEWCASTLE FLOOD (Newcastle)** A flash flood kills 167 people and destroys many quayside homes.

**1342AD - DAVID BRUCE TAKES DURHAM (Newcastle and Durham City)** Baliol is deposed as King of Scotland and replaced by David II who attacks Newcastle but cannot break the walls. David seizes Durham after a seven day siege before returning to Scotland.

**August 1346AD - HARTLEPOOL PROVIDES SHIPS FOR CALAIS SIEGE (Hartlepool)** Newcastle, Hartlepool and Bamburgh provide ships for the siege of Calais following victory over the French at Crecy. Newcastle provides 17 ships, 314 men; Hartlepool 5 ships, 145 men; Bamburgh 1 ship, 9 men

**October 17 1346AD - BATTLE AT NEVILLES CROSS (Durham City)** Scots under David II attack Hexham and Blanchland and head for Durham. Assembling at Bearpark they battle with English forces at Nevilles Cross. Scots outnumber the English but are defeated. David is discovered hiding under a bridge on the River Browney and is held prisoner for eleven years.

**1349AD - NEWCASTLE FIRE (Newcastle)** A great fire destroys many houses. Meanwhile, the Black Death is sweeping the North and in some cases wipes out entire villages.

**October 17 1357AD - DAVID BRUCE RANSOMED (Berwick)** King David II is handed over to the Scots for ransom by the English in the Treaty of Berwick. The Scots never pay the fee.

**1371AD - KING DAVID BRUCE DIES (Edinburgh)** David II, son of Robert Bruce, dies at Edinburgh Castle and is succeeded by Robert II, a less effective king, who reigns until 1290.

Nevilles Cross

# Hotspur and the Percys

1377AD to 1461AD

Warkworth Castle, Northumberland. Harry Hotspur's Castle

**HOTSPUR AND THE PERCYS 1377AD TO 1461AD** The Percys were the most powerful Northumberland barons in the Middle Ages and in the north were matched only by the Nevilles of Durham and Yorkshire. As Earls of Northumberland they were chief defenders of the Border and held the great Northumberland castles at Alnwick, Warkworth, Bamburgh and Prudhoe. The most famous Percy was 'Harry Hotspur', who fought against the Scottish Earl of Douglas at the Battle of Otterburn in 1388.

**1377AD - PERCY BECOMES EARL (England)** At Richard II's coronation, the Yorkshire based baron, Henry Percy, becomes 'first' Earl of Northumberland, a title revived from Anglo-Saxon times.

**1378AD - NEVILLE BUILDS RABY CASTLE (Staindrop and Raby)** John Neville is granted a licence to build a castle at Raby by Bishop Thomas Hatfield. A market and an annual fair are granted to nearby Staindrop.

**1381AD - PERCYS OF PRUDHOE (Northumberland coast)** Last year John of Gaunt, Earl of Lancaster, Lieutenant of the Marches, inherited Dunstanburgh Castle. This year the Percys inherited Prudhoe Castle.

**1384AD - SCOTS SEIZE BERWICK (Northumberland and Durham)** Ford Castle is taken by the Scots. Wark and Cornhill Tower are destroyed before the Scots raid Durham and Cumberland.

**August 6 1388AD - SCOTS ATTACK NEWCASTLE AND DURHAM (Newcastle and Brancepeth)** Scots under William Douglas raid Durham as far as Brancepeth. On return the Scots engage in a skirmish at Newcastle. English forces under Harry 'Hotspur' Percy were safe behind Newcastle's walls.

**August 19 1388AD - BATTLE OF OTTERBURN (Otterburn, Redesdale, Northumberland)** While the Scots under Douglas encamp at Otterburn on return to Scotland, Harry Hotspur headed north from Newcastle to attack them. Hot-headed Hotspur does not wait for the Bishop of Durham's troops to join him. In the darkness Hotspur's troops attack Scottish servants and camp followers by mistake. This group fight back and alert the main force of Scots. Hotspur loses over a thousand troops in the battle, Douglas only 200. Hotspur's men flee but Douglas is killed despite his victory. Hotspur and his brother Ralph Percy are taken prisoner by the Scots and are later released on ransom.

**1389AD - LUMLEY CASTLE (Lumley, County Durham)** Tynemouth priory is plundered by Scots under the Earl of Murray. Meanwhile Lumley Castle is being built by Ralph, Lord Lumley.

**1397AD - RABY NEVILLES BECOME EARLS OF WESTMORLAND (Raby)** The Nevilles of Raby Castle gain the title Earls of Westmorland.

**1399AD to 1400AD - RICHARD II IMPRISONED AT KNARESBOROUGH (Knaresborough)** King Richard II, criticised for 'favouritism', is imprisoned by Parliament at Knaresborough Castle and is later moved to Pontefract Castle where he is murdered or starved to death. Henry IV, son of John of Gaunt, Duke of Lancaster, usurps the throne with the support of Henry Percy, Earl of Northumberland. King Henry raids Scotland in the summer.

**1402AD - BATTLE OF HUMBLETON HILL (Newcastle and Wooler)** Scots under Earl Archibold Douglas attack Newcastle before retreating. They are stopped by the English under Earl Percy at Humbleton Hill near Wooler and are defeated in battle. Later, the Percys fall into disagreement with the English king over Scottish prisoners taken in the battle and rebel against him.

**July 21 1403AD - HOTSPUR KILLED (Shrewsbury and York)** Harry Hotspur Percy is killed in battle at Shrewsbury fighting against Henry IV. Hotspur had raised a rebellion in Cheshire but the king intercepted him before he could join the forces of his father, the Earl of Northumberland. King Henry orders that Hotspur's head be sent to his widow in Northumberland. On August 11 Hotspur's father, Henry Percy, submits to the king at York.

**June 5 1405AD - SCROPE EXECUTED (York)** Earl Henry Percy joins a rebellion against the king organised by Richard Scrope, Archbishop of York, but Scrope is captured and executed at York. Percy takes refuge in Scotland after the rebellion is defeated.

**1406AD - SCOTTISH KING CAPTURED (Flamborough Head, Yorkshire)** King James I of Scotland, aged eleven, is captured by pirates off Flambourough Head. James was heading south to safety in France. James is imprisoned in various parts of England for the next eighteen years.

**1408AD - PERCY LIMBS ON TYNE BRIDGE (Bramham Moor and Newcastle)** Percy, Earl of Northumberland, is killed in battle at Bramham Moor in West Yorkshire fighting Henry IV. Percy's limbs are placed on the Tyne Bridge at Newcastle as a warning to rebels. Hotspur's son Henry succeeds as Earl.

**1413AD - HENRY V CROWNED (England)** Henry IV dies and is succeeded by his son King Henry V.

**July 22  1414AD - BATTLE AT YEAVERING (Northumberland)** The Scots are defeated in a battle at Yeavering near Wooler, by Sir Robert Umfraville.

**1417AD - PERCY IS BORDER WARDEN (Northumberland)** Henry V appoints Earl Henry Percy as Warden of the East and Middle Marches. He will have responsibility for maintaining control in the Northumberland sections of the Border.

**1417AD - WOMEN ARRESTED FOR DRESSING AS MEN AT CUTHBERT'S SHRINE (Durham Cathedral and Newcastle)** Two Newcastle women were arrested after dressing up as men to visit St. Cuthbert's shrine at Durham Cathedral. According to Benedictine rules, women are not allowed to approach the shrine. As punishment Matilda Burgh and Margaret Usher have to walk in a procession at Newcastle dressed in men's apparel.

**1419AD - SCOTS CAPTURE WARK (Northumberland)** Scots capture Wark on Tweed Castle from Richard Ogle.

**1422AD - HENRY VI ASCENDS TO THRONE (England)** King Henry V dies and is succeeded by his son Henry VI as King of England. He is the third monarch from the Royal House of Lancaster.

**March 28  1424AD - HOSTAGES EXCHANGED (Durham City)** James, King of Scotland, an English prisoner since 1406, is given freedom in exchange for English hostages at Durham City. The Treaty of Durham is signed in the hope of bringing peace to the Borders. James spends a month in the hospitality of the Bishop of Durham before he is escorted to the Abbey of Melrose for the exchange.

**1428AD - ALNWICK PLUNDERED (Northumberland)** Alnwick is plundered by the Scots.

**1429AD - CATHEDRAL TOWER HIT BY LIGHTNING (Durham City)** After a dreadful storm, a bolt of lightning hit the belfry tower of Durham Cathedral today, causing a fire.

**December 15  1430AD - TRUCE RENEWED (York)** The Anglo-Scottish truce is renewed.

**1434AD - TOWN WALLS FOR ALNWICK (Northumberland)** The King gives permission for town walls to be built at Alnwick.

**September 10  1436AD - DOUGLAS DEFEATS PERCY AT BATTLE AT PIPER DENE (Northumberland)** Scots, under William Douglas, Earl of Angus, defeat the English under Henry Percy in a minor skirmish.

**1448AD - HENRY VISITS CUTHBERT'S SHRINE (Durham City)** Henry VI makes a pilgrimage to the shrine of St Cuthbert at Durham.

**1455AD - EARL KILLED AT ST. ALBANS (Hertfordshire)** Henry Percy, Earl of Northumberland, is killed in battle at St Alban's, fighting for the Lancastrian cause. It is the first battle in the Wars of the Roses.

**1460AD - KING KILLED AT ROXBURGH (Roxburgh near Kelso)** At the Siege of Roxburgh Castle James II, King of Scotland, is killed by an exploding canon.

Alnwick Castle. The lion is a symbol of the Percy family

# Wars of the Roses

1455AD to 1508AD

King Richard III and his queen Anne Neville of Middleham Castle

**WARS OF THE ROSES AND HENRY VII 1455AD TO 1508AD** The Wars of the Roses were fought between the Royal Dynasties called Lancaster and York and have nothing to do with rivalry between the counties of Yorkshire and Lancashire. The weak and insane Henry VI was challenged and defeated by the 'Yorkist' Edward, who was victorious at Towton near York in 1461. King Henry and his Queen, Margaret, were exiled and although Margaret managed to capture Alnwick, Dunstanburgh and Bamburgh Castle she lost three battles in Northumberland. Her only hope came when the powerful Richard Neville of Middleham in North Yorkshire switched his allegiance to the Lancastrians, but the Yorkists remained in power until the reign of Henry Tudor in 1485.

**21 December 1460AD - BATTLE OF WAKEFIELD (Near Wakefield)** Richard, Duke of York, is defeated and killed by Lancastrian forces near Wakefield. Richard takes refuge in nearby Sandal castle but is killed when he finally emerges. Yorkist support will now focus on Richard's son Edward.

**30 December 1460AD - DUKE'S HEAD DISPLAYED AT YORK (York)** Richard, the Duke of York's head is displayed on Micklegate Bar in York, topped with a paper crown as a sign of mockery.

**March 29 1461AD - EDWARD IV VICTORIOUS AT TOWTON (Yorkshire)** Yorkists are victorious in a heavy snowstorm at the Battle of Towton (near York and Leeds) and Edward of York is crowned Edward IV. Lancastrian supporter Earl Henry Percy is among those killed. The Lancastrian castle at Alnwick is acquired by John Neville, brother of 'Warwick'.

**October 25 1462AD - LANCASTRIANS CAPTURE BAMBURGH AND ALNWICK (Northumberland)** After a long siege, the Lancastrian, Margaret of Anjou, queen of the deposed Henry VI, captures Bamburgh and Alnwick Castle with the support of the French and Scots.

**January 1463AD - NEVILLE ATTACKS ALNWICK (Alnwick)** Richard Neville, of Middleham castle, besieges the Lancastrians in Alnwick castle, who eventually retreat, despite Scottish reinforcements.

**April 3   1463AD - ROSES BATTLE AT HEXHAM (Hexham)** The first Battle of Hexham takes place between Yorkists under John Neville, Lord Montagu, and the Lancastrian supporters of Margaret. The owner of Bamburgh, Ralph Percy, switches allegiance to the Lancastrians. The Lancastrians are defeated and flee to Scotland.

**April 25   1464AD - ROSES BATTLE AT HEDGELEY MOOR (Northumberland)** A battle takes place at Hedgeley Moor, near Wooler. The Yorkist, John Neville, is attacked by Lancastrians. Neville defeats his attackers, who include Sir Ralph Percy and Sir Ralph Grey.

**May 5  1464AD - ANOTHER ROSES  BATTLE AT HEXHAM (Hexham)** A second Wars of the Roses battle takes place at Hexham. The Lancastrians, under Margaret, are defeated again by John Neville.

**May   1464AD - NORTHUMBERLAND'S LANCASTRIAN CASTLES SURRENDER (Bamburgh, Dunstanburgh and Alnwick.)** The Lancastrian held castles of Bamburgh, Dunstanburgh and Alnwick surrender to King Edward IV.

**May 27  1464AD - NEVILLE EARL OF NORTHUMBERLAND (York)** John Neville, Lord Montagu, is appointed as Earl of Northumberland.

**July   1464AD - SCOTS RETREAT FROM NORHAM (Northumberland)** James III of Scotland retreats from Norham-on-Tweed after the arrival of John Neville and Richard Neville, the Earl of Warwick. James had invaded England to support the Lancastrians.

**1465AD - HENRY CAPTURED (Lancashire)** Exiled King Henry VI is captured at Clitherhoe by the Yorkists.

The Middleham Jewel, believed to have belonged to Richard III

**1465AD - FUTURE KING LIVES IN WENSLEYDALE (Middleham Castle, Wensleydale)** Richard, Duke of Gloucester, (later Richard III) lives at Middleham Castle. It is the home of Richard Neville, known as 'Warwick the Kingmaker', whose brother George Neville has just been appointed Archbishop of York.

**1467AD - NEVILLE AND KING FALL OUT (England)** Richard Neville of Middleham Castle falls out with Edward IV over foreign policy. Neville switches allegiance to the Lancastrians. The king dismisses Richard's brother, George Neville, as Archbishop of York because of his Yorkist support.

**August 1469AD - EDWARD IV IMPRISONED AT MIDDLEHAM (Middleham, Wensleydale)** King Edward is imprisoned at Middleham Castle by Richard Neville, Earl of Warwick. Edward was captured by Richard's brother George, in Northamptonshire. In September, Edward is thought to have escaped from captivity in Yorkshire, but he may actually have been released by Richard Neville.

**1471AD - NEVILLE THE KINGMAKER KILLED (Barnet, London)** Richard Neville, 'the Kingmaker' of Middleham Castle, is killed fighting against King Edward at the Battle of Barnet, near London. Meanwhile, former King Henry VI is killed during imprisonment in the Tower of London

**1477AD - RICHARD GAINS BARNEY (Barnard Castle)** Richard, Duke of Gloucester (later Richard III), takes possession of Barnard Castle. It becomes one of his favourite residences.

**August 24 1482AD - RICHARD TAKES BERWICK (Northumberland)** Richard, Duke of Gloucester, takes Berwick from the Scots, without resistance. Berwick has remained in English hands ever since.

**1483AD - RICHARD III LOCKS PRINCES IN THE TOWER (The Tower of London)** Edward IV dies and is succeeded by his son Edward V, who becomes king. The young Edward is never actually crowned, but is imprisoned in the Tower of London with his brother, by Richard who becomes King Richard III. The two princes are never seen again.

**April 9 1484AD - KING'S SON DIES AT MIDDLEHAM (North Yorkshire)** Richard III's only son dies at Middleham Castle in North Yorkshire.

**July 1484AD - RICHARD SETS UP NORTHERN COUNCIL (West Yorkshire)** Richard III has set up a northern council at Sandal, Yorkshire, under his nephew John de la Pole, the Earl of Lincoln.

**August 22 1485AD - HENRY TUDOR IS KING (Leicestershire)** The Battle of Bosworth Field takes place in Leicestershire. Richard III is killed and the victorious Welshman, Henry Tywdr (Tudor), is crowned Henry VII, King of England.

**1487AD - HENRY TUDOR STAYS AT NEWCASTLE (Newcastle)** King Henry VII stays for some time in Newcastle while investigating persons involved in a rebellion against him. Last year Henry visited York for the same purpose.

**1496AD - CASTLE DESTROYED (Northumberland)** King James IV of Scotland destroys Twizel Castle in Northumberland. James invaded to support the Perkin Warbeck rebellion, a failed attempt by the Yorkists to overthrow Henry Tudor.

**July 1503AD - KING'S DAUGHTER STAYS AT DURHAM (Durham City)** Margaret Tudor, the eldest daughter of Henry VII, who is due to marry the King of Scotland, has stayed at Durham where she has been entertained by Bishop Fox in the Great Hall of the castle.

**1503AD - MARGARET AT BERWICK (Newcastle)** Margaret Tudor has arrived in Berwick on her way to Scotland to marry King James IV. She also visited Northallerton, Darlington, Durham, Newcastle, Morpeth and Alnwick during her journey north to Edinburgh.

**1508AD - RENOVATIONS AT BERWICK (Northumberland)** Henry VII encourages renovations to fortifications at Berwick.

# Reform and Rebellion

1509AD to 1603AD

Queen Elizabeth I

**REFORM AND REBELLION 1509AD TO 1603AD** From the late fourteenth century individuals, like the North Yorkshire born John Wycliffe (1320-1384), challenged the rule of the Roman Catholic church and set in motion the religious changes which resulted in King Henry VIII's break with Rome. King Henry is best known for his six wives, but it was the refusal of the Pope to annul Henry's first marriage that led to the establishment of the Protestant Church of England. Henry destroyed the old church and its monasteries and although the north rebelled in the Pilgrimage of Grace, it was heavily crushed. Henry's daughter Queen Elizabeth I (1558-1603) likewise crushed the Catholic Rising of the North in 1569. The hopes of the Catholic North in Tudor times were temporarily raised by the Marys - 'Bloody Mary', Queen of England (1553-1558) and Mary, Queen of Scots (1583-1586).

**1509AD - KING HENRY VIII CROWNED (Britain)** Henry VIII is crowned King of England in succession to his father Henry VII

**September 9  1513AD - BATTLE OF FLODDEN FIELD (Northumberland)** The English, under the Earl of Surrey, have defeated and killed King James at the battle of Flodden Field, near Branxton, in North Northumberland. The Scots lost 12earls, 15 lords, an archbishop and a number of clan chiefs.

**1523AD - WOLSEY BISHOP OF DURHAM (North)** Henry VIII's chief adviser, Cardinal Thomas Wolsey, becomes Bishop of Durham. He is already Archbishop of York (Since 1514) but has yet to visit his diocese there. His favourite Rushes are planted at Auckland Castle ready for his appearance but he never visits Durham.

**1530AD - WOLSEY ARRESTED AT YORK (York)** Wolsey is arrested at York on the orders of King Henry VIII, on suspicion of treason. Wolsey only came north to be Archbishop after he was stripped of the position of Lord Chancellor by King Henry. Wolsey later dies at Leicester, during transportation to London for imprisonment.

**1532AD to 1534AD - ENGLISH RAVAGE SCOTLAND (Northumberland)** The Earl of Northumberland ravages the Scottish Middle March in 1532 and in 1534. In 1534 the English destroy 192 Scottish bastles, towers and churches.

**1536AD - PILGRIMAGE OF GRACE (North)** The Pilgrimage of Grace takes place. It is a Northern rebellion of Catholics against Henry VIII's anti-Catholic reforms, with marches and demonstrations centred on Lincolnshire and York. Rebels, including gentry and commoners, march from throughout Yorkshire to York to hear the address of pilgrimage leader Robert Aske. Support also comes from Barnard Castle and Bishop Auckland and other places further north. On December 8, the Duke of Norfolk, on behalf of Henry, promises the rebels a pardon. The Duke's promises were designed to subdue the rebellion and will not be kept. Robert Aske and the Abbot of of Jervaulx are among those who will be executed in the following years.

**1538AD - COVERDALESMAN TRANSLATES BIBLE (England)** Miles Coverdale, of Coverdale, Yorkshire, translates the Bible into English.

**December 31  1538AD - COUNCIL OF THE NORTH MOVES TO DARLINGTON (Darlington)** The Council of the North has been moved to Darlington, to keep peace and administer the affairs of the Border Country.

**1538AD to 1540AD - MONASTERIES DISSOLVED (England)** Wealthy monasteries, like Rievaulx and Whitby, are stripped of their wealth and power by King Henry. Monks are pensioned off and the monasteries and their land are sold to whoever wants them.

**November 24  1542AD - BATTLE OF SOLWAY MOSS (Cumbria-Scotland)** James V and 10,000 Scots are defeated by a small army of English.

**1544AD - COUNCIL MOVES TO BARNEY (Barnard Castle)** The Council of the North established at Darlington in 1538 has moved to Barnard Castle because of the threat from plague.

**27 Feb 1545AD - BATTLE AT ANCRUM MOOR (Scotland)** Henry VIII's forces are scattered by the Scots on Ancrum Mooor.

**1547AD - KING EDWARD VI (England)** Henry VIII's ten year old son Edward becomes king of England. He rules under the protectorship of John Dudley, Earl of Warwick (later Duke of Northumberland).

**1553AD - NEWCASTLE TRIES TO ANNEX GATESHEAD (Newcastle)** Newcastle annexes Gateshead from the Bishop of Durham but it terminates on the death of Edward VI. A plan to establish a Bishopric at Newcastle out of part of the Bishopric of Durham is also ended by Edward's death. Nicholas Ridley would have been appointed as Bishop.

**1553AD - BLOODY MARY IS QUEEN (England)** Mary I, Roman Catholic daughter of Henry VIII and Catherine of Aragon, becomes Queen of England. She becomes known as Bloody Mary because of her ruthless persecution of Protestants. The Northumbrian born Nicholas Ridley is one of many burnt at the stake in Oxford (1555).

**1558AD - QUEEN ELIZABETH (Britain)** Elizabeth I ascends to the throne of England following the death of Mary, Queen of England. She is the daughter of Henry VIII's second wife, Anne Boleyn, who was beheaded in 1563.

**February 22 1560AD - TREATY OF BERWICK (Berwick Northumberland)** A treaty is signed between English and Scottish Protestants agreeing to expel French Catholic forces established north of the border.

**1561AD - FIRST PROTESTANT BISHOP AT DURHAM (Durham City)** James Pilkington is the first Protestant Bishop of Durham. He removes all superstitious books and statues of idolatry from the cathedral.

**1568AD - SCOTS QUEEN HELD IN WENSLEYDALE (Wensleydale)** Mary, Queen of Scots, seen as a dangerous focus for Catholic rebellion, has been imprisoned on the orders of her cousin Queen Elizabeth. Mary is imprisoned at Castle Bolton in Wensleydale for a time, but will be held in many other places throughout the north in the coming years.

**November 1569AD - RISING OF THE NORTH (Raby Castle and Brancepeth)** The Nevilles of Durham and Percys of Northumberland plot to overthrow Elizabeth I and reinstate Roman Catholicism in 'The Rising of the North'.

Cardinal Wolsey became Archbishop of York in 1514 and Bishop of Durham in 1523

Their rebellion supports Thomas Howard, Duke of Norfolk. The rising is planned at meetings in Brancepeth and Raby Castle. The rebels capture Durham and reinstate Catholic mass in the cathedral before marching south to Tutbury, near Nottingham, where Mary Queen of Scots is imprisoned. During the journey many rebels lose nerve and flee. George Bowes, a steward of Elizabeth, defends his castle at Barnard Castle against the rebels but is defeated.

**December 8 1569AD - ROOKHOPE RYDE (Weardale and Tynedale)** Tynedale mosstroopers raid Weardale while many Weardale men assist with the Rising of the North. The remaining Weardale men see them off.

**November 1572AD - REBELS EXECUTED THROUGHOUT THE NORTH (Durham City and Newcastle)** The Rising of the North gained support throughout the North but is a failure and many of the rebels flee to Scotland. Brancepeth and Raby are confiscated from the Nevilles by the Crown and sixty persons are executed at Durham in 1570 for their part in the rising. Many other executions occurred throughout the North in nearly every town and village from Wetherby to Newcastle. This year Charles Neville of Raby was executed at York for his major part in the rising

**1586AD - MARY EXECUTED (Fotheringhay Castle, Northamptonshire)** Mary, Queen of Scots is executed at Fotheringhay Castle on Elizabeth's orders.

**1594AD - PRIESTS AND CATHOLICS EXECUTED (Durham City, Newcastle, Gateshead and Darlington)** Four years ago three Roman Catholic priests were executed at Durham. They are among the first of many executed throughout the reign of Elizabeth I, who has forbidden Roman Catholic Priests from practising in the country. Last year, a member of the Lambton family was executed at Newcastle for being a Roman Catholic priest. This year, John Speed, a layman, was executed at Durham for assisting Roman Catholic priests. John Bost, a Roman Catholic priest, has also been executed in the city. Similar executions take place at Gateshead and Darlington.

**1603AD - ELIZABETH DIES** Elizabeth I has died and is succeeded by James VI of Scotland, son of Mary, Queen of Scots. James becomes the first king of both England and Scotland.

# The Border Reivers

1400AD to 1611AD

## THE BORDER REIVERS 1400AD TO 1611AD

**THE BORDER MARCHES** Tudor times were an age of culture and discovery, but in Northumberland lawlessness ruled. Constant war forced people to live by raiding and thieving and on both sides of the border. 'Border Reiver' families, like the Armstrongs, Robsons and Charltons, raided and thieved from each other.

**THE TYNEDALE LIBERTY** From Norman times Tynedale was an independent Liberty, often held by the Scottish Kings. The Liberty was abolished by Henry VIII in 1495 and from this time the Tynedale clans or 'Graynes', like Robson, Milburn and Charlton, increasingly became a law unto themselves. Even Tynedale priests were described as 'evil and irregular' and Thomas Wolsey closed the Tynedale churches in 1524. Lord Dacre, a Guardian of the Marches, arrested ten principal thieves in the area in 1518 but he begged relief from the office in 1524 due to poor pay and conditions.

**CASTLES, PELES AND BASTLES** Northumberland has more castles than any part of England and a list compiled in 1415 found over 100 towers and castles. Fortifications included stone Pele (Peel) Towers with walls 3-4 feet thick and fortified farmhouses called Bastles. Most were inhabited by reivers but 'Vicar's Peles' were inhabited by local clergy. A small scattering of Pele towers can also be found in Durham, including Ludworth Tower, which dates from 1422.

**THE CHARLTON SPUR IN THE DISH** The Charltons often assembled for lunch at Hesleyside Hall in North Tynedale, where the lady of the house would bring a salver and dish for her husband and retainers. The salver was sometimes lifted to reveal a dish containing a riding spur. It meant the larder was empty and that they must ride, reive and steal cattle or sheep if they wished to be fed. This practice is commemorated in a famous painting at Wallington Hall near Morpeth.

**THE ARMSTRONG CLAN** Thirty members of this mainly Scottish family were hanged at Newcastle in 1532, but it did not stop hundreds of Armstrongs settling in Cumbria in 1549. The most famous reiving Armstrong was 'Kinmont Willie' who invaded Tynedale in 1579. He made off with 80 cattle and one thousand sheep.

Legend says Armstrongs are descended from a Scotsman called Fairbairn who lifted a fallen King of Scotland to his horse during a battle, using only one strong arm.

**THE ROBSON CLAN** The arch enemies of the Tynedale Robsons were the Grahams of Liddesdale in Scotland. The Robsons once stole scab-infected sheep from the Grahams and brought them into Northumberland. Scab spread through the Robson flock, so the Robsons returned to Liddesdale, caught seven Graham family members and hanged them. They left a note saying; 'The Neist time gentlemen cam to tak their schepe, they are no te' be scabbit!

**THE FOOTBALL CRAZY REIVERS** Charlton, Milburn and Robson are famous footballing names of the twentieth century and it is worth noting that football was a very popular sport among the reivers in early times. In 1599 a six-a-side football match involving the Armstrongs at Bewcastle (Cumbria) was interrupted by enemies. A member of the Ridley clan had his throat cut and a Robson was killed. A great football match took place between the men of Tynedale and Redesdale at Kielder Castle in 1790. Final score Tynedale 3 Redesdale 2.

**APOSTLE OF HOUGHTON-LE-SPRING** English people once feared the Borders and were wary of travelling north of the Tees, let alone the Tyne. Bernard Gilpin, 'Apostle of the North', Rector of Houghton from 1557, had no fear. A formidable man, 'tall,lean with a hawk like nose', he preached to the Border folk and there is evidence to suggest the reivers feared him.

**RAIDS AND MURDERS** Border reiving raids are too numerous to list but include the Raid of Reidswire at Carter Bar in 1575. This was a border fray at a peace-making meeting in which George Heron, Keeper of Tynedale, was murdered. The fray was provoked by the Border warden John Forster and rivalry between the Crozier and the Fenwick families. Durham generally escaped Border raiding, but on December 8 1569, Tynedale and Cumbrian reivers raided Weardale while the Weardale men were away supporting the rebellion called the Rising of the North. Those that remained fought off the invaders and the raid was recorded in a ballad called the Rookhope Ryde.

The Spur in the Dish
A nineteenth century painting by William Bell Scott

**BATTLE OF FLODDEN FIELD SEPTEMBER 9th 1513** The Battle of Flodden Field was a major conflict between the English and Scottish crowns, rather than a Border reiving feud, but it was a Borderland murder that provided an excuse for King James IV of Scotland to invade England. James was invading England in support of France where King Henry VIII was at war, but James claimed he was seeking revenge for the murder of Robert Kerr, a Border warden murdered by the Northumbrian, John Heron, in 1508. The Scots were defeated by the English under the Earl of Surrey at Flodden and King James was killed. The Scots lost twelve earls, fifteen lords, an archbishop and a number of clan chiefs. It was the bloodiest battle ever fought against the Scots on English soil and was commemorated in the Scottish ballad 'Flowers of the Forest'

**THE FLODDEN FIELD REIVERS** Amidst the slaughter at the Battle of Flodden in 1513 it is interesting to note the attitude of the Border Reivers in the English and Scottish armies. As the fight progressed, reivers from both sides, notably the dales of Tyne and Teviot, gathered under the leadership of Lord Home and stripped the slain of possessions and plundered the baggage of both armies as the night of fighting continued. National identity was seemingly a low priority for the Border Reivers.

**BORDER BALLADS** Border Reivers, like Dark Age warriors, were famous for their ballads glorifying raiding and revenge. The Northumbrian historian G.M. Trevelyan said "It was not one ballad-maker alone but the whole cut throat population who felt this magnanimous sorrow, and the consoling charms of the highest poetry."

**TRANSPORTATION AND THE END OF RAIDING** James I united Scotland and England in 1603 and brought peace to the Border, but Border people did not immediately adapt to new lifestyles. In 1606 James resorted to transportation of Border families to military service in Ireland. Newcastle Keelmen assisted members of the Graham family to return the following year, but commisioners at Carlisle continued to round up a hundred of the worst criminals for Irish transportation. Reivers who dared to return were hanged at Newcastle.

**THE LAST RAIDS** In 1611 Elliots and Armstrongs of Liddesdale raided Tynedale against the Robsons. Lionel Robson of Leaplish was murdered with members of his family while others were shot in the arms and legs as a form of intimidation. It is sometimes called the last Border raid, but in 1649 a Newcastle man recorded that "the men of Tynedale and Redesdale come down from the dales and carry away horses and cattle so cunningly that it will be hard for any to get them or their cattle except that they be aquainted with some master thief, who for safety money may help them to their stolen goods, or deceive them".

**EIGHTEENTH CENTURY REIVING** Some eighteenth century members of Border society continued to live by the old ways. A horse thief described in 1701 how the Keeper of Tynedale encouraged raiding in Durham or Scotland to reduce crime in his area, and in 1725 a bigamist-robber called Charlton of Tynedale was executed at Durham for killing his illegal wife. In 1732 horse thieves called John and James Graham were executed at Durham.

**TYNESIDE KEELMEN AND THE REIVERS** As the Border way of life ended in the seventeenth century, Border people sought work in the coal mines of Tyneside and Durham and a great many became Keelmen, ferrying coal on the Tyne and Wear. It was a far cry from 1554 when Newcastle merchants banned Tynedale men from working there. Keelmen formed a community outside Newcastle's walls at Sandhill and wore distinctive clothes, including Border-style blue bonnets as recalled in the famous 'Keel Row' ballad.

Flodden Field Memorial Cross

168

# Elizabethans and Stuarts

1560AD to 1714AD

King Charles I

**ELIZABETHANS AND STUARTS 1560AD TO 1714AD** Plagues, witch trials and fires are familiar aspects of Elizabethan and Stuart life but perhaps the greatest disruption was caused by the Civil War in the mid 1600s. In 1640 Charles I summoned Parliament to raise funds for a war against the Scots, but Parliament, not called for eleven years, naturally refused him the money. Charles was defeated by the Scots at Newburn on Tyne in 1640 and the Scots seized the region. This increased the tensions between King and Parliament, which resulted in the English Civil War.

**1560AD - ELIZABETHAN DARLINGTON (Darlington)** Darlington, like many Northern towns, is an agricultural centre and most of its inhabitants are employed in farm-related industries like weaving, leather tanning and fulling. Unfortunately, Darlington is also renowned for unpaved streets and will come to be known as Darnton I' the Dirt.

**1571AD - HARROGATE SPA (Harrogate)** A spring is discovered at Harrogate which will attract many tourists.

**1579AD - NEWCASTLE PLAGUE (Newcastle)** Plague is so bad at Newcastle that the Mayor of Newcastle writes to Yarmouth warning ships not to visit Newcastle for coals.

**1582AD - HARTLEPOOL WITCHCRAFT (Hartlepool)** A sorcerer from Hart near Hartlepool is serving pennance by sitting in Durham Market Place, Hart Church and Norton church while wearing a paper hat.

**May 7 1585AD - DARLINGTON FIRE (Darlington)** 273 houses are destroyed in a Darlington fire. The fire affects High Row and Skinnergate, leaving 800 people homeless. Figures may have been exaggerated to encourage charitable donations, but flames could be seen from Roseberry Topping.

**1588AD - PLAGUES (North)** A Hartlepool plague killed 89 last year. 1,726 die in Newcastle this year.

**1590AD - GRAMMAR SCHOOLS (The North)** Yarm Grammar School is established. Recently established schools include Newcastle (1525), Berwick (1559), Guisborough (1561) and Darlington (1567).

**1597AD - MORE PLAGUE (The North)** Plague has ravaged Newcastle, Darlington (killing 340), Aycliffe, and Chester-le-Street. It will return to Durham and Darlington next year.

**1603AD - KING JAMES MARKS UNION OF THE CROWNS (Britain)** James VI of Scotland becomes James I, King of Scotland and England, following the death of the childless Elizabeth I.

**November 1605AD - GUNPOWDER PLOT (London)** Guy Fawkes of York is chief among those implicated in a plot to blow up the Houses of Parliament. Fawkes is tortured and executed.

**1606AD - REIVERS TRANSPORTED (Northumberland)** King James begins the transportation of Border Reivers to Ireland. The Border raids will come to an end over the next five years.

**1607AD - SKINNINGROVE MERMAN (Cleveland coast)** A merman is reputedly caught by the fishermen of Skinningrove.

**1610AD - SUNDERLAND MUST PAY NEWCASTLE (Sunderland)** Around 14,700 tons of coal a year is being exported from Sunderland to London but following a petition from Newcastle, the king orders that part of Sunderland's coal revenue must be paid to Newcastle's merchants.

**1620AD - SCARBOROUGH SPA (Scarborough)** Scarborough's development as a holiday resort begins with the discovery of a spa.

**1636AD - NEWCASTLE PLAGUE (Newcastle)** 5,037 are said to have died of plague at Newcastle after spreading there from North Shields in 1635. Grass is said to have grown in Newcastle's streets.

**1638AD - CHARLES STRENGTHENS NEWCASTLE (Britain)** Charles I, who became King in 1625, strengthens Newcastle's defences against the Scots whom he believes to be plotting against him. The following year he makes peace with the Scottish army, near Berwick. On his return to London, skirmishes continue in the north between his York based troops and the Scots.

**1640AD - BATTLE OF NEWBURN ON TYNE (Newburn, near Blaydon Tyneside)** On August 20 Scots under General Leslie invade England and cross the Tyne, west of Newcastle. Charles' army are defeated in battle. English losses are light but they flee and the garrison at Newcastle is deserted.

**August 29 to August 30 1640AD - SCOTS SEIZE NEWCASTLE AND DURHAM (North)** Newcastle and Durham are seized by the Scots. The Newcastle coal trade ceases and shops in Durham and Newcastle are looted. Charles negotiates a truce at York and the Scots disband on receipt of £60,000 in 1641.

**January 14 1643AD - COAL SHIPS BANNED (Newcastle)** Last year Hull came out in support of the Parliamentarians and banned Charles from entering. Parliament has now banned London coal ships from sailing to Newcastle unless Newcastle also agrees to support the Parliamentarians.

**June 30 1643AD - BATTLE AT ADWALTON MOOR (West Yorkshire)** Parliamentarian troops under Fairfax are defeated by Royalists, despite support in Leeds and Bradford. Royalists now control all of Yorkshire except Hull.

Guy Fawkes, a native of York, was among those involved in the Gunpowder Plot of 1605

**3 February to 6 February 1644AD - SCOTS REACH NEWCASTLE (Alnwick)** In January Scots, under Leslie, invaded England once again. The Scots encamp at Corbridge and outside Newcastle. Heavy Ordnance is delivered to the Scottish camp at Newcastle via Blyth.

**22 February to 8 March 1644AD - SCOTS MOVE TO SUNDERLAND (Sunderland)** The Scots leave six regiments at Newcastle while the rest make their way to Sunderland, where there is Parliamentarian support. They camp temporarily at Ebchester and Chester-le-Street before entering Sunderland on March 4th. On March 8th a skirmish takes place near Sunderland, possibly at Boldon, between Scots and Royalists under the Marquess of Newcastle, but terrain prevents battle.

**13 March 1644AD - SCOTS BESIEGE SOUTH SHIELDS (South Shields)** Part of Sunderland's Scottish garrison moves towards Durham City seeking provision in the countryside, but finds the land destroyed by Royalists. The garrison is struggling because provisions delivered from Scotland are being captured and forced into the Tyne. The Scots turn their attention to South Shields and capture the town after a siege on March 19.

**24 March 1644AD - SCOTS WON'T FIGHT AT HYLTON (Sunderland)** After marching troops from Newcastle to Durham, Royalist soldiers of the Marquess of Newcastle fail to engage the Scots in battle at Hylton. Canon is fired but the Scots remain at safe distance. On returning to Durham the Royalist rear is attacked by a small party of Scots, possibly on Gilesgate Moor. In April the Scots extend their quarters south to Quarrington Hill and Easington.

**11 April to 20 April 1644AD - ARMIES JOIN YORK SIEGE (York)** Parliamentarian troops besiege the Royalist garrison at York and the Royalist troops of the Marquess of Newcastle move south to defend it. They travel via Bishop Auckland, Barnard Castle and Piercebridge. At the same time, Scottish troops in east Durham head south via Ferryhill. Skirmishes occur near Darlington during the journey. On April 20, the Marquess arrives at York while the Scots joined the Parliamentarian troops of Fairfax at Tadcaster.

# Cromwell
# to Queen Anne

1560AD to 1714AD

Oliver Cromwell

**CROMWELL TO QUEEN ANNE 1560AD TO 1714AD** The Battle of Marston Moor near York in July 1644 was a turning point in the Civil War. By the end of October the Royalist strongholds of York and Newcastle were taken by Parliamentarian forces and the Royalist hold on the North was ended. When Charles finally surrendered in 1646, Newcastle became his place of imprisonment. He would be executed in London three years later. Parliament ruled the country until 1660 when the Stuart monarchy returned. The Stuarts ruled the nation until the death of Queen Anne in 1714.

**July 2  1644AD - MARSTON MOOR (Near York)** Parliamentarians and Scots inflict a heavy defeat on the Royalists in a night battle at Marston Moor. 3,000 Royalists are killed. On 16 July, York is taken by Parliamentarians after a long siege.

**August 13  1644AD -  NEWCASTLE AND SUNDERLAND (Newcastle)** The Scots, fresh from Marston Moor, capture and occupy Stockton Castle. Other Scots head for Newcastle, which falls under siege. The town is defended by the mayor, John Marley. Scottish 'blue caps' and 'cull cuckolds' of Parliamentarian Sunderland are resented by Newcastle. Sunderland is challenging Newcastle's Royalist coal monopoly, which has been criticised by Parliament.

**October 22  1644AD - NEWCASTLE TAKEN (Newcastle)** After a ten week siege Scots capture Newcastle, penetrating its walls with gunpowder on October 20. The castle held out for longer until its occupant, John Marley, surrendered today. Newcastle's coal trade comes to a standstill during Scottish occupation of the town. Tynemouth castle also surrenders on October 27.

**May 13  1646AD - CHARLES SURRENDERS (Newark, Nottinghamshire)** Charles surrenders to the Scots on May 9 and is escorted to Newcastle for imprisonment. He considers a list of propositions regarding increased Parliamentary powers. Scots leave Newcastle in February 1647 after receiving £200,000 from Cromwell for the prisoner.

**October 1  648AD - ROYALIST RISING (Northumberland)** A Royalist rising takes hold in Scotland and the North. Raby is besieged and Berwick captured. Cromwell retakes Berwick on October 18 and visits Newcastle (19-22 Oct), Durham (23 Oct) and Barnard Castle at Blagraves (24 Oct).

**1648AD - COLLIERIES FLOODED (Washington)** Collieries on the Wear (near Washington) are drowned out by a severe storm.

**January 30  1649AD - CHARLES BEHEADED (London)** King Charles is accused of treason and executed on Cromwell's orders. Cromwell abolishes the monarchy and makes himself Lord Protector, ruler of England.

**March 26  1649AD - NEWCASTLE WITCH TRIAL (Newcastle)** 27 out of 30 suspected witches are found guilty of witchcraft at Newcastle and 14 are executed on the Town Moor. One man is executed for being a wizard. Newcastle Council had suggested all witches be brought to trial, so magistrates sent for a Scottish witch finder called Cuthbert Nicholson. The Newcastle bellman invited people to report suspected witches. 30 women were brought to the Town Hall and stripped to their waist. Nicholson pushed a pin under their clothes to pierce their skin. If they did not bleed they were declared witches. Nicholson was later arrested in Scotland for trickery and executed. He confessed responsibility for the deaths of 220 women. He was paid twenty shillings for each witch captured.

**March 28  1649AD - LEVELLER LILBURNE IMPRISONED (Tower of London)** John Lilburne, founder of 'The Levellers' political group, is imprisoned by Cromwell. Lilburne is from East Thickley, Bishop Auckland. The Lilburnes are important Sunderland merchants and his uncle is the Sunderland Mayor. Lilburne, once a friend of Cromwell now criticises Cromwell's reforms as not radical enough. Lilburne has much support among Cromwell's New Model Army and is seen by Cromwell as a dangerous threat.

**July 1  650AD - CROMWELL'S COLLEGE (Durham)** Cromwell suggests a college at Durham would be 'a matter of great importance to promoting learning and piety in these rude and ignorant partes'. Cromwell will sign a writ of privy seal for a University at Durham but it is suppressed by objections from Oxford and Cambridge in 1657.

**September 3  1650AD - DUNBAR BATTLE (Dunbar)** After months of pursuit, a battle raged between Cromwell and the Scots under the former Parliamentarian General Leslie. Scots outnumber English 2 to 1 but Cromwell launches a surprise attack and defeats them. 10,000 Scots are captured and 3,000 imprisoned in Durham Cathedral. Cathedral woodwork is destroyed by the prisoners for firewood but a clock featuring a thistle is spared.

**1652AD - CASTLES DESTROYED (Durham and Stockton)** Durham and Stockton Castles, former properties of the Bishops of Durham, have suffered under Cromwell's regime. Durham Castle was sold to Thomas Andrews, Lord Mayor of London, for £1267 in 1649 and he severely defaced the property. This year Cromwell ordered the destruction of Stockton Castle.

**1658AD to 1660AD - MONARCHY RETURNS (Coldstream on Tweed)** On Sep 3 1658 Cromwell died and was succeeded by his son Richard, who proved a weak leader. Support grew in Parliament for restoring the monarchy and crowning Charles II. General Monck, Duke of Abermarle, led Scottish troops from Coldstream to London and successfully negotiated the coronation of King Charles II. A section of his army becomes the 'Coldstream Guards'.

**1665AD - PLAGUE (Gateshead and Sunderland)** Plague hits the North again at Gateshead and Sunderland.

**1669AD - CROFT SPA (Croft on Tees)** A small spa is opened at Croft near Darlington.

**1673AD - STORMY SEAS (The North)** Around 40 ships are destroyed in northern storms off the North East coast.

**1675AD - JOLLY RANT (Newcastle)** A pestilent disease called 'Jolly Rant' kills 924 people in Newcastle.

**1675AD - DURHAM MPs (County Durham)** Durham sends its first MPs to the House of Commons with two MPs for Durham City and two for the county. One MP dies of smallpox four days after his election.

**1688AD - WILLIAM AND MARY (Britain)** Dutchman King William III (of Orange) becomes King of Britain in joint rule with his wife Queen Mary II

**1697AD - NORTHERN MP BEHEADED (London)** Northumberland MP, Sir John Fenwick, is beheaded for plotting against King William.

**1698AD - SUNDAY SCHOOL (Stockton)** Britain's first Sunday School is established in Finkle Street, Stockton.

**April 23 1699AD - FIVE INCH HAIL (Durham)** Hail stones five inches in diameter fall on Durham and its surrounds.

**1700AD - CASTLE HOWARD (Yorkshire)** Castle Howard is being built by John Vanbrugh and is constructed on the site of Henderskelfe Castle which recently burnt down.

**1702AD - KING KILLED (Britain)** William III dies after falling from a horse which once belonged to the Northumberland MP John Fenwick, whom he executed in 1697. William is succeeded by Queen Anne.

**1712AD - STOCKTON PARISH (Stockton)** Stockton, an agricultural port, gains independent parish status. It was previously part of Norton.

**1714AD - ANNE DIES (Britain)** Queen Anne dies and is succeeded by George I.

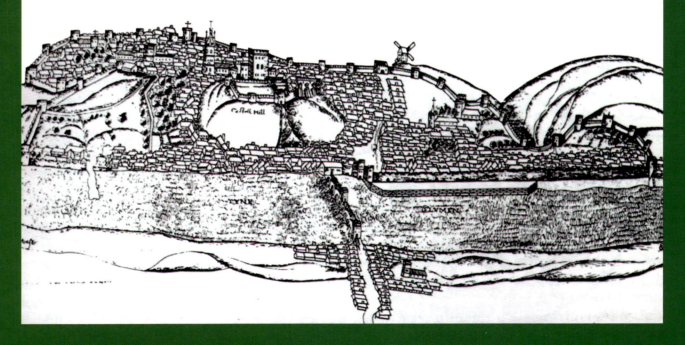

Newcastle in 1590

# Coal and Industry

1500AD to 1800AD

Causey Arch, the world's oldest surviving railway bridge

**COAL AND INDUSTRY 1500AD TO 1800AD** Coal dominated the region's industry in the seventeenth and eighteenth century and the world's first railways emerged, using horse-drawn wagons to carry coal from the local mines to Newcastle. Industries like iron, glass and salt-making also grew under the influence of coal production.

**TYNE AND WEAR - THE REGION'S FIRST COAL DISTRICT** Seventeenth century mining was concentrated around Tyneside and the Washington area of Wearside. It spread to the Hetton area after 1800 but was not significant in south-west Durham until after 1825. 7,000 pitmen worked in the region in 1787, growing to 10,000 by 1810. Coal mines were opening in the region at places like Newbottle (1774), Lumley (1776) Washington F Pit (1777) and Penshaw (1791).

**THE NEWCASTLE KEELMEN** Keelmen ferried coal on keel boats to collier ships on the Tyne. They formed a distinct community in the Sandgate area of Newcastle and demonstrated against poor wages in the 1650s and 70s. In the late 18th century coal staithes enabled coal to be loaded directly from rail wagons onto ships. This threatened the Keelmens' livelihood and the Newcastle and Sunderland Keelmen often resorted to vandalising the staithes which would ultimately bring an end to their trade.

**THE WORLD'S FIRST RAILWAYS** Seventeenth Century Colliery railways called 'Newcastle Roads' enabled coal mines to be opened further away from the Tyne and Wear. These were the first railways in the world and were operated by horse drawn wagons called Chaldrons filled with coal. The first recorded railway 'The Whickham Grand Lease Way' of 1620 ran from Whickham to Dunston on Tyne via Lobley Hill, but other railways may have existed in the area. A railway existed near Blyth from at least 1693 and a railway supplied coal staithes on the Wear near Washington. In North West Durham the Tanfield railway of 1725 claims to be the oldest existing railway in the world and the associated Causey Arch of 1727 is the world's oldest surviving railway bridge.

**EARLY ENGINES** From 1580 deeper mines around Tyneside used horse driven engines or gin-gans to pump out water. Standing 'Fire Engines' of the type developed by Newcommen in 1712 appeared in the region around 1715 at Byker, Washington Fell and Oxclose Collieries. Scotsman James Watt made improvements to this kind of engine in 1769. In 1753 Michael Menzies of Chartershaugh Colliery (Wearside) invented a machine for raising coal, called the Menzie.

**MINE HAZARDS AND SAFETY** As mines got deeper, safety became a problem. In 1662 a petition was handed to Parliament signed by 2000 pitmen regarding mine ventilation, as colliery gas was claiming victims. Later mine deaths included 69 at Fatfield (1708), 80 at Bensham (1743), 39 at Fatfield (1767), 23 at Chartershaugh (1773), and 30 at Picktree in 1794. Pit ponies used underground from 1750 were often victims. Roof safety was also a problem and pillars supporting roofs were first recorded in the region at Chartershaugh Colliery in 1738.

**THE COAL OWNERS** In 1547 Newcastle's population was 10,000 and powerful merchants called The Hostmen controlled the mines and coal export. By 1615, 200 ships carried coal to London and another 200 supplied other parts of the country. Newcastle had a virtual monopoly on exporting coal with considerable control over rival ports like Sunderland. By the eighteenth century control of the northern coal trade had fallen into the hands of a cartel of wealthy coal-owning families called the Grand Allies who were the Russells of Brancepeth, Brandlings of Gosforth, Liddells of Ravensworth (near Gateshead) and the Bowes family who

Lambton Staithes, Sunderland circa 1815

were the Earls of Strathmore. William Russell, a Sunderland banker who bought Brancepeth castle in 1796, was the country's wealthiest commoner.

**SUNDERLAND COAL** Sunderland, described in 1559 as a little-used port, was a late developer in exporting coal and was second to Newcastle. By 1609 Sunderland exported 14,700 tons of coal a year and the Newcastle merchants felt threatened enough to petition the king and order a levy. By the mid seventeenth century Sunderland was a major rival to Newcastle. North of the Tyne, Seaton Delaval was developed as a port by the Delaval family from 1628 and nearby Blyth was a port of the 1600s which developed further in 1722.

**COAL FROM THE TEES** The ports of the Tees and Whitby to the south lay oustide the coalfield but were able to benefit from the coal trade. Whitby was the home to much shipping and a certain James Cook (later Captain Cook) worked on Whitby colliers, shipping coal from the Tyne and Wear to London in 1746. Stockton shipped coal from at least 1622 and by 1795 had easily eclipsed Hartlepool and Yarm as a port. The flat Tees vale prompted suggestions that a coal canal might benefit Stockton and Darlington trade and proposed canals were surveyed by Robert Whitworth in 1767 and Ralph Todd in 1796. Neither was built and by 1810 the idea of building a railway was suggested instead. It was an idea that led to the Stockton and Darlington Railway of 1825.

**IRON AND STEEL** Ambrose Crowley opened a nail making works at Sunderland in 1682, moving to Winlaton in 1691, and William Hawks established an iron works at Gateshead in 1647 for ship anchors and chains. Simple iron works existed near Stockton High Street from 1765 and the region's first Blast Furnace was at Lemmington on Tyne in 1797. A more unusual metal industry came to Shotley Bridge in 1687 when Lutheran swordmakers from Solingen in Germany sought refuge from persecution.

**SALT AND GLASS** Salt was made at Sunderland from at least 1511 and a mine opened at nearby Offerton in 1589 to supply coal for heating brine. South Shields was the region's most important salt town, where the industry caused terrible pollution. North and South Shields had around 200 salt pans in 1767 consuming 1000 tons of coal a year, creating horrendous fumes. In 1798 John Losh leased a supply of brine from

A Georgian view of Stockton

**THE GEORGIAN NORTH 1714 TO 1800** The Georgian era stretches from 1714 to 1838, although the early part of the nineteenth century is also called the Regency era. The Georgian era was the age of Industrial Revolution, world exploration and a new style of architecture.

**November 1715 - GEORDIES NOT JACOBITES (Newcastle)** George I, a German protestant, was crowned king of England last year despite objections from Scottish 'Jacobite' rebels who support James Stuart, the 'Old Pretender'. Leading rebel, Tom Forster of Bamburgh, marches an army into England. Every Northumberland town supports him except Newcastle which declares for King George. Newcastle folk are now said to be called 'Geordies'. The Jacobites are defeated at Preston later this month.

**1716 - CAPABILITY BROWN BORN (Northumberland)** Future landscape gardener Lancelot Brown is born at Kirkharle near Morpeth.

**1727 - GEORGE II (Britain)** George II becomes King of Britain. Like his father King George I, he prefers Germany to Britain.

**1727 - DEFOE VISIT (Newcastle)** Daniel Defoe visits Newcastle and says 'They build ships here to perfection'.

**1736 - NEW TEETH (Bishop Auckland)** A 108 year old Bishop Auckland woman has been given a new set of teeth.

**1739 - TURPIN HANGED (York)** The notorious Yorkshire highwayman Dick Turpin is hanged for murder.

**June 9 1740- NEWCASTLE RIOT (Newcastle)** A riot breaks out in Newcastle over rising corn prices. The militia open fire killing one. Seven men are later transported.

**April 17 1741 - FARMER'S WIFE GOES BESERK (Fishburn)** A farmer's wife called Charlton went berserk at a farm near Fishburn killing her 14 year old son with a cleaver before killing her two younger children. She then committed suicide after stabbing herself below the ear. All this happened while her husband was trying to get a cow out of a ditch. The coroner recorded a verdict of lunacy.

**May 1742 - WESLEY AT NEWCASTLE (Newcastle)** John Wesley, the founder of Methodism, preaches at Newcastle and records 'I was surprised; so much drunkenness, cursing and swearing, even from mouths of little children, do I never remember to have seen and heard before on so small a compass of time.' Newcastle will become one of his favourite places to preach.

**1745 - NO JACOBITE SUPPORT (North East)** Scottish Jacobites supporting Bonnie Prince Charlie rebel against George II. There is little North East support so the Jacobites march south through Cumbria avoiding troops stationed at Framwellgate Moor and Newcastle. The Jacobites later retreat and will be defeated at Culloden near Inverness.

**1759 - STOCKTON PRESS GANG (Stockton)** John Wesley is interrupted by a press gang raid during his sermon in the High Street at Stockton.

**1760 - SHAFTO MP (County Durham)** Bobby Shafto (of the song) becomes an MP for County Durham.

**January 1760 - PRESS GANG (North Shields)** 60 men are captured by Press Gangs but manage to take control of the ship that captured them and sail into Scarborough where they escape.

**March 9 1761 - HEXHAM MASSACRE (Hexham Market Place)** Troops open fire on the crowd after The Riot Act was read to Allendale miners demonstrating against army conscription methods. Forty men are killed on the spot. A 74 year old man is later hanged for his part in the riot, but it is discovered he was not in Hexham on the day of the riot.

**8am on July 13 1764 - ICE ROCKS SHOWER HARTLEPOOL (Hartlepool)** Ice crystals with a 5 inch circumference shower Hartlepool for 15 minutes.

**November 1765 - STORMS KILL KEELMEN (Tyneside)** Storms kill 30 keelmen and leave 53 Tyneside children fatherless.

**1767 - DIXIELANDER OF DURHAM (America)** Cockfield's Jeremiah Dixon surveys the Mason-Dixon line which gives its name to 'Dixieland'.

**1768 - ELSIE MARLEY (Chester-le-Street)** Elsie Marley, landlady of the White Swan, Picktree, falls to her death in a pit.

**1769 - JAMES COOK (The World)** James Cook, who was born at Marton near Middlesbrough in 1728, has been placed in charge of HM Bark Endeavour to explore new lands. He journeys to Tahiti, New Zealand and Australia where he named a great bay Botany Bay. Cook once lived on a farm at the foot of Cleveland's Roseberry Topping.

**November 17 1771 - GREAT FLOOD (The North)** A flood hits the North destroying every major bridge on the Tyne, Wear and Tees.

**1772 - COOK VOYAGE (The World)** James Cook sets sail on a second voyage in search of the great southern continent, sailing as far south as the Antarctic Circle.

**1774 - BACKHOUSE BANK (Darlington)** Jonathan Backhouse establishes a bank in Darlington's High Row

**August 21 1776 - POSTMAN EXECUTED (Newcastle)** A South Shields postman was executed on Newcastle Town Moor for stealing a letter from Newcastle Post office containing two 50 pound notes.

**1779 - JAMES COOK MURDERED (Hawaii)** Cleveland born Captain James Cook's third great sea voyage ends in disaster when he is murdered on Hawaii following an affray between his crew and natives.

**1779 - AMERICAN BOMBER (Alnmouth)** American Privateer John Paul Jones bombs Alnmouth from his boat just off the coast.

**1782 - MARSDEN GROTTO (South Shields)** Quarryman 'Jack the Blaster' makes himself a home at Marsden Rock.

Captain James Cook

**1788 - GEORGIAN THEATRE (Richmond)** Richmond's Georgian theatre opens.

**December 9 1790 - STOCKTON EARTHQUAKE (Stockton)** Residents of Stockton report a great earthquake.

**1790 - BEWICK BOOK (Newcastle)** The Newcastle engraver Thomas Bewick publishes his History of Quadropeds.

**1790 - WORLD'S FIRST LIFEBOAT (South Shields)** William Wouldhave and Henry Greathead invent the world's first lifeboat called The Original, at South Shields.

**July 17 1792 - SEDGEFIELD HAILSTORM (Sedgefield)** Sedgefield's streets are filled with 2 feet of hail damaging many houses and windows.

Stockton's Georgian Town Hall

# Farming

100AD to 1900AD

The Durham Ox

## FARMING 100AD TO 1900AD

**THE REGION'S FIRST FARMERS** Some of the earliest farmers in the region practiced Transhumance - moving livestock from uplands to valleys according to the season. This was carried out by the Ancient Britons in pre-Roman times and later by the Norwegian Vikings. Circular sheep folds in Weardale dating from the 13th century show the continuation of this practice in later periods. Anglo-Saxon farmers preferred lowland farms and villages, which they called 'tons' and 'hams' and the Danes called their farming settlements 'thorpes' and 'bys'. Girsby near Darlington means 'Pig Farm village' and demonstrates that some farms specialised in early times. In medieval times monasteries dominated the agricultural scene and farmed vast areas, particularly in Yorkshire, where Fountains Abbey owned around 15,000 sheep.

**FARM TOWNS AND VILLAGES** In the medieval lowlands the Open-Field System was practiced in which there were usually three large arable fields surrounding a village employing a crop rotation system. Each year one field was left fallow to allow soil recovery while the other two grew rye, wheat, oats or barley. Fields were ploughed by teams of oxen and the area one ox could plough for sowing each season was known as a Bovate or Oxgang. Bonded men cultivated the land as servants to a local lord. Beyond the fields was pasture land for cows and sheep or perhaps woodland providing fuel in the form of charcoal. During Scottish raids village greens may have provided shelter for livestock.

**MEDIEVAL FORESTS** Vast areas of upland were designated forests, set aside for hunting and belonging to the King. Medieval forests were vast open fields and commons often inhabited by peasants and subjected to special forest laws. In County Durham the Medieval Prince Bishops owned a hunting forest in Weardale between Eastgate and Westgate and hunted here every autumn. Royal forests included the Forest of Galtres near York, the Forest of Pickering and extensive forests in Northumberland. In addition there were around sixty deer parks in North Yorkshire from which deer were released into forests before a hunt. Deer parks and forests caused resentment among farmers as they often encroached upon agricultural land. Some areas of forest were however reclaimed for farmland in medieval times and were known locally as Riddings.

**ENCLOSURE** Apart from Demesnes, special areas of land or special features directly held by the Lord of the Manor, medieval farmland was not enclosed. There were some enclosures after the Black Death in 1348, but it was in Tudor times that enclosures began to increase as a result of local agreements. At this time enclosures were not yet enforced by Acts of Parliament. Lowland villages of Yorkshire and east Durham were affected by these early enclosures and fields formerly divided into strips were permanently enclosed with neatly cut hedges.

**LATER ENCLOSURES** From about 1750 Acts of Parliament increased enclosure in upland areas to meet the demand from growing towns and the increasing cost of grain. Dry stone walls became a feature of the dales as the uplands were enclosed. Most upland remained in pasture but in some cases land was cultivated for the first time, often fertilised with lime extracted from nearby lime kilns.

**BREEDING - CATTLE AND SHEEP** Breeds of farm animals developed in the region include the Shorthorn cattle, which were a significant development of the Durham Ox (or Ketton Ox) bred by Charles and Robert Colling near Darlington around 1796. Other famous  livestock breeders from the Darlington area were Matthew and George Culley, who moved to Northumberland in 1767 to farm at Fenton, near Wooler. They developed a strain of sheep called Border Leicester by crossing the region's Teeswater Sheep with Bakewell Dishleys. Border Leicesters could be fattened quickly for the town market.

**DOGS AND HORSES** Famous breeds of working dogs developed in the region include the Border Collies, which have herded sheep along both sides of the Scottish border for at least 300 years. Terriers, bred for hunting, have strong northern links, including the Border Terrier, Yorkshire Terrier and the Bedlington Terrier, first bred in the Northumberland mining town of that name. North Yorkshire is particularly noted for its horse breeding including the famous Cleveland Bays.

Field ploughing in Medieval Times

# The Locomotive Age

1800AD to 1828AD

Opening of the Stockton and Darlington Railway, illustrated by John Dobbin

**THE LOCOMOTIVE AGE 1800 TO 1828** Early colliery railways of the 1700s used horse-drawn wagons to haul coal to the Tyne and Wear. Later, stationary engines hauled coal along inclined railways, but locomotives, effectively steam engines on wheels, were the next stage of development. Locomotives were developed at collieries like Wylam, Killingworth and Hetton by George Stephenson and William Hedley and eventually led to the developments of The Stockton and Darlington Railway of 1825.

**1801 - TWENTY FIVE PEOPLE LIVE IN MIDDLESBROUGH (Middlesbrough)** Middlesbrough, a farmstead of four houses, has a population of only twenty five. Stockton's population is 3,700, Hartlepool 993, Darlington 4,700 and Yarm 1,300. Middlesbrough will grow as a result of railway developments.

**1805 - TREVITHICK AND STEPHENSON (Cornwall)** Last year, Cornish engineer Richard Trevithick invented a locomotive for use on rails. It follows his development of a road locomotive in 1801. Meanwhile George Stephenson becomes an employee at Killingworth Colliery.

**1810 - S & D RAILWAY IDEA (Stockton on Tees)** In a meeting at Stockton Town Hall, Leonard Raisbeck, Recorder of Stockton suggests a railway might be an alternative to a canal for moving south Durham coal to Stockton.

**1810 - TEES SHORT CUT (Stockton on Tees)** It takes as long for ships to travel from the Tees estuary to London as it does for them to journey from the estuary to Stockton. The Tees Cut, a short canal, reduces this journey time.

**1814 - PUFFING BILLY AND BLUCHER BUILT (Wylam on Tyne and Killingworth)** Last year the Puffing Billy and Wylam Dilly locomotives were developed by William Hedley at Wylam colliery. This year George Stephenson has built his first locomotive 'the Blucher' at Killingworth Colliery.

**1815 - SAFETY LAMP INVENTED (Britain)** A miner's safety lamp has been invented by Humphry Davy and George Stephenson. It should reduce the number of colliery gas explosions.

**1815 - BYRON WEDDING (Seaham)** The Poet Lord Byron marries at Seaham Hall.

**March 20  1815 - KEELMEN RIOT (Sunderland)** Keelmen at Sunderland riot and pull down a small railway bridge leading to coal staithes on the Wear.

**October 18 1816 - CORN RIOT (Sunderland)** Corn riots occur at Sunderland. There were also riots here in 1807.

**1816 - HARTLEPOOL IN DECLINE (Hartlepool)** Sharp's 'History of Hartlepool' describes the little fishing community as 'a place that had seen better days now facing a continuing decline'.

**1818 - STANHOPE RIOT (Stanhope)** A riot breaks out between lead miners and the Bishop of Durham's men over Weardale gaming rights.

**February 12  1820 - RAILWAY MEETING AT YARM (Yarm)** In 1818 George Overton surveyed the possible route of a horse tramway through south Durham to the Tees. The idea develops into the Stockton and Darlington Railway. A meeting held at Yarm decides in favour of a railway.

**1820 - EDENS SELL PRESTON (Yarm)** The Eden family sell Preston on Tees to David Burton Fowler of Yarm.

**1820 - PLANS FOR PORT AT SEAHAM (County Durham)** Engineer William Chapman prepares a plan for developing a port (Seaham harbour) on the Durham coast for Lord Londonderry. The following year Londonderry buys the Seaham Estate.

**1821 - RAILWAY GETS ROYAL ASSENT (London)** The Stockton and Darlington Railway has gained the Royal assent.

**1822 - HETTON RAILWAY COMPLETE (Hetton)** George Stephenson's Hetton Colliery railway is complete - it is the largest in the world and will be worked by locomotives. It will serve as a model for the future Stockton and Darlington Railway. Hetton Staithes are built on the River Wear for loading coal into ships.

**May 23 1822- FIRST SECTION OF RAILWAY (Stockton)** George Stephenson is appointed the engineer for the Stockton and Darlington Railway project by Darlington businessman Edward Pease. The first section of rail is laid today near St John's Well at Stockton by Thomas Meynell of Yarm.

**February 2 1823 - SNOW BLOCKS MAIL (The North)** Snow blocks roads and prevents mail from reaching or leaving Durham or Newcastle for a week. Mail reaches Darlington but north-bound coaches find it impossible to proceed beyond Rushyford.

**1823 - ROBERT STEPHENSON'S WORKS AT NEWCASTLE (Newcastle)** George Stephenson's son, Robert establishes an engineering works in Newcastle.

**1823 - COAL PORT FOR HARTLEPOOL (Hartlepool)** Plans are discussed to bring waggonways to Hartlepool from local collieries in south east Durham to develop Hartlepool as a coal port. Hartlepool is little more than a fishing community.

**August 3 1825 - SEAMAN RIOT (Sunderland)** A riot breaks out among seamen in Sunderland in a dispute with coal owners. The Newcastle Militia opens fire killing four men.

**September 27 1825 - RAILWAY HISTORY MADE (Darlington)** The opening of the Stockton and Darlington Railway, the world's first public railway, took place today. A crowd of 40,000 turned out to see the procession of waggons hauled by the famous Locomotion Number One from Shildon to Stockton via Darlington. The train included fee-paying passengers, on this, the world's first public railway. Over 300 passengers travelled on the train, increasing to 600 as the journey progressed. Most passengers travelled in Chaldron waggons, fitted with seats, but local dignitaries travelled on a specially made carriage called 'The Experiment'. The railway is the most significant event in the history of Teesside and will bring increasing industrial growth to the area and spur on the birth of Middlesbrough.

**1826 - BOWES RAILWAY (Gateshead)** The Bowes Colliery Railway is built near Gateshead.

Painting of the Locomotion Number One

**1827 - MAN OF THE MATCH (Stockton on Tees)** John Walker of Stockton on Tees invents the friction match. On the 17 April the first ever friction matches went on sale in Stockton.

**1828 - PORT CLARENCE RAILWAY GIVEN GO-AHEAD (Stockton on Tees)** The Clarence Railway has obtained an act enabling a railway to be built linking Port Clarence to Stockton, and from there to Shildon and collieries further north. Port Clarence and the Clarence Railway are named after the Duke of Clarence who will later become King William IV.

**1829 - ROCKET WINS TRIAL (Rainhill, Lancashire)** George Stephenson's Rocket is victorious at the Rainhill locomotive trials in Lancashire.

Former Stockton and Darlington Railway Ticket Office at Stockton

# A Town is born

1828AD to 1839AD

Joseph Pease, the founder of Middlesbrough

**A TOWN IS BORN 1828 TO 1839** The most remarkable event of the late 1820s was the birth of Middlesbrough. In 1829 Middlesbrough was a small riverside farm purchased by a Darlington businessman called Joseph Pease who bought the farm and developed a town and coal port. Over seventy years Middlesbrough would see one of the most extraordinary population growths ever known in British history. Further north the new town of Seaham Harbour was also born, while Hartlepool was transformed from a fishing community into one of Britain's busiest ports.

**August 2  1828 - PEASE SURVEYS MIDDLESBROUGH (Darlington)** Darlington's Quaker industrialist Joseph Pease has sailed up the River Tees to view the farmland site of Middlesbrough as the potential setting for a new port. This evening he recorded in his diary that he could see the day when 'The bare fields would be covered with a busy multitude, and numerous vessels crowding to the banks denoting a busy seaport'.

**November 28  1828 - HARBOUR AT SEAHAM (County Durham)** A harbour is begun at Seaham by the Marquess of Londonderry. The first stone is laid on 28 November.

**1829 - MIDDLESBROUGH IS BORN (Middlesbrough)** Joseph Pease and Partners have bought the Middlebrough farmland estate of  William Chilton of Billingham from the tenant farmer John Whinfield Parrington. The land by the Tees will be used for the building of a new town. Middlesbrough currently has a population of only thirty people. The Stockton and Darlington railway has been extended to Middlesbrough which it reached on 27 December 1830.

**August 22  1830 - MIDDLESBROUGH'S FIRST CHILD (Middlesbrough)** John Richardson Chapman is the first child to be born in Middlesbrough.

**1830 - SECOND SHORT CUT ON TEES (Stockton on Tees)** A second cut of 1,100 yards has been made across a loop in the River Tees. This canal has been made at Portrack near Stockton and stretches from Blue House Point to Newport. Portrack is situated on a hazardous meander on the Tees where large ships had to be tugged by men or horses towards the port of Stockton. This is called 'racking' and is the reason Port - rack acquired its name.

**1831 - MIDDLESBROUGH'S POPULATION IS 154 (Middlesbrough)** Middlesbrough's population is 154, tiny compared to the population of neighbouring Stockton on the north side of the river where 7,000 people live.

**1831 - NEW MEMBERS (The North)** The Northumbrian born government minister Earl Grey introduces a government reform bill which creates many new MPs. Sunderland, Gateshead, South Shields and Tynemouth elect MPs for the first time.

**1831 - MIDDLESBROUGH BOOMS (Middlesbrough)** In January, William Fallows, who has organised the shipping of coal from Middlesbrough staithes, made the first shipment of coal in his ship called The Sunnyside. At the end of the year 151,000 tons of coal had been shipped from the new port.

**1831 - BIG PLANS FOR HARTLEPOOL (Hartlepool)** The Hartlepool Dock and Railway Company has been established at the instigation of Christiopher Tennant of Yarm and Rowland Burdon of Castle Eden. The two businessmen want to develop the old fishing community into a busy coal port.

**1831 - MIDDLESBROUGH POTTERY (Middlesbrough)** Middlesbrough Pottery is started.

**1831 - SUNDERLAND CHOLERA (Sunderland)** An Asiatic cholera epidemic hits the country after it is unwittingly introduced by a sailor at Sunderland.

**July 25 1831 - COAL FROM SEAHAM (County Durham)** The first coal is shipped from Seaham Harbour by the Lord Seaham collier brig.

**1833 - TEESSIDE'S FIRST CHEMICAL WORKS (Teesside)** Chemical works have been founded at Urlay Nook near Egglescliffe on Teesside by Robert Wilson of Yarm. The company is engaged in the manufacture of sulphuric acid and fertilisers.

**1833 - MONASTERY SITE FOUND (Hartlepool)** A cemetery has been discovered at Hartlepool. It is thought to be that of the Anglo-Saxon monastery of St Hilda.

**1833 - MIDDLESBROUGH'S FIRST SHIP BUILT (Middlesbrough)** A shipyard has been opened in the newly born town of Middlesbrough by a Mr Laing. The first ship to be lauched was called 'The Middlesbro'.

**1833 - CLARENCE RAILWAY BUILT (Teesside)** The Clarence Railway has been opened. It is linked to Clarence Staithes at Billingham on Tees.

**1834 - MIDDLESBROUGH SHIP LAUNCHED (Middlesbrough)** The Otnaburgh has been launched at Middlesbrough by boat builder J.G.Holmes.

**1835 - HARTLEPOOL SHIPS COAL (Hartlepool)** The Hartlepool Dock has opened and has commenced shipping coal from its newly deepened harbour. The first vessel engaged in this purpose was The Britannia owned by leading citizen and historian of Hartlepool Sir Cuthbert Sharp.

**1835 - SHIPYARD ESTABLISHED (Hartlepool)** Thomas Richardson of Castle Eden and John Parkin of Sunderland have established a shipyard at Hartlepool. The yard is based near the High Street in Old Hartlepool. The first ship to be built was called The Castle Eden.

**1836 - DURHAM UNIVERSITY (Durham)** The remaining privileges and revenues held by the Prince Bishops of Durham have been abolished and their castle at Durham has passed to the recently established University of Durham, following the death of the Bishop William Van Mildert. Durham University was established in 1832.

**1837 - CONSETT IRON ORE DISCOVERED (County Durham)** Iron Ore is discovered at Consett.

**1837 - MORE PLANS FOR HARTLEPOOL (Hartlepool)** Christopher Tennant, who built the Clarence Railway has gained an Act of Parliament for The Great North of England Clarence and Hartlepool Junction Railway. Mr Tennant has plans to further develop the industrial growth of Hartlepool as a port.

**1838 - FIRST SCHOOL (Middlesbrough)** Middlesbrough's first school has opened in Stockton Street for the education of 120 boys and 100 girls.

**1838 - RAILWAYS CONTINUE TO EXPAND** The Stanhope and Tynedale Railway is completed in 1834 linking Weardale - Consett - South Shields, while The Sunderland and Durham Railway opened in 1836. This year Newcastle and Carlisle have been linked by rail.

**1838 - SHIP ENGINES FROM HARTLEPOOL (Hartlepool)** The building of ships' engines is begun at Hartlepool.

**1839 - DURHAM COAL FROM HARTLEPOOL (Hartlepool)** County Durham's Cornforth and Garmondsway Moor Collieries have commenced shipping coal at Hartlepool. A new railway has been built this year called the Stockton and Hartlepool Railway linking Hartlepool with the coalfield. Instigated by Christopher Tennant, who died before its completion, the railway has been taken over by a Stockton solicitor called Ralph Ward Jackson.

**1839 - NEWCASTLE DEVELOPMENT (Newcastle)** From 1835, Newcastle develops a new town centre. Builder Richard Grainger and architect John Dobson build in grand classical style on the site of gardens which were formerly part of a country estate. Developments take place to the north and east of the existing, largely medieval town and include the Grainger Market, Royal Arcade, Grey Street, Grainger Street and Clayton Street. The developments are backed by the town clerk John Clayton and reinforce Newcastle's status as the region's principal town.

Middlesbrough as it appeared in 1832

# The Northern Coalfield

1800AD to 1900AD

Miners strike at Hebburn in 1892

**THE NORTHERN COALFIELD 1800 TO 1900** During the period 1800-1900 coal mining rapidly expanded in the region and over 200 pits were sunk in County Durham alone. The coal ports of Tyne, Wear and Tees were growing and new industries demanded the use of coal. Mines came to be deeper and deeper but safety was increasingly an issue as many miners lost their lives in horrific colliery disasters. The increasing workforce of coal miners formed into unions fighting for better pay and conditions.

**COAL STAITHES** Tyneside coal ports continued to be important and new docks opened in the 1850s like the NER Tyne Dock at Jarrow of 1859. Iron and engineering developments increased demand for coal and the ever-growing network of colliery railways brought coal to Tyneside staithes. Foremost were the massive staithes at Dunston on Tyne, built by the NER from 1890 to 1893 and still in existence today.

**SUNDERLAND COAL** Sunderland continued to grow as a coal-port and shipbuilding town in the nineteenth century. Coal was brought by rail to Wearside staithes from mines near Washington, Chester-le-Street, Durham and Hetton. A number of Sunderland docks were built in the period 1837 to 1868. From 1831 a nearby rival coal port at Seaham Harbour was developed by Lord Londonderry, but it would never develop the vast range of industries present at Sunderland.

**HARTLEPOOL COAL** In the early 1800s Hartlepool was a fishing community with a silted harbour and was not involved in coal export until the 1830s when railways brought coal from Cornforth, Garmondsway, Cassop and Trimdon. Hartlepool was developed by Christopher Tennant of Yarm from 1831 whose Stockton and Hartlepool Railway boosted trade. Tennant died before completion of the railway in 1839 and it was taken over by the Stockton solicitor Ralph Ward Jackson. In 1841 Jackson opened the Victoria Dock, linked it to the railway and Hartlepool soon shipped more coal than any northern port. In the 1840s Hartlepool railways carried more coal than any other in the North East, with 27 per cent of all coal shipped from the region passing along its tracks.

**ENGLAND'S FOURTH PORT** Ralph Ward Jackson was frustrated by restrictions on business at Hartlepool's Victoria Dock and obtained an act in 1844 for the formation of Hartlepool West Harbour Dock Company. This dock was the first stage in the growth of West Hartlepool.

By 1862 the two Hartlepools shipped merchandise to the value of more than three times as much as that of all North-East ports put together, beating Newcastle, North and South Shields, Sunderland, Stockton and Middlesbrough. Hartlepool was the fourth busiest port in the country behind Liverpool, London and Hull and overtook Hull for a time in the 1890s. By 1881, Old Hartlepool's population was 12,361 and newly born West Hartlepool had a population of 28,000.

**MIDDLESBROUGH COAL** Middlesbrough Dock opened on May 12 1842 to export coal but was a small dock of 5 acres. Until that time coal was shipped from Middlesbrough via staithes on the riverside. The dock was built in response to competition from Hartlepool's deep dock, which threatened Middlesbrough's early coal trade. As the decade progressed, iron making replaced coal export as Middlebrough's main industry.

Hebburn Colliery, 1844

**UNIONS AND STRIKES** In 1830 the region's coal miners established a Union under the guidance of Thomas Hepburn and the following year negotiated a 10 per cent increase in wages and a reduction in working hours for boys. A mass meeting of Northumberland and Durham miners was held on Newcastle Town Moor that year and the following year the miners went on stike. In the 1840s the miners organised themselves on a national basis in the Miners Association of Great Britain and Ireland with its headquarters at Newcastle from 1843. In 1848 successive depression in the coal industry weakened the union but it recovered in the later part of the century.

**DURHAM MINERS' GALA** The Durham Miners' Union was formed on November 20 1869 after a meeting of mine leaders at the Market Hotel in Durham's Market Place. Their first Annual Gala was held at Durham's Wharton Park on August 12 1871 but moved to the racecourse in 1873. Enormous crowds attended the galas and on July 3, 1875 the LNER Railway Company withdrew all trains from Bishop Auckland, Lanchester and Newcastle to Durham. It claimed its railways could not cope with the huge quantity of passengers travelling to the gala. The real reason may have been political.

**COAL OWNERS AND CANDYMEN** Businessmen made their fortune from the region's mines and were often unscrupulous or uncompromising over pay and conditions. Coal owners usually owned the miners' homes and often evicted those who protested. The notorious 'Candymen', or Down and Outs from dockside areas often helped with eviction. Many coal owners like the unpopular Marquess of Londonderry were aristocrats.

**COLLIERY DISASTERS** There were around 30 major colliery disasters in Durham and Northumberland in the period 1800-1899, claiming the lives of more than 1,500 men and boys. Gas explosions were the major danger, although some incidents were caused by collapsing mines. The six worst disasters of the period in terms of numbers killed were:- 204 killed at Hartley near Blyth (1862), 164 at Seaham (1880), 102 at Wallsend (1833), 95 at Haswell (1844), 92 at Felling (1812), 76 at Burradon (1860) and 74 at Trimdon in 1882. Many pit ponies were also killed in the disasters including 181 killed in the 1880 Seaham disaster.

**SAFETY** Colliery disasters highlighted the need for improvements in safety. As mines got deeper safety became more of an issue. The major danger was from gas explosions caused by naked flames on miners' lamps. In 1815 Humphry Davy and George Stephenson developed the Miners' Safety lamp. This reduced the danger of explosion and enabled coal owners to explore ever-deeper mines. The cage, for the movement of miners underground, was introduced to collieries for safety reasons in 1834, and in 1862 an Act of Parliament made it compulsory for every colliery to have two shafts for the purposes of safety. In 1867 John Dalglish, General Manager of Earl Vane's Durham collieries, organised a system of voluntary inspection of pits by his workmen. This system was made compulsory by an Act in 1887.

**DEEP COAL** East Durham Coal lay deep below the Magnesian Limestone which dominates the east of the county. Coal was first proved to exist here by the sinking of a pit at Haswell in 1811 but the first great deep pit in the region was sunk at Hetton in 1821. Sunk to a depth of 147 fathoms (over 1000ft), it became one of the most productive pits in the region as well as a focus for some of Stephenson's important locomotive developments. Monkwearmouth Colliery followed shortly afterwards and was shipping coal from 1835 with a seam 1,590 feet below the surface. Harton near South Shields became the deepest Tyne pit in 1841 (1,290 feet). Monkwearmouth, 1,700 ft in 1846 was the deepest coal mine in the country.

Hetton Colliery in the 1820s

# Lead Mining

## 1750AD to 1850AD

Kilhope Wheel, Weardale

**LEAD MINING 1750 TO 1850** From about 1750 to 1850 lead mining was big business and Britain was the world's leading producer. The North Pennine Lead field comprising Teesdale, Weardale, South Tynedale and the Derwent valley formed the most important lead producing area in the country. Lead mining was also carried out in the Yorkshire dales, particularly in neighbouring Swaledale and Arkengarthdale.

**EARLY LEAD MINING IN THE NORTHERN DALES** There is evidence that the Romans mined lead in the region and during the later Anglo-Saxon age Bede records that lead miners from Swaledale often haggled with Catterick merchants over the price of lead. The Prince Bishops of Durham exploited lead and silver deposits in Durham's dales while monasteries mined and smelted lead in the Yorkshire Dales. In Henry II's reign lead was shipped from South Tynedale to Windsor. German metallurgists introduced new lead extracting skills to the North from at least 1400AD. In the 16th century Sir William Bowes owned extensive lead mining interests in Teesdale and Weardale and operated a smelting mill, but it was not until the late 17th century that the industry really developed.

**THE LEAD COMPANIES** The Blacketts, a Tyneside coal owning family, were mining lead in the Allendales near Hexham in 1684. A few years later they leased land in Weardale from the Bishop of Durham. Lead mines owned by the Blacketts included Burtree Pasture in Weardale, Coalcleugh in the West Allen, and Allenheads Mine. The London Lead Company was mining around Alston from 1696 and in the following century extensively mined in the Derwent Valley, Weardale and Teesdale. The company was noted for its social welfare and built houses, schools and libraries for its workers. It was the first company to introduce the five day week. From 1880 Middleton in Teesdale was its Northern headquarters. The company operated Teesdale mines until it folded in 1905.

**LEAD INDUSTRY** Growing towns and the industrial revolution stimulated the demand for lead for use in roofing, piping, casting, building materials, lead shot, paint-bases and glazing. Lead works began to open on Tyneside at places like Elswick, Hebburn, Blaydon, Bill Quay and Byker Bridge. Newcastle was the main point of export for lead from the Durham dales (including Teesdale), but Stockton was often used for exporting Swaledale lead. Until the growth of railways in the dales around 1860 lead was usually carried to port by teams of Galloway ponies along packhorse routes.

**HUSHING** The earliest methods of extracting lead were simple bell pits or through Hushing, an open cast technique. Hushing involved damming streams and then releasing the water by directing it into a man-made trench in order to remove vast quantities of peat and soil from suspected layers of lead. This created artificial valleys up to half a mile long and sometimes as deep as 100 feet. Many can still be seen in the lead mining dales of the region, particularly Weardale.

**MINING METHODS** By the late eighteenth century the preferred method of mining was to dig stone tunnelled shafts called Levels into the hillsides along a vein. The lead was hauled from the mines along wooden rails (later iron) by horses. Lead mines were well drained and much safer than coal mines in terms of flooding. The lead ore was stripped of its waste products outside the mines, often by boys, and then washed and crushed before transportation to a smelting mill where the lead would be produced in the form of ingots along with any silver.

**ROOKHOPE CHIMNEY** Smelting mills were erected throughout the dales and served several mines. Horizontal condensing tunnels were often built such as the mid nineteeth century Rookhope Chimney. Here a two mile long horizontal tunnel eventually led to a vertical chimney. It served partly to redirect polluting fumes away from the workers but also allowed the formation of lead and silver deposits from the fumes to collect on the walls which were scraped free and collected by lead workers.

**WATER WHEELS** In the late eighteenth and early nineteenth century hydraulic machinery was extensively used in mines, dressing floors and smelt mills and there was an extensive network of man made mill races, streams and channels. Water power was increasingly used in the 1870s. Weardale's Kilhope Mine (opened 1860) saw the introduction of a great 30 feet diameter wheel in 1878 by Blackett Beaumont. It hauled tubs of ore up to the crushing mill while other wheels worked the crushing machines, jiggers, buddles and separators. Mill races drove the wheels and the mill race was linked to other plants at Burtree Pasture and Westgate.

**SILVER MINING** The lead-ore from mines in Allendale and Weardale was particularly rich in silver in the early nineteenth century but by the end of the 19th century it had been thoroughly worked. One of the most important silver mines was that at Allenheads between Stanhope and Alston. It was closed in 1896, but was once the largest silver mine in the world. Silver could be extracted from the lead ore (when it was present) using a special process called crystalization developed at Blackett's Lead Works at Blaydon on Tyne in 1833.

**THE END OF LEAD MINING 1850-1900** By the 1850s, the best lead ore had been mined in Britain and there was cheap competition from the United States, Germany and most significantly from Spain. Ironically, many of these foreign developments were backed with British capital and expertise. Many Northern mines closed in the 1870s and some miners sought work abroad, notably in the United States. Lead mining companies folded or sold their interests to new, smaller companies like the Weardale Lead Company of 1883. This company continued mining at places like Rookhope, but lead mining was virtually dead by the 1900s. The only consolation was that former lead mining waste products like Witherites, Barytes and Fluorspar acquired commercial uses in the twentieth century.

The remains of Rookhope Chimney in Weardale

# The Age of Iron

1839AD to 1879AD

Middlesbrough Ironmaster John Vaughan

**THE AGE OF IRON 1839 TO 1879** Small scale iron making had been important since ancient times and was mined in the Dales from at least the 12th century in simple blast furnaces called Bloomeries. It was not, however, until the nineteenth century that the industry really began to develop in the region. The growth of railways and demand from shipbuilding were major causes of this development, at first on Tyneside, but this was later eclipsed by great iron works at Middlesbrough and Consett in the 1840s and 50s.

**1840 - IRONMASTERS (Newcastle)** John Vaughan, iron works manager at Walker on Tyne, and Henry Bolckow, a German accountant who has settled at Newcastle, become business partners. They aim to establish a new ironworks. Joseph Pease sells them land at Middlesbrough. Meanwhile, ironworks open at Thornaby, and last year at Hartlepool.

**1841 - CONSETT IRON (Consett)** Consett Iron Works is established as Derwent Iron Company. Iron Ore was discovered here in 1837. Meanwhile iron rolling mills and Puddling furnaces are founded by Vaughan and Bolckow at Middlesbrough using Scottish pig iron.

**1842 - MORE IRON (North)** The Weardale Iron company is founded. Meanwhile blast furnaces are erected at Walker by Losh, Wilson and Bell using Whitby iron ore.

**1844 - GILKES AND WILSON (Middlesbrough)** Isaac Wilson and Edgar Gilkes take over the Tees Engine works. The works will build iron railways. Meanwhile Bell Brothers take over a blast furnace at Wylam and Robert Stephenson builds an iron bridge over the Tees, replacing an earlier one used by the Stockton and Darlington Railway.

**1845 - HACKWORTH WORKS (Shildon)** Timothy Hackworth establishes a locomotive works at Shildon.

**1846 - BLAST FURNACES (County Durham)** Middlesbrough's Vaughan and Bolckow build blast furnaces at Witton, where there is a good supply of coking coal. Whitby iron stone is imported into Middlesbrough, transported to Witton, and returns to Middlesbrough as pig iron for processing in forges, foundries and rolling mills.

**1847 - TYNESIDE WORKS (Elswick)** W.G Armstrong establishes a factory at Elswick making hydraulic machinery.

**1850 - ESTON IRON (Cleveland)** This year iron is found in the Eston Hills near Middlesbrough by John Vaughan and will replace the use of Whitby ironstone.

**1851 - MIDDLESBROUGH FURNACE (Middlesbrough)** The first blast furnace on Teesside is erected at Middlesbrough. The whole iron making process is now carried out here.

**1853 - IRONMASTER MAYOR (Middlesbrough)** Henry Bolckow becomes the first mayor of Middlesbrough. A number of ironworks are being established in the area and Darlington Forge has been established to serve the marine and electrical industry.

**1854 - RAILWAYS AND IRON (North)** Expanding railways are important to the demand for iron. The London railway reached Gateshead in 1844, extending to Berwick in 1848. Iron railway bridges include Newcastle's High Level Bridge (1848) and Berwick's Royal Border Bridge. The North Eastern Railway Company is formed this year. It gradually swallows up smaller railways and develops docks.

**1855 - ARMSTRONG'S CANON (Newcastle)** William G Armstrong invents the first successful breech loading canon.

**1855 - TEESSIDE SUPPLIES LONDON PIPING (Teesside)** Practically all London's water piping is presently made of Teesside cast iron. Meanwhile Liverpool's Bernhard Samuelson provides land for an iron works at South Bank and a new community develops there.

**1856 - SHEFFIELD THREAT (England)** The Bessemer Steel-making process is developed, a setback for Middlesbrough as local iron ore is unsuitable. Steel is in demand and Sheffield, with its existing industry, dominates the market for a time.

**1858 - FAMOUS BRIDGE MODIFIED (Sunderland)** Sunderland's Georgian Iron Bridge is extensively modified by Robert Stephenson. The bridge resembles the famous Iron Bridge of Coalbrookdale, in Shropshire.

**1860 - STOCKTON IRON (Stockton)** The Malleable Iron Works of South Durham Steel and Iron Company are opened by C.Furness. There are 32 blast furnaces in Middlesbrough, over the Tees.

**1862 - DARLINGTON WORKS (Darlington)** Darlington Railway Locomotive Works are established.

**1864 - CONSETT IRON COMPANY (Consett)** Derwent Iron Company becomes Consett Iron Company Ltd.

**1864 - RAILWAY KING DIES (York)** Sunderland born 'Railway King' George Hudson dies. He played a very important part in developing the Northern railway network, most of which converges on York.

**1866 - HEAD WRIGHTSON (Thornaby)** Engineer Thomas Wrightson, who trained at William Armstrong's Tyneside engineering works, teams up with the Teesside engineering company Head Ashby & Co. Head's firm started as a Thornaby foundry, established in 1840.

**1871 - ENGINEERS' STRIKE (North East)** Northern Engineers strike over working hours. The Tyneside Works of Armstrong and Hawthorn are badly affected but Robert Stephenson's Locomotive Works is not. Management at Charles Palmer's in Jarrow persuade employees to continue working, promising to accept deals negotiated by strikers at other factories.

**1874 - MIDDLESBROUGH FIRST FOR IRON (Middlesbrough)** Middlesbrough is the number one iron town in England. One third of the nation's output originates here and is exported all over the world. About 95 blast furnaces now exist in the town. Meanwhile Palmers of Jarrow are presently obtaining royalties for Cleveland Coast iron mining.

**1875 - DORMAN LONG (Middlesbrough)** Arthur Dorman and Albert de Lande Long establish an ironworks and will play a part in converting Teesside's ironworks to steel making. Meanwhile Bolckow and Vaughan open a Bessemer steel plant at Eston, helping Middlesbrough compete with Sheffield. High grade iron ore has to be imported from Spain as local ore is unsuitable.

**1876 - SWING BRIDGE (Newcastle)** Newcastle's Swing Bridge is built by Armstrong, replacing the stone bridge of 1781. It allows ships to move downstream.

**1878 - CLEVELAND BRIDGE (Darlington)** Cleveland Bridge Engineering Company Ltd are established at Darlington.

**1878 - BOLCKOW DIES (Middlesbrough)** Ironmaster Henry Bolckow dies. He was Middlesbrough's first mayor and its first MP in 1868.

**1879 - NEW METHODS FOR MIDDLESBROUGH (Middlesbrough)** New steel making methods enable the use of Teesside ore. This is a great boon to Middlesbrough's industry.

Sunderland's old iron bridge can be seen in the rear of this picture

# Shipbuilding

1790AD to 1899AD

The 'Middlesbro', the first ship built in Middlesbrough

**SHIPBUILDING 1790 TO 1899** Shipbuilding has long been one of the region's most important industries. In 1294 Newcastle built a galley for the King's fleet and ships were built at Sunderland from at least 1346, and at Stockton from at least 1470. The early ships were built of wood but in the nineteenth century there was a move towards building ships of iron.

**SUNDERLAND SHIPBUILDING** Sunderland developed as a coal port but it was Sunderland's place as the largest shipbuilding town in the world that gave the town its fame. The first recorded shipbuilder was Thomas Menville at Hendon in 1346. By 1790 Sunderland was building around nineteen ships per year. It became the most important shipbuilding centre in the country in the 1830s and by 1840 there were 65 shipyards. Over 150 wooden vessels were built at Sunderland in 1850 when 2,025 shipwrights worked in the town. A further 2,000 were employed in related industries. Sunderland's first iron ships were built from 1852 and wooden shipbuilding ceased here in 1876. Sunderland shipbuilders included Austin and Son 1826, William Pickersgill 1851 and William Doxford 1840.

**TEESSIDE SHIPS** In 1678 Stockton was building ships of 200 burthen and Yarm had an early shipbuilding trade at around this time, but it was in the late eighteenth century that shipbuilding really began to develop. Between 1790 and 1805 Thomas Haw of Stockton was a builder of ships for the Napoleonic wars, but Middlesbrough shipbuilding did not begin until 1833 when a wooden sailing ship called 'The Middlesbro' was built. Teesside's first iron ship was a screw steamer called 'The Advance', built at South Stockton (Thornaby) in 1854, and Teesside's first steel was 'Little Lucy' built in 1858. One famous Teesside-built ship was the 377 feet long Talpore, built by Pearse & Co of Stockton in 1860. It was a troop ship for the River Indus, and was the world's largest river steamer at the time.

**HARTLEPOOL SHIPS** Thomas Richardson of Castle Eden and John Parkin of Sunderland established a shipyard at Old Hartlepool in 1835 and built The Castle Eden ship. The shipbuilding company of William Gray was established here in 1862 and Gray became one of the most influential men in the town. He was the first mayor of West Hartlepool in 1887. William Gray shipbuilders won the Blue Ribband prize for maximum output in 1878, 1882, 1888, 1895, 1898 and 1900. The yard closed in 1961.

**TYNESIDE YARDS** South Shields born Charles Mark Palmer established a yard at Jarrow in 1851 and built its first iron collier 'The John Bowes' in the following year. It was the first ever sea-going screw collier and was built for John Bowes of Barnard Castle for shipping coal to London. Palmers were also famed for building the first rolled armour plates for warships in 1854. William Smith & Co launched the 1600 ton Blenheim in 1848. W.G.Armstrong, the famous northern engineer, gained interests in the Tyneside shipbuilding firm of Mitchells in 1882 and the company of W.G.Armstrong, Mitchell & Co was formed. The yard built battleships as well as a ship called The Gluckauf, which was arguably the world's first oil tanker. It was launched by the yard in 1886.

**SWAN AND HUNTER** Scotsman Charles Mitchell started building ships at Walker on Tyne in 1852 and purchased a 6.5 acre site at Wallsend in 1873 to soak up excess orders from his Walker shipyard. The new yard failed financially and was handed to his brother-in-law Charles Swan. Charles and his brother Henry were directors of the Wallsend Slipway Company, a repair yard established by Mitchell in 1871. In 1878 Charles arranged a partnership with Sunderland shipbuilder George Hunter, but in 1879 Charles died after falling overboard from a channel steamer whilst returning from the continent with his wife. Hunter went into temporary partnership with Swan's wife before becoming Managing Director in 1880. Swan Hunters built their first steel ship at Wallsend in 1884 and their first Oil Tanker in 1889.

**THE MAURETANIA** Most early ships built on the Swan Hunter yard were smaller ships, like colliers and barges, but in 1898 it built its first ocean liner 'The Ultonia'. It would build a further 21 liners in the period 1898-1903. The most famous ship ever launched was undoubtedly 'The Mauretania', a Transatlantic ocean liner launched on 20th September 1906. The ship was 790 feet long with a beam of 88 ft and a gross tonnage of 31,938 tons. It carried 2000 passengers on its maiden voyage on 16 Nov 1907 and captured the Blue Ribband for the fastest crossing of the Atlantic, a record held for twenty-two years.

**STEAM TURBINES** A major pioneering development in marine engineering was the steam turbine, invented by Charles Algernon Parsons. He patented the first steam turbine on Tyneside in 1884. Parsons, born in Ireland in 1854, was the youngest son of the Earl of Rosse and a keen inventor who worked as Junior Partner in the Tyneside engineering firm of Clarke Chapman. In 1894 Parsons' Marine Turbine Company launched 'The Turbinia', a famous vessel powered by electric turbines.

**YARD CLOSURES 1909-1979** Shipyard closures in the twentieth century took place during economic slumps and occurred in two phases, between 1909-1933 and 1960-1993. Early closures included Smiths Dock at North Shields in 1909, which became a ship repair yard, Armstrongs of Elswick in 1921, Richardson Duck of Stockton (1925), Priestman's of Sunderland (1933) and Palmers of Jarrow and Hebburn (1933). There were 28 North East closures in this period of which 14 were on the Tyne, 7 on the Wear, 6 on the Tees and 1 at Hartlepool. Six shipyards closed in the 1960s including W.Gray of Hartlepool (1961), Short Brothers of Sunderland (1964) and The Blyth Shipbuiding Company (1966). There were five closures in the region in the 1970s including the Furness yard at Haverton Hill, near Stockton, in 1979.

The Mauretania

**THE REGION'S LAST SHIPYARDS 1979-1993** In the 1980s and 90s there were nine remaining shipyards, but closures continued with Hawthorn Leslie's Yard at Hebburn 1981. Further closures followed and in 1987 closure of the Smiths Dock Company Shipyard at Middlesbrough brought an end to shipbuilding on the Tees with a loss of 1,295 jobs. The following year shipbuilding ended in Sunderland with the closure of the Doxford Pallion and Austin & Pickersgill Yards. Tyneside's Neptune Yard was closed in the same year, leaving only Swan Hunter Shipbuilders at Wallsend. This was the region's last shipyard and it closed in 1993.

Wearmouth shipbuilding and colliery, Sunderland 1842

# Chemicals and Glass

**BRUNNER MOND** A number of salt works were established at Haverton Hill, near Billingham, in 1882 by Bell Brothers of Port Clarence, who became the first firm to begin large scale salt production on Teesside. Salt workers were brought in from Cheshire and housed at Haverton Hill. The salt-making interests of Bell Brothers were bought by Brunner Mond & Co of Cheshire in 1890, who became the great giants of Teesside chemical making in the late nineteenth and early twentieth century. Meanwhile rationalization of chemical firms in 1891 left only four works on Tyneside.

**SALT MAKING AT GREATHAM** Salt-making in and around Greatham (between Hartlepool and Billingham) had been important in medieval times but by the sixteenth century the industry was eclipsed by South Shields, on the Tyne. In 1894 the industry returned to Greatham in a big way with the establishment of the Greatham Salt and Brine Company by George Weddell. The works were later purchased by the famous salt making company Cerebos in 1903.

**THE BILLINGHAM CHEMICAL WORKS** The Chemical Industry was established at Billingham in 1918 by the government for the production of synthetic ammonia. It was intended for use in the making of bombs for the war. The seven hundred acre Grange Farm at Billingham was chosen for the site. The war was over by the time the plant opened and it had to adapt to new manufacturing. The plant was taken over by Brunner Mond in 1920 and manufactured synthetic ammonia and fertilisers. Brunner Mond merged with other great chemical manufacturers in 1926 to form ICI. From 1928 Anhydrite or Dry Gypsum was mined from 700 feet below Billingham for use in the making of fertilisers.

**PLASTICS AND NYLON** The making of plastics commenced at Billingham in 1934 and a new plant was established the following year for making oil and petrol from cresote and coal, through a process called hydrogenation. In 1946 another great chemical works opened on Teesside at Wilton, on the south side of the Tees. Further lands were purchased by ICI in 1962 at Seal Sands, where land had been reclaimed from the sea.

**PETRO-CHEMICALS** Coke ovens used in the making of chemicals at Billingham were replaced in 1962 by new plants utilising the steam naptha process which enabled the use of crude oil. This proved to be a much cheaper process of making ammonia on Teesside. From 1964 to 1969 four great oil refineries were erected at the mouth of the Tees by Phillips Petroleum (2), ICI and Shell. Their main purpose was to supply the Billingham chemical industry. A 138 mile long pipeline was built in 1968, linking chemical works on Teesside with chemical plants at Runcorn, for the transportation of ethylene.

**BREWERIES** A chemical industry of an altogether different kind, but linked to the demand for glass, was of course the beer brewing industry. Major beer brewers in the region were Tetley's, established in Leeds 1822, Vaux Breweries at Sunderland 1837, The Lion Brewery at Hartlepool (later Camerons)1852 and the Newcastle Breweries, established in 1890.

Felling Chemical Works 1837

**GLASS MAKING** Glass had long been an important industry in the North since stained glass glaziers were introduced to Wearmouth and Jarrow monastery way back in 674AD. Sunderland and Tyneside were once again noted for glass making from the seventeenth century, and from the nineteenth century glass making was particularly important. In 1827 about two fifths of all English glass was made in the Tyneside area and in 1845 South Shields was making more plate glass than anywhere else in England. Sunderland was also rising to prominence as a glass making centre. James Hartley's Wear Glass Works were opened in Sunderland in 1836 and by 1865 one third of the sheet glass in England was supplied by his Sunderland works. Sunderland is now home to Britain's National Glass Centre.

Salt making in the North East in the eighteenth century

# The Electric Light Years

## 1878AD to 1899AD

**1879 - U.S PRESIDENT VISITS SUNDERLAND (Sunderland)** U.S.President Ullyses Grant visits Sunderland and opens the Central Museum and Library.

**1880 - SWAN LAMPS AT CRAGSIDE (Northumberland)** Sir William Armstrong has installed Swan's light bulbs in his house at Cragside.

**1881 - BENWELL LAMPS (Newcastle)** A company has been formed and established at Benwell for the manufacture of Joseph Swan's newly patented electric lamps. It is thought to be the world's first light bulb factory.

**1880 - EDISON TAKES SWAN TO COURT (England and America)** Thomas Edison has threatened to take Joseph Swan to court over an alleged infringement of patent in the development of a successful electrical light bulb, but it becomes clear that the two inventors have coincidentally made their developments at the same time.

**1883 - EDISON-SWAN LIGHT COMPANY FOUNDED (Tyneside)** The Edison & Swan United Electric Light Company has been formed. The American inventor Thomas Edison has teamed up with Tyneside industrialist Swan after at first accusing Swan of copyright infringement. Both men developed an electric light at around the same time.

**1883 - NEWCASTLE ELECTRICAL WORKS (Newcastle)** J.H.Holmes opens an electrical works at Portland Road, Newcastle.

**1883 - ARMSTRONG GIVES DENE TO CITY (Newcastle)** Lord Armstrong has given Jesmond Dene to the new city of Newcastle. It was part of his town centre estate.

**1884 - ELECTRICAL SWITCH (Newcastle)** J.H.Holmes of Newcastle has manufactured the first quick break electrical switch.

**1884 - THE FIRST STEAM TURBINE (Tyneside)** Charles Algernon Parsons has patented the first steam turbine on Tyneside. Parsons, born in Ireland in 1854 is the youngest son of the Earl of Rosse and is a keen inventor. He currently works as a Junior Partner in the Tyneside firm of Clarke Chapman.

**1884 - CRAGSIDE COMPLETE (Northumberland)** Cragside House, with it vast estate near Rothbury, has been completed by Norman Shaw for Lord Armstrong.

**1889 - PARSONS OPENS HEATON WORKS (Tyneside)** Parsons has opened his own works at Heaton for the manufacture of turbines. Parsons Turbines will change the world and enable the wide scale production of electricity. He will be known as 'the Man who invented the Twentieth Century'.

**1889 - LIGHT COMPANY REGISTERED (Newcastle)** The Newcastle and District Electric Light Company has been registered.

**1890 - FORTH BANKS POWER STATION (Newcastle)** The Forth Banks Power Station Newcastle has started work.

**1894 - TURBINE COMPANY SET UP (Tyneside)** The Marine Steam Turbine Company is set up by Charles Parsons at Wallsend.

**1894 - ARMSTRONG BUYS BAMBURGH (Northumberland)** Lord Armstrong has purchased Bamburgh Castle.

**1897 - ARMSTRONG WHITWORTH WORKS (Tyneside)** Armstrong's works become Armstrong Whitworth & Co. They will achieve prominence in the manufacture of arms.

**1897 - TURBINIA DEMONSTRATION (Spithead)** Parsons Turbinia vessel is demonstrated at the naval review at Spithead.

**1898 - MIDDLESBROUGH GOES ELECTRIC (Middlesbrough)** Electric lighting has been introduced to Middlesbrough this year. Electric trams are replacing horse drawn trams in the town.

Joseph Swan's Lamp

Cragside House near Rothbury, one of the earliest houses lit by electricity

# The Victorian Age

1837AD to 1901AD

A Victorian view of the old Tyne bridge at Newcastle

**THE VICTORIAN AGE 1837 TO 1901** The Victorian Age was a period of great changes and developments in the region. It was an age of increasing travel, booming leisure, tourism and political reform. It was also a period of booming industry and rapidly expanding towns.

**June 20 1837 - VICTORIA (Britain)** Queen Victoria ascends to the throne.

**September 7 1838 - GRACE DARLING RESCUE (Farne Islands)** Lighthouse Keeper's daughter Grace Darling rescues survivors from a wreck off the Farne Islands. Grace becomes famous overnight, receives offers of marriage and even has a play written about her. She dies of consumption in 1842.

**1839 - CANADA REPORT (Canada)** John George Lambton, Earl of Durham, the new Governor General of Canada compiles the Durham Report laying down the future of Canada as an independent country.

**1840 - MIDDLESBROUGH CHURCH (Middlesbrough)** Middlesbrough's first church is built. Its first school was built in 1838.

**1841 - BAINBRIDGE STORE (Newcastle)** Weardale's Emerson Bainbridge establishes Bainbridge's general drapers in Market Street.

**1844 - PENSHAW MONUMENT (Penshaw)** Penshaw Monument is erected in honour of John George Lambton, Earl of Durham.

**1844 - OLD SHIRES ABOLISHED (North)** The County Durham districts of Bedlingtonshire, Norhamshire and Islandshire, become part of Northumberland.

**1846 - FARM DEMOLISHED (Middlesbrough)** The original Middlesbrough farm is demolished.

**1847 - SEASIDE TRIPS (Coast)** Railways extended to the coast make the seaside a more accessible place of recreation. Railways reach Redcar in 1846 and Tynemouth this year.

**1847 - RAILWAY REACHES BERWICK (Berwick)** The London railway reached Gateshead in 1844 and Berwick this year. Robert Stephenson's Royal Border Bridge is built.

**1849 - BARNEY CHOLERA (Barnard Castle)** 143 people die of Asiatic Cholera.

**1850 - NEWCASTLE STATION (Newcastle)** John Dobson's magnificent Central Station is opened.

**1850 - ANCIENT FINDS (Weardale)** A Bronze Age discovery is made at Heathery Burn cave in Weardale. One of the earliest known wheels is discovered.

**1851 - IRISH AND SCOTS (North)** Many incoming workers originate from Wales, Scotland and Ireland. One fifth of Tyneside's population is Irish and one fifth Scottish. Sunderland has 4,000 Irish and 2,300 Scots in the town employed mainly in the ship yards. Many coal miners from these nations have found work in the region's coal mines. Teesside's rapidly increasing population also includes many Irish, Welsh and Scots.

**1853 - NEWCASTLE CHOLERA (Newcastle)** Cholera kills 1500 people.

**October 6  1854 - THE GREAT FIRE OF TYNESIDE (Newcastle)** At one o' clock this morning a fire at a Gateshead worsted factory spread to an adjoining warehouse containing a lethal range of chemicals and 3000 tons of Brimstone. Crowds gathered along the Tyne and at quarter past three the building exploded, sending off debris 'like flying fish'. The explosion was heard far off in Berwick and is said to have damaged houses as far away as Shields. Miners at Sunderland came to the surface in alarm and the glow from the fire could be seen at Smeaton near Northallerton. Flying debris set alight ships and caused a second fire to break out on Newcastle's side of the river destroying medieval quayside buildings. Hundreds were made homeless and at least fifty died. Most bodies were incinerated and unidentifiable.

**1857 - VIADUCT AND STATION (Durham)** Durham railway station and viaduct are built. Many stations and viaducts are built in the Victorian era.

**1862 - INFANT HERCULES (Middlesbrough)** Gladstone describes Middlesbrough as an infant Hercules during a visit.

**1862 - ROWNTREES' CHOCOLATE (York)** Rowntrees begin manufacturing chocolate.

**1862 - BLAYDON RACES SONG (Newcastle)** Music Hall is a popular form of entertainment and entertainers include Geordie Ridley. Tyneside's 'National Anthem' The Blaydon Races, is first sung by Ridley at Balmbra's Music Hall in Newcastle.

**1867 - HARTLEPOOL TREASURE (Hartlepool)** A hoard of Spanish silver dollars is revealed beneath the sands at Seaton Carew following a heavy storm.

**1868 - SALTBURN BY THE SEA (Saltburn)** The railway reached Satburn in 1860 and The Zetland Hotel was built to accomodate tourists. Saltburn is developed as a resort by Henry Pease of Darlington and a pleasure pier has been built.

**1869 - BOWES MUSEUM (Barnard Castle)** John Bowes starts the Bowes Museum. It is completed in 1892.

**1871 - UNIVERSITY ACQUIRES COLLEGE (Newcastle)** Durham University acquires Newcastle School of Medicine and the Newcastle College of Science.

**1871 - MIDDLESBROUGH POPULATION (Middlesbrough)** Middlesbrough's amazing rise in population has been as follows 1830 (40), 1841 (5,463), 1851 (7,431), 1861 (19,416), 1871 (39,563).

**1873 - LEAZES PARK (Newcastle)** Newcastle's Leazes Park opens. Many public parks are opening in the region's towns.

**March 24 1873 - MARY ANN COTTON (Durham)** Mary Ann Cotton is hanged at Durham Jail for poisoning her son Charles at West Auckland. She is said to be responsible for 21 deaths including her mother, 3 husbands, 1 lover and a number of children including her own.

Grey Street, Newcastle - a Victorian view

**1878 - HANCOCK MUSEUM (Newcastle)** The Hancock Natural History Museum opens.

**1882 - NEWCASTLE CITY (Newcastle)** The town of Newcastle becomes a city. St Nicholas' Church becomes a cathedral. Meanwhile the original Fenwick's store opens in Newcastle's Northumberland Street.

**1883 - MUSIC HALL DISASTER (Sunderland)** 182 children are killed by suffocation at Victoria Hall Theatre in Sunderland due to crushing by an inward opening door.

**1884 - MARKS AND SPENCER (Leeds)** Michael Marks opens a Penny Bazzar in Leeds, with everything priced at a penny, in 1884. Marks was a Lithuanian Jew who had entered the country via Stockton on Tees. He will later establish a partnership with a Mr Spencer in Wigan.

**1885 - BERWICK LOSES STATUS (Berwick)** Special references to Berwick in acts of parliament are abolished.

**1887 - DARLINGTON STATION (Darlington)** Darlington's Bank Top station opens. It becomes the town's main station.

**1896 - WOMEN AT UNIVERSITY (Durham)** The first women students are admitted to Durham University.

**1898 - SMALL POX (Middlesbrough)** Small pox kills 202 people in Middlesbrough.

**August 15  1900 - POLICE CHASE (Newcastle)** The world's first pursuit of a criminal by motor car takes place at Newcastle. A car is borrowed by a policeman who orders the driver to chase a drunken horse-rider. The chase lasts one mile. Cars have become increasingly popular in the 1890s.

**January 22  1901 - VICTORIA'S DEATH MARKS END OF AN ERA (Britain)** Queen Victoria dies at her home on the Isle of Wight. She is succeeded by her son Edward VII.

252

Iron and Coal
A nineteenth century painting of Tyneside industry by William Bell Scott

# A New Century and World War One

**1901AD to 1919AD**

The victims of the Washington Glebe Colliery disaster, February 20 1908

**A NEW CENTURY AND WORLD WAR ONE 1901 TO 1919** The Industrial importance of the region was no more apparent than during the First World War, when military engineering and expertise were of great importance. The coastal towns of the region were bombed by German battleships, while far away in Europe many North East soldiers lost their lives.

**January 22 1901 - KING EDWARD VII (Britain)** Edward VII succeeds Victoria as King of Britain.

**1901 - STEPHENSON WORKS MOVE (Darlington and Newcastle)** Robert Stephenson & Co move their locomotive works from Newcastle upon Tyne to Darlington due to lack of space for expansion.

**1901 - TOWN POPULATIONS (The North East)** 91,302 people live in Middlesbrough. Seventy years ago it was little more than a farm inhabited by twenty five people. The population of Newcastle upon Tyne is over 215,328, Sunderland's population 146,077.

**1901 - 100,000 MINERS (Durham and Northumberland)** 100,000 coal miners work in the Durham coalfield and a further 37,000 are employed in the Northumberland coalfield.

**1903 - HUGH MACKAY CARPETS (Durham City)** Hugh Mackay begin manufacturing carpets in Durham City.

**1903 - NEWCASTLE SMALLPOX (Newcastle)** A smallpox epidemic hits Newcastle.

**1903 - CEREBOS BUY SALT WORKS (Hartlepool)** Cerebos buy the Greatham salt works near Billingham.

**1905 - VICTORIA FALLS BRIDGE BUILT (Darlington)** Cleveland Bridge and Engineering of Darlington build the Victoria Falls Bridge in Africa.

**1905 - LEAD COMPANY LEAVE TEESDALE (Middleton in Teesdale)** The London Lead Company have ceased operating in Teesdale.

**1906 - DOXFORD SHIPS (Sunderland)** Doxfords are thought to be the world's busiest shipbuilders, building an average of one ship every two weeks in this year.

**October 14 1906 - 24 DIE IN WINGATE DISASTER (Wingate, County Durham)** Twenty four men were killed in an explosion at Wingate Colliery.

**February 20 1908 - GLEBE DISASTER (Washington)** Fourteen men were killed in an explosion at Washington Glebe Colliery.

**February 16 1909 - 168 IN WEST STANLEY EXPLOSION (West Stanley, County Durham)** 168 men are killed in an explosion at Burn Pit Colliery, West Stanley. 59 of the deaths were boys aged under 20. There were 36 survivors.

**1909 - ENGLAND'S FIRST LABOUR COUNCIL ASSEMBLES (Durham City)** England's first all Labour County Council assembles at the Shire Hall in Durham City under the leadership of Peter Lee.

**May 6 1910 - GEORGE V ASCENDS TO THRONE (England)** George V is the new King of England.

**1910 - SMITHS DOCK ESTABLISHED (Middlesbrough)** Smiths Dock is established at South Bank, Middlesbrough by a North Shields firm established on Tyneside in 1899.

**January 17 1911 - TRANSPORTER BRIDGE OPENS (Middlesbrough)** The Transporter Bridge is opened across the River Tees at Middlesbrough by Prince Arthur of Connaught. The bridge was started in 1906 and built at a cost of £68,026. It was designed and built by Cleveland Bridge and Engineering of Darlington with the assistance of Sir William Arrol & Company of Glasgow. The Transporter Bridge was the idea of Alderman McLaughlin and has an advantage over a conventional bridge in that it does not restrict shipping.

**1911 - 200,000 MINERS (Durham and Northumberland)** 152,000 coal miners work in the Durham coalfield and a further 54,000 are employed in the Northumberland coalfield.

**1912 - FORMER EDITOR DIES ON TITANIC (Darlington)** The Northumbrian born social reformer W.T.Stead dies on board the Titanic. Stead had been a one time editor of the Northern Echo in Darlington.

**June 1913 - SUICIDAL SUFFRAGETTE (Epsom)** The North East born Suffragette, Emily Davison is killed after throwing herself in front of the King's horse during the Derby. Emily is protesting for womens' rights.

**August 4 1914 - WAR BREAKS OUT (Europe)** Britain declares war on Germany. Thousands of miners and other workers from across the North East enlist in the armed services. On Tyneside, thousands of men join battalions of either the Durham Light Infantry or Northumberland Fusiliers. Many Teessiders will join the North Yorkshire regiment of the Green Howards.

**December 16  1914 - BATTLESHIPS BOMB HARTLEPOOL, WHITBY AND SCARBOROUGH (The North)** German battleships have bombarded Hartlepool. 112 civillians and 9 soldiers have been killed. 340 buildings were destroyed. The Hartlepool and Teesside area is a prime target for the Germans because of the making of munitions, bridges and other resources for the war effort in the area. Dorman  Long at Middlesbrough, for example, will be responsible for the manufacture of millions of shells. Lloyd George has described the war as an 'engineers war'. Scarborough and Whitby have also been shelled.

**1914 to 1918 - ARMAMENTS BOOM (North East)** The First World War brings a huge increase in the demand for armaments constructed by the Armstrong Whitworth factory at Elswick. The naval yards of Armstrong Mitchell at Low Walker, Hawthorn Leslie at Hebburn and Palmer at Jarrow also benefit from manufacturing for the war effort.

**October 23  1915 - MINERS' HALL OPENED (Durham City)** A new Durham Miners' Hall has opened at Redhills in the north west of the city. The building replaces the Old Miners' Hall in North Road.

**November 27 1916 - ZEPPELIN SHOT DOWN (Hartlepool)** A German Zeppelin is shot down a mile off Hartlepool by a pilot from Seaton Carew aerodrome.

**November 11  1918 - ARMISTICE DECLARED (Europe)** At the eleventh hour of the eleventh day of the eleventh month fighting ceased in the Great War. Declarations of peace are read out in towns and cities across the North.

**1918 - BILLINGHAM CHEMICAL WORKS (Billingham)** A Chemical works is established at Billingham for the production of synthetic ammonia intended for making bombs for the War. As the War is now over the plant will have to adapt to new manufacturing.

**1919 - MIDDLESBROUGH STEEL (Middlesbrough)** Middlesbrough is producing one third of the nation's steel output. Britain's total steel output is ten million tons, 3.35 million tons of which comes from Middlesbrough's nine steel plants.

Illustration depicting a bombing raid on Hartlepool, December 16 1914

# The 20s and 30s

1920AD to 1939AD

**1928 - THE TYNE BRIDGE (Middlesbrough and Newcastle)** The Tyne Bridge is built by Dorman Long of Middlesbrough and is opened on Tyneside on Oct 10th by George V.

**1928 - ANHYDRITE MINED (Billingham)** Anhydrite Mining commences at Billingham. Anhydrite, also known as dry gypsum, can be used in the production of fertilisers. The mine beneath Billingham consists of miles of grid-like subterranean streets 700 feet below the surface.

**1928 - ARMSTRONG VICKERS MERGE (Elswick)** Armstrong's factory at Elswick on Tyne has been forced to merge with the firm of Vickers of Sheffield. The factory has been unable to diversify since the end of the war.

**1928 - FLYING SCOTSMAN (North)** The Flying Scotsman locomotive service begins operating on the LNER London-Edinburgh route.

**1929 - INDUSTRIAL MERGER (Middlesbrough)** Dorman Long of Middlesbrough absorb neighbouring industrial giants Bolckow and Vaughan.

**1929 - MACDONALD MP (Seaham)** Ramsay Macdonald is elected MP for Seaham Harbour.

**1930 - SHIPYARD CLOSURES (The North)** There have been 19 shipyard closures in the region in the last decade. The closures result in the loss of thousands of jobs and contribute to heavy unemployment throughout the region.

**1931 - JARROW UNEMPLOYMENT (Jarrow)** About 80% of Jarrow's workforce is unemployed. Unemployment is caused by a slump in demand caused by the end of the war and the huge number of unemployed men returning from service.

**June 19 1932 - PALMER LAUNCHES LAST SHIP (Jarrow)** The Palmer Shipyard launches its last ship at Jarrow - the HMS Duchess.

**1932 - SYDNEY HARBOUR BRIDGE (Middlesbrough)** The Sydney Harbour Bridge is completed by Dorman Long of Middlesbrough for shipment in sections to Australia.

**1932 - 5000 WORKERS AT BILLINGHAM (Billingham)** 5000 workers are now employed by the chemical industry at Billingham.

**1933 - HAWTHORN LESLIE REDUCES WORKFORCE (Hebburn)** Hawthorn Leslie has reduced its workforce by about a fifth over the last two years. It now employs around 1000 people. Many industrial firms have had to take similar actions.

**1933 - SHIPYARD CLOSURES (The North)** There were 6 shipyard closures in the region from 1931 to 1933 further increasing unemployment.

**February 28  1934 - NEWPORT BRIDGE OPENS (Middlesbrough)** The Duke and Duchess of York open the Newport Lifting Bridge at Middlesbrough. It was built by Dorman Long.

**1935 - BILLINGHAM PLASTICS (Billingham)** A new chemical plant is established at Billingham for making oil and petrol from creosote and coal through a process called hydrogenation. The making of plastics was established here last year.

**1936 - T.V.T.E ESTABLISHED (Team Valley, Gateshead)** The Team Valley Trading Estate is established to encourage the light industries in the region. It is a recognition of the dangers of relying too heavily on a small number of manufacturing industries which employ many people. The region had been designated a Special Area in the Special Areas Act of 1934.

**October 5 to October 31 1936 - JARROW MARCH (Jarrow)** Two hundred unemployed men marched 274 miles from Jarrow to the House of Commons in protest against recession. They arrive in London on October 31st.

**1937 - SCANDINAVIAN FERRY (Tyneside)** A regular ferry service commences from the mouth of the Tyne to Bergen and Oslo in Norway.

**May 12 1937 - GEORGE VI CROWNED (London)** George VI is crowned at Westminster Abbey. In December last year King Edward VIII abdicated because of his love for American divorcee Wallis Simpson.

**1937 - UNIVERSITY SPLITS (Newcastle and Durham)** Reorganization of Durham University recognised two divisions; Durham and Newcastle. The Newcastle colleges are grouped under the title King's College.

**1937 - CINEMA BOOM (The North)** Many cinemas, a popular craze, are built in the region throughout the 1930s including 4 at Gateshead, 5 in Sunderland and 15 in Newcastle.

The Tyne Bridge under construction

# World War Two and the late 40s

1939AD to 1949AD

A squadron of spitfires over Catterick

**WORLD WAR TWO AND THE LATE 40s 1939 TO 1949** Like the great war of 1914-18, the Second World War brought a huge loss of life to the forces of the region who were fighting abroad, while at the same time placing a great demand on the manufacturing industries of the region. Many lives were lost back home, where the great industrial centres of Tyne, Tees and Wear were a constant victim of the bombing raids of German aircraft. Even non-industrial cities like York were in danger and were targetted specifically because of their rich heritage in the so called Baedeker raids, aimed at demoralising our nation by the destruction of its history. The North remained resilient and proud throughout.

**September 3 1939 - NATION AT WAR (Britain)** Neville Chamberlain announces that the Nation is at war with Germany.

**1940 - BOMBS HIT TEESSIDE (Middlesbrough)** Some of the first German bombs to hit England at the beginning of World War Two have hit the South Bank Road area of Middlesbrough. The Oxford Palace Music Hall in Feversham Street, Middlesbrough (opened in 1867) has been destroyed by a German bomb. In June a bomb hit the car of the Transporter Bridge.

**1941 - RAF STATIONS (The North)** Goosepool RAF Station has been established at Middleton St George. It will later become Teesside Airport. This is one of many RAF stations throughout the region.

**1941 - NEWCASTLE GOODS STATION BOMBED (Newcastle)** Newcastle Goods Station has been severely destroyed in a German bombing raid. Railway stations, engineering works, iron and chemical works are major targets for German bombing raids. The Germans are making detailed plans of industrial sites on the Tyne, Wear and Tees which they intend to bomb.

**June 26 1942 - 13 DIE IN MURTON COLLIERY DISASTER (Murton)** Thirteen men are killed in an explosion at Murton Colliery.

**1942 - YORK SUFFERS BAEDEKER RAID (York)** York has been bombarded in one of the so called Baedeker raids which are particularly aimed at cities with outstanding architectural features.

**May 8  1945 - V.E. DAY (Europe)** Victory in Europe was declared today.

**1945 - REMEMBERING THE WAR (The North)** During World War Two there were 298 air raids on the Northern region. Hundreds of civilians have lost their lives as a result of the raids, but thousands more North Easterners lost their lives fighting in Europe.

**June 8  1946 - NORTH CELEBRATES VICTORY (Durham City)** Victory Day celebrations have been taking place throughout the region. In Durham events in the city included hymns in the market place, boating and boat races, children's sports, a grand cricket match, dancing in the Town Hall and a prize for the best decorated house. The cathedral and castle were floodlit from dusk to 2am.

**1946 - ICI START WILTON WORKS (Middlesbrough)** I.C.I start building The Wilton Works near Middlesbrough on the south side of the Tees. The works will compliment their extensive works at Billingham on the north side of the river where around 11,000 workers are now employed.

**1947 - NEW TOWNS (North East)** The New Towns of Newton Aycliffe and Peterlee have been established. Peterlee is named after a County Durham miners' leader.

**August 22  1947 - 21 DIE IN LOUISA COLLIERY DISASTER (Stanley)** Twenty one men were killed in an explosion at the Louisa Colliery.

**1947 - COAL MINES NATIONALISED (Britain)** The coal mines of Great Britain are 'Nationalised' and will now come under the control of the government controlled National Coal Board (NCB). Mines were previously controlled by private companies.

**1948 - DHSS AT LONGBENTON (Tyneside)** The Department of Health and Social Services has established its huge records centre at Longbenton near Newcastle. The service sector will increasingly become a major employer in the North in the later part of the twentieth century.

A German bomber brought down near Whitby

A VE Day celebration in Darlington

# The 50s and 60s

1950AD to 1969AD

The A1(M) Motorway

**THE 50s AND 60s 1950 TO 1969** The 1950s saw the advent of many things we now take for granted today. Rock 'n' Roll music, colour television, motorways, the contraceptive Pill and concrete architecture. The Conservative Prime Minister and former Stockton MP, Harold Macmillan claimed we'd 'never had it so good'. On the industrial front, oil refineries were opening at the mouth of the Tees but there was an ever increasing closure of coal mines in County Durham.

**May 29 1951 - 81 DIE IN EASINGTON EXPLOSION (Easington)** 81 men are killed in an explosion at Easington Colliery.

**1952 - ANDY CAPP (Hartlepool)** Cartoon character Andy Capp is created by Hartlepool cartoonist Reg Smythe.

**June 2 1953 - ELIZABETH II (Durham City)** Queen Elizabeth II has been crowned

**April 6 1955 - PRIME MINISTER EDEN (Britain)** Anthony Eden, the new Prime Minister of Great Britain, was born at Windlestone Hall, County Durham and is a member of a well known Durham family.

**1959 - 1950S COLLIERY CLOSURES (County Durham and Northumberland)** Collieries which have closed in Durham and Northumberland over the last decade include;- Axwell Park, Bildershaw, Blaydon Burn Bessie, Blaydon Burn Mary, Castle Eden, East Hedleyhope, Greencroft Tower, Harbour House, Little Burn, Montague (Newcastle), New Brancepeth, New Delaval, New Hartley, Ramshaw, South Shildon and Throckley Isabella.

**January 1959 - TYNE TEES TELEVISION (Newcastle)** Tyne Tees Television begins broadcasting to the region.

**1962 - BILLINGHAM FESTIVAL (Billingham)** Billingham International Folklore Festival is established.

**1962 - OIL REPLACES COAL AT BILLINGHAM (Billingham)** Coke ovens at Billingham Chemical works have been replaced by new plants utilising the Steam Naptha process which uses crude oil. This is a much cheaper process for producing ammonia.

**1962 - NEW DOCK (Middlesbrough)** Tees Dock opens, superceding the old Middlesbrough Dock, further downstream.

**1962 - NEW ICI PLANT (Teesside)** ICI have purchased land at Seal Sands near the mouth of the Tees for the development of a new chemical plant.

**1962 - NEW DEVELOPMENTS (The North)** Throughout the 1960s many urban redevelopments took place in the region. A number of these developments are carried out by the Northern Economic Planning Council under the leadership of T.Dan Smith.

**1963 - NEWCASTLE UNIVERSITY GOES ALONE (Newcastle)** Durham University's King's College, Newcastle has become the University of Newcastle upon Tyne and will now be independent of the University of Durham.

**1963 - BEECHING REPORT (Britain)** Many of the region's branch railways will close, on the advice of a Railway Report undertaken by Doctor Beeching.

**1963 - KILLINGWORTH AND CRAMLINGTON (Killingworth)** Northumberland County Council begins the construction of Cramlington New Town. Last year Killingworth new town was begun.

**1964 - WASHINGTON TOWN (Washington)** Washington New Town is being built to soak up the increasing populations of Tyneside, Sunderland and neighbouring villages. It will be divided into certain districts or villages, each with an assigned number.

**1965 - MOTORWAY OPENS (Darlington)** Darlington bypass is the first section of the new A1(M) motorway which will become the main routeway through the North East.

**1966 - DARLINGTON WORKS CLOSED (Darlington)** Darlington railway workshops have closed, bringing an end to an important industrial era in the town.

The Durham Miners Gala in the 1950s

Newcastle United FC won the FA Cup in 1951, 1952 and 1955

**1966 - HARTLEPOOLS MERGE (Hartlepool)** The Hartlepool Order merges Old Hartlepool with West Hartlepool.

**1966 - SLUM CLEARANCE (The North)** Throughout the 1960s slum clearances and urban redevelopments will take place in the region's urban areas. Clearance of Cannon Street and Newport Road in Middlesbrough took place this year.

**1966 - WORLD CUP (Britain)** Ayresome Park, Middlesbrough and Roker Park, Sunderland are venues for World Cup football matches. England will eventually defeat Germany in the World Cup Final at Wembley with a team which includes the Ashington born brothers Jack and Bobby Charlton.

**1966 - SHIPYARD CLOSURES (The North)** Between 1960 and 1966 there were six shipyard closures in the region.

**January 1 1967 - T.H.P.A ESTABLISHED (Teesside)** The Tees Conservancy Commission is replaced by the Tees and Hartlepool Port Authority who will be responsible for managing the whole port area.

**1967 - STEEL MERGER (Middlesbrough)** Dorman Long becomes part of British Steel Corporation.

**October 19 1967 - TYNE TUNNEL (Tyneside)** The Tyne Tunnel is officially opened by Her Majesty the Queen. Work has been carried out on the tunnel since 1961. It is a continuation of the A1(M) mortorway.

**April 1968 - TEESSIDE CREATED (Teesside)** The County Borough of Teesside is created, uniting the Durham towns of Stockton and Billingham with the Yorkshire towns of Redcar, Thornaby and Middlesbrough.

**1968 - OIL REFINERIES AT TEESMOUTH (Middlesbrough)** In the past four years three oil refineries have been built at the mouth of the River Tees to supply the chemical industry.

**1968 - DLI DISBANDS (Durham)** The Durham Light Infantry is disbanded.

**1968 - PORT OF TYNE (Tyneside)** The Port of Tyne Authority is established, replacing the Tyne Improvement Commission.

**1969 - LAST COLLIERY ON NORTH BANK CLOSES (Tyneside)** The Rising Sun Colliery has closed at Wallsend. It is Tyneside's last colliery on the north bank of the river.

**1969 - 1960S COLLIERY CLOSURES (County Durham and Northumberland)** Collieries which have closed in Durham and Northumberland over the last decade include;- Addison Colliery, Barcus Close, Barlow Towneley, Beamish Mary, Bedlington F, Bedlington Doctor, Bowburn, Brancepeth, Brandon, Burnopfield, Cambois, Chester South Moor, Choppington A, Chopwell, Clara Vale, Crofton Mill (Blyth), Crookhall (Lanchester), Deaf Hill (Trimdon), Dean and Chapter (Ferryhill and Chilton), Dinnington, East Tanfield, East Walbottle, Esh, Hamsterley, Handenhold, Harraton, Harton, Hazlerigg, Heworth, High Marley Hill, Kimblesworth, Lambton D, Lanchester, Leasingthone, Linton, Lumley Sixth, Longhirst (Ashington), Mainsforth, Malton (Lanchester), Middridge (Ferryhill), Newbiggin, New Shildon, Pelton, Randolph, Ravensworth Anne (Gateshead), Ravensworth Park, Ravensworth Shop, Rising Sun (Wallsend), Roddymoor, Ryhope, Seghill, Sherburn Hill, South Pelaw, Staindrop Field House, Stanley Burn, Stanley Cottage, Stargate, Tanfield Lea, Thrislington, Trimdon Grange, Tudhoe Mill, Tudhoe Park, Ushaw Moor, Washington F, Waterhouses, West Auckland, West Thornley, Wheatley Hill, Whitburn, Wingate Grange and Witton.

Horden Colliery - closed in 1986

# Pits and Politics

## 1970AD to 1989AD

David Jenkins, a controversial Bishop of Durham

**PITS AND POLITICS 1970 TO 1989** One of the most important political changes of the 1970s was the establishment of the new counties of Cleveland and Tyne and Wear which swallowed up the most populous chunks of Northumberland, Durham and North Yorkshire. Coal mines continued to close in the 70s and 80s and the big political issue of the 1980s was mine closures and the Miner's Strike of 1984. By the end of 1980 there were only six collieries left in the land between Tyne and Tees.

**1970 - BEAMISH MUSEUM (County Durham)** The North of England Open Air Museum has been established at Beamish by Mr Frank Atkinson. The museum will bring to life the social and economic history of the region.

**1970 - RESERVOIR OPENS (Teesdale)** Cow Green reservoir opens in Teesdale, supplying homes and industries on Teesside.

**1970 - MONSANTO (Teesside)** Monsanto textiles establish a plant at Seal Sands for production of acylonite for making acrylic fibre.

**1971 - THE SERVICE SECTOR (Tyneside)** About 53 per cent of Tyneside employment is now in the service sector. Manufacturing and heavy industry no longer dominate the Tyneside scene.

**1972 - POWER STATION COMMENCES SUPPLY (Hartlepool)** Hartlepool Nuclear Power Station has commenced supplying electricity. Its construction began in 1968.

**April 1  1974 - TYNE AND WEAR AND CLEVELAND CREATED (The North)** Local Government reforms have considerably changed the shape of County Durham's boundaries. Gateshead, Jarrow, Blaydon, South Shields and Sunderland have all been moved from County Durham into the new county of Tyne and Wear. Most of the Tyneside area north of the Tyne has been moved from Northumberland into Tyne and Wear. In southern County Durham, Hartlepool has been moved into the newly created County of Cleveland which includes most of the old borough of Teesside, created in 1867, plus areas of rural North Yorkshire including Guisborough.

**1974 - METRO SYSTEM STARTED (Tyneside)** The building of the Metro Rapid Transport System commences on Tyneside.

**September 27  1975 - RAILWAY CELEBRATIONS (Darlington)** The 150th anniversary celebrations of the Stockton and Darlington Railway have been held. The Duke of Edinburgh visited the celebrations at Preston Park and opened the North Road Station Museum in Darlington.

**1976 - KIELDER RESERVOIR (Tynedale)** The construction of the Kielder Dam has begun in North Tynedale. The resulting reservoir in North Tynedale has been built primarily to supply the thirsty industries of Teesside.

**1979 - 1970S COLLIERY CLOSURES (County Durham and Northumberland)** Collieries which have closed in Durham and Northumberland over the last decade include;- Adventure Pit (Rainton), Bardon Mill, Bedlington A, Blackburn Fell (Gateshead), Burradon, Elemore, Fishburn, Hylton, Kibblesworth, Langley Park, Medomsley, Metal Bridge, Nettlesworth, Shotton, Silksworth, Thornley, Usworth, Washington Glebe and Whitworth Park (Spennymoor).

**May 4  1979 - THATCHER IS PM (Britain)** Mrs Thatcher has been elected as Britain's first woman Prime Minister.

**1979 - SHIPYARD CLOSURES (The North)** Between 1974 and 1979 there were five shipyard closures in the North East of England. There are now only 8 shipyards left in the region.

**1980 - DOCK CLOSES (Middlesbrough)** The Tees and Hartlepool Port Authority have closed Middlesbrough Dock to commercial traffic. The Dock is scheduled for redevelopment.

**1980 - CONSETT WORKS CLOSE (Consett)** The Consett Steel Works are closed on economic grounds.

**1980 - METRO OPENS (Tyneside)** The first section of railway line for Tyneside's Metro Rapid Transport System is offically opened. It runs from Newcastle's Haymarket to Tynemouth.

The Austin and Pickersgill shipyard in Sunderland

Durham Cathedral - a World Heritage site

**1981 - SERVICE SECTOR INCREASES (Tyneside)** Tyneside employment in the service sector is now 63 per cent.

**July 16  1983 - 100th MINERS' GALA HELD (Durham City)** The 100th Durham Miners' Gala was held today in Durham. The gala has been held every year since 1871 with the exception of the war periods 1915-1918 and 1940-45.

**1984 - WAGON WORKS CLOSE (Shildon)** The Shildon Wagon Works are closed on economic grounds. The works were responsible for building most of Britain's railway freight wagons.

**March 12  1984 - MINERS' STRIKE (Britain)** Mines across the country are out on strike in protest over pit closures.

**1984 - JENKINS IS BISHOP (County Durham)** David Jenkins becomes the new Bishop of Durham. Jenkins is noted for his outspoken and controversial beliefs, including doubts over the resurrection of Christ and the Virgin birth. He is consecrated at York Minster.

**July  1984 - MINSTER FIRE (York)** A major fire destroys parts of York Minster after it is hit by lightning.

**1984 - WORLD'S MOST BEAUTIFUL BUILDING (Durham City)** As a celebration of the 150th anniversary of the Royal Institute of British Architects, a panel of 50 architectural experts vote Durham Cathedral the most beautiful building in the world.

**1986 - TEES IS NUMBER THREE (Teesside)** The port of Tees is the third largest port in the UK in terms of tonnage shipped.

**September  1986 - NISSAN OPENS (Washington/Sunderland)** A Nissan Car plant, the first Japanese company to establish a factory in Britain, has been established near Sunderland.

**1987 - WORLD HERITAGE SITE (Durham City)** Durham Cathedral and Castle are declared a World Heritage Site, one of only a few selected sites designated as such in this country by UNESCO.

**1987 - SHIP RESTORED AT HARTLEPOOL (Hartlepool)** The restoration of H.M.S Warrior is completed at Hartlepool.

**1987 - DEVELOPMENT CORPORATIONS (Tyne and Wear and Teesside)** Two new development corporations - The Teesside Development Corporation and The Tyne and Wear Development Corporation are established. They will invest millions of pounds into developing the region's two major urban areas.

**1987 - SHIPYARD CLOSURES (Middlesbrough)** The 15,000 tonne North Islands was launched on 15th October last year and will be the last ship ever to be launched on the Tees at Smiths Dock, South Bank, following the closure of the historic shipyard. 1,295 people have lost their jobs.

**October 1987 - METROCENTRE (Gateshead)** The MetroCentre, Europe's largest shopping and leisure complex, is opened. It is the brainchild of former Coal Board Surveyor, John Hall, later to become Sir John Hall.

**1988 - SUNDERLAND SHIPBUILDING ENDS (Sunderland)** The Austin and Pickersgill Shipyard has closed at Sunderland bringing an end to shipbuilding in a place which once described itself as the largest shipbuilding town in the world. There have been seven shipyard closures in the 1980s and only one now remains - the Swan Hunter Yard on the Tyne at Wallsend.

**1980 to 1989 - COLLIERY CLOSURES (County Durham and Northumberland)** Collieries which have closed in Durham and Northumberland over the last decade include;- Ashington, Bearpark, Blackhall, Boldon, East Hetton, Eccles (Backworth), Eden and South Medomsley, Eppleton, Herrington, Horden, Houghton, Marley Hill, Sacriston, Seaham, Shilbottle, South Hetton and Woodhorn.

Kielder Reservoir

# Sport

1700AD to 1999AD

West Auckland FC - World Cup winners

**EARLY FOOTBALL** No evidence supports the belief that Romans introduced football to the region although some annual Shrove Tuesday matches like Alnwick, Chester-le-Street and Sedgefield may have pre-Norman origins. Football is recorded as early as 1280 when a man was killed during a match near Morpeth, but organised football teams did not appear until the 1870s. Middlesbrough FC was formed by cricket players in 1876, Sunderland in 1879 and Newcastle United in 1892 by uniting Newcastle West End FC with Newcastle East End. Darlington formed in 1861 (re-formed 1883) and West Hartlepool of 1881 became Hartlepool United in 1908. In 1888 Sunderland and Middlesbrough were troubled by rival break-away teams called Sunderland Albion and Middlesbrough Ironopolis but both folded before the century was out.

**EARLY SUCCESS** Success came early to the region with Sunderland winning the championship three times in the 1890s under manager Tom Watson who later established Liverpool as a force. Sunderland peaked too early to benefit financially but Newcastle reaped rewards for successes in the first decade of the 1900s being champions three times and reaching the FA Cup Final three times before winning it on a fourth attempt in 1910.

**FAMOUS FOOTBALLERS** Famous footballers included Sunderland's Alf Common, the world's first £1000 player, signed by Middlesbrough in 1905. Other greats were Charlie Buchan, George Camsell and Hughie Gallacher. In the 30s Wilf Mannion, Raich Carter and Bob Gurney shot to fame, the last two being joint top scorers for Division One in the 1935-36 season. Heroes of the 40s, 50s and 60s included Joe Harvey, Jackie Milburn, Len Shackleton and Brian Clough while Newcastle's Malcolm Macdonald was a great name of the seventies. Goalscorers attract fame, but goalkeeper Jim Montgomery's double save, which helped Sunderland win the 1973 FA Cup Final, is often remembered. Players of the 80s and 90s include local born internationals like Peter Beardsley, Paul Gascoigne, Chris Waddle and Alan Shearer.

**WEST AUCKLAND'S WORLD CUP** From time to time amateur football sides like Bishop Auckland find fame and success but the most extraordinary feat of any side was surely that achieved by West Auckland FC in 1910. In that year the team were invited to take part in a competition in Italy to compete for the soccer World Cup. West Auckland won the competition against some of Europe's biggest sides and defeated the mighty Juventus 2-0 in the final. West Auckland successfully defended the title the following year.

**HORSE RACING** Early races were mentioned in 1613 at Woodham near Aycliffe and were held at Newcastle's Killingworth Moor from 1632, moving later to the Town Moor. The 'Pitmen's Derby' or Northumberland Plate was held from 1833 and moved to Gosforth in 1882. Georgian races were held at places like Barnard Castle, Bishop Auckland, Blaydon, Chester-le-Street, Darlington, Durham, Gateshead, Hebburn, Heighington, Lanchester, Ryton, Sedgefield, South Shields, Stockton, Sunderland, Tanfield, Whickham and Witton Gilbert. A 1740 Act banned smaller meetings but some meetings like Durham survived into the late nineteenth and early twentieth century.

**YORKSHIRE RACING** Racing may have taken place at York since Roman times and York's Knavesmire has held races since at least 1731. Middleham claims to have trained horses since the reign of Henry VIII. Doncaster has held the St Leger race since 1776 and Catterick has held races since 1783. Thirsk Race Course opened in 1855 and racing was recorded at Ripon as early as 1664. At Redcar, horse races were held on the beach until the present racecourse opened in 1872. The remains of a Georgian grandstand can be found at Richmond where a meeting was once held.

**THE BLAYDON RACES** The Blaydon Races, a popular musical hall song first sung by Geordie Ridley at Balmbra's Music Hall in Newcastle in 1862, gives an idea of some of the characters attending the old meetings. These races were held on an island in the middle of the Tyne and were last held on 2nd September 1916. A riot broke out after the winning horse was disqualified and the event was discontinued.

**ROWING** Football is now the big spectator sport in the region but for much of the nineteenth century it was rowing. There were many organised teams or schools, particularly on Tyneside, competing against each other and against rowers from the Wear, Tees, Thames and Mersey. Rowing was extremely popular and attracted crowds of thousands. Rowers, like the keelman Harry Clasper, were great celebrities. Rowing was also a great tradition in Durham City where an annual regatta was established in 1834 (before Henley Regatta) and has been held continuously ever since.

**GOLF** Golf is probably a Scottish import but is said to have been played by St Cuthbert on the dunes of the Northumberland coast. The region's oldest Club was Alnmouth, founded in 1869 - the fourth oldest in the country. The nine hole course is now Alnmouth Village Club.

The Great North Run

Golf appeared in Durham in 1874 at Seaton Carew while across the Tees at Redcar, the Cleveland Golf Course of 1887 is the oldest in Yorkshire. Tyneside Golf Club at Ryton dates from 1880 but there may have been earlier courses in the region. During the Civil War King Charles played 'Goff' in the fields near Newcastle during imprisonment in the town.

**CRICKET** Cricket has long been a popular sport in the North East and is said to date back to Elizabethan times. Yorkshire County Cricket Club was formed in 1863 and Durham County Cricket Club was established in 1882. After many years of success in the Minor Counties Championship, Durham joined Yorkshire in the Senior Counties Championship in 1990.

**ATHLETICS** Athletics is a sport of rising popularity since the international success of Tyneside athletes Brendan Foster in the 1970s and Steve Cram in the mid 1980s. Both athletes won international medals and broke world records in middle and long distance running. Brendan Foster was the man behind the establishment of the annual Great North Run, one of the best known half marathons in which thousands of participants run from Newcastle to South Shields.

Alf Common, of Sunderland and Middlesborough, was the first £1000 footballer

# The 1990s - Towards a New Millennium

Tony Blair visiting his old school in Durham

**TOWARDS A NEW MILLENNIUM** The last ten years of the second millennium saw the closure of County Durham's last coal mine, ending an era of at least eight-hundred years. A huge football stadium was built in its place as one of many modern developments carried out in the 1990s. Aimed at rejuvenating the region and its economy, most new developments were concentrated in the old riverside areas of the Tyne, Wear and Tees, which had once been at the forefront of the region's manufacturing economy. Today the major industries which dominated the region throughout the nineteenth and twentieth century have declined or disappeared, leaving the region to adjust to new technologies, new forms of employment and a new way of life.

**1990 - NATIONAL GARDEN FESTIVAL (Gateshead)** The National Garden Festival has been held at Gateshead. Its site stretches from the River Tyne towards Dunston and includes the Dunston Coal Staithes which are reputedly the world's largest wooden structure. The festival is designed to regenerate derelict industrial land for future use.

**July 1991 - DAWDON COLLIERY CLOSES (Dawdon)** Dawdon Colliery in eastern County Durham has closed.

**November 1991 - MURTON COLLIERY CLOSES (Murton, County Durham)** Murton Colliery in East Durham has closed.

**1992 - SUNDERLAND IS A CITY (Sunderland)** The town of Sunderland has become a city. The last town in the North East to gain this status was Newcastle in 1882.

**1992 - NEW UNIVERSITIES (The North)** The government has given permission for Teesside Polytechnic to become the University of Teesside. Sunderland Polytechnic will also become a University and Newcastle Polytechnic becomes the University of Northumbria.

**1992 - FIRST CLASS CRICKET FOR DURHAM (Durham City)** Durham County Cricket Club has joined the first class cricket league.

**April 1993 - EASINGTON COLLIERY CLOSED (Easington, County Durham)** Easington Colliery in East Durham has closed.

**1993 - CATHEDRAL CELEBRATES 900 YEARS (Durham City)** Durham Cathedral is celebrating its 900th year. The construction of the cathedral was commenced in the year 1093 by the Prince Bishop William St Carileph.

**May 1993 - TYNESIDE'S LAST COLLIERY CLOSES (South Shields)** The Westoe Colliery at South Shields, Tyneside's last remaining colliery is closed.

**June 1993 - VANE TEMPEST CLOSES (Seaham, County Durham)** The Vane Tempest Colliery at Seaham in County Durham has closed.

**June 1994 - DURHAM COALFIELD'S LAST COLLIERY CLOSES (Wearmouth, Sunderland)** Wearmouth Colliery at the mouth of the River Wear in Sunderland, the last colliery in the County Durham Coalfield, has closed, signalling the end of an era in the land between the Tyne and Tees.

**July 1994 - HISTORIC QUAY (Hartlepool)** Hartlepool's historic quay has opened. The quay, developed by Teesside Development Corporation, is a reconstruction of an eighteenth century seaport, which brings Britain's maritime heritage to life.

**April 22 1995 - £50m TEES BARRAGE OPENS (Stockton on tees)** The £50 million pound Tees barrage has been opened at Stockton. The barrage has created a ten mile stretch of clean water from Worsall near Yarm to Stockton and has enabled the creation of a purpose built white water course for canoeists.

**August 26 1995 - RIVERSIDE STADIUM OPENS (Middlesbrough)** Middlesbrough Football Club has played its first game in the £16 milllion, 32,000 all seater Cellnet Riverside Stadium at the grand opening. The opening was celebrated with a 2-0 victory over Chelsea.

The Sunderland Stadium of Light

**1995 - DURHAM 1000 YEARS OLD (Durham City)** Durham is 1000 years old. It was in the late summer of 995 AD that the monks carrying the coffin of St Cuthbert established a settlement at 'Dun Holm' as the final resting place of their saint.

**May 1997 - BLAIR IS PM (Britain)** Tony Blair, MP for Sedgefield, who grew up in Durham City, is elected Prime Minister of Great Britain. He will live in Downing Street and at his home near Trimdon, County Durham.

**July 30  1997 - STADIUM OF LIGHT OPENS (Sunderland)** The first match has been played at Sunderland Football Club's new stadium. Named the Stadium of Light, the ground is built on the site of the Wearmouth Colliery, the last colliery in the County Durham coalfield  which closed in 1994.

**February 15 1998 - ANGEL OF THE NORTH (Gateshead)** The Gateshead Angel, a sculpture by Turner Prize winner, Antony Gormley OBE, has been erected. It weighs 300 tonnes. It was built by Hartlepool Steel Fabrications. It will rapidly become one of the best known landmarks in the region.

**1999 - TOWARDS A NEW MILLENNIUM (The North East)** The North East celebrates the coming of a New Millennium.

# The North East of England

1900AD to 1999AD

Angel of the North

**INDUSTRIAL CHANGES** The dramatic industrial developments of the nineteenth century were in many ways eclipsed by the rapid technological and social changes of the twentieth century. The contrast between 1900 and 1999 is startling. At the beginning of the century most North Easterners were employed in heavy industries and coal mining employed over 100,000 people. By 1999 the service sector dominated the region's employment and only one coal mine at Ellington, in Northumberland, remained. This is scheduled for closure in the year 2000. Mining reached its peak in 1923, but after that, employment in coal mining and related heavy industries fell into gradual decline. The pit waste heaps which once dominated the landscape of the Northumberland and Durham coalfields have now all gone.

**UNEMPLOYMENT** The two world wars provided a temporary boost for manufacturing, with an increasing demand for armaments, but in the inter-war years heavy unemployment was rife. In towns like Jarrow, where industries like shipbuilding had been of great importance, unemployment reached as high as 80%. In 1934 Tyneside was designated a special area to encourage light industries and the Team Valley Trading Estate was established here in 1936 to encourage change. In this same year the famous Jarrow March for jobs took place, highlighting the still desperate need for jobs in the region. Unemployment throughout the century would have a major effect on the North East because the region had relied on only a small number of large manufacturing industries. Today economic planners recognise the need for manufacturing industry, but also emphasise the need for a greater variety of smaller, lighter industries.

**SYMBOLS OF THE NORTH** Despite economic changes, the region continued to play an important role in world manufacturing in the early twentieth century. Great ships were built on the Tyne, Tees and Wear, notably the ocean liners of the Tyne. Civil Engineering, especially bridge building also made an impact. In 1911 the famous Transporter Bridge became Teesside's most famous landmark, while the Tyne Bridge of 1928 became the symbol of the Tyne. The Tyne Bridge would serve as a model for the larger, internationally famous Sydney Harbour Bridge, itself constructed by a Middlesbrough firm. Indeed every populated continent of the world has impressive examples of North-Eastern built bridges.

**URBAN REGENERATION** The later part of the twentieth century saw many urban re-developments which literally changed the face of the region. Slums were cleared, and new houses were erected. In certain areas like central Gateshead, blocks of concrete flats were erected and in town centres modern civic centres replaced Victorian town halls. T.Dan Smith, Chairman of the Northern Economic Council, talked of creating a new Brasilia at Newcastle. New Towns were created at places like Peterlee and Washington to bring new and better houses for the region's increasing population. New industries like Nissan were attracted to neighbouring sites. Business parks and industrial estates increasingly appeared close to centres of population, while Regional Development Companies made great improvements to derelict riverside sites. Disused land by the Tyne near Gateshead became the site of the MetroCentre, Europe's largest shopping and leisure complex, while Middlesbrough's old dock and Sunderland's last colliery became locations for superb football stadiums overlooking the Tees and Wear.

**TRANSPORT AND TECHNOLOGY** Some of the biggest changes in the region in the twentieth century have been in transport and technology. The region can be proud that its pioneering electricity developments of the late nineteenth century were the first seeds of the electronic and technological revolution of the late twentieth century. Similarly the locomotives and railways of the eighteenth and nineteenth century paved the way for the development of the motor car in the twentieth century. Indeed the earliest cars of the late nineteenth and early twentieth century were steam cars. The motor car dominates the North East today as much as any western region. The region's railway network has however shrunk and the tram cars of the early twentieth century towns have completely disappeared. Nevertheless, the Tyneside Metro system, which opened in 1980, demonstrates that rail transport can still be revived in new ways.

**THE REGION'S IDENTITY** The decline in heavy industry may have dented the region's identity, but the North East still retains a distinct character of its own. The age of broadcasting has reinforced aspects of the region's culture and at the same time made the region better known to other parts of the world. The gritty, romantic novels of the Tyneside author Catherine Cookson immortalise the working class life of Tyneside in times gone by. Her books have been adapted as television productions and are exported across the world. The same can be said of Alf Wight, the Sunderland born vet, who under the alias James Herriot recorded his adventurous working life in North Yorkshire. The music industry has also found talent in the region including international rock stars like Sting, Mark Knopfler and Chris Rea. However, a quite different figure, with an ever-increasing international fame is the 65 feet tall Angel of the North at Gateshead. With its magnificent wingspan of 175 feet, the Angel erected in 1998 now complements the Tyne Bridge and Durham Cathedral as a symbol of the region's pride and identity.

Newcastle - A view of the New Millennium

Index

305

Ad Caprae Caput (Gateshead), 39

Aegelwine, Bishop of Durham, 83, 89, 90

Aelle, King of Deira, 27, 28, 60

Aethelfrith, King of Northumbria, 28, 31, 32, 37

Agricola, 5, 14, 19, 20

Agricultural, 171, 180, 186, 195

Agriculture, 171, 186, 193, 195, 206

Ailred, abbot of Rievaulx, 117

Air raids, 268, 269

Alan the Red, 91, 122

Alcuin, 56, 57

Aldborough, 9, 15

Aldfrith, King of Northumbria, 45, 49

Aldhun, Bishop of Durham, 77, 79

Alexander, King of Scotland, 97, 127, 128, 129, 130

Alfred the Great, 61, 62

Alfwold, 56, 57

Alhred, King of Northumbria, 56

Alkali manufacture, 235

Allendale, 190, 219

Alnmouth, 45, 191, 290

Alnwick, 95, 98, 111, 122, 127, 128, 134, 141, 147, 149, 150, 153, 154, 156, 174, 289

Ammonia, 237, 261, 273

Andy Capp, 273

Angel of the North, 298, 300, 302

Angles, 21, 23, 25, 26, 27, 31, 33, 61

Anglo-Saxons, 14, 26, 31, 32, 48, 60, 61, 62, 64, 67, 71, 73, 83, 90, 91, 92, 101, 106, 107, 109, 110, 123, 147, 195, 206, 217

Anhydrite, 236, 262

Anno Domini, 48, 51

Antonine Wall, 8, 9, 10

Apostle of the North, 165

Armaments, 257, 301

Armistice, 257

Armstrong, William George, 224, 225, 226, 230, 241, 242, 243

Arthur, 19, 23, 26

Ashington, 277

Aske, Robert, 160

Athelwald Moll, 55, 56

Athletics, 292

Atkinson, Frank, 281

Augustinians, 98, 106, 109, 110, 111

Austin and Pickersgill, 229, 283, 286

Austin Pickersgill, 232

Australia, 191, 261, 263

Aycliffe, 56, 65, 171, 290

Ayresome Park, 277

Baedeker raids, 267

Bainbridges Store, 247

Baliol family, 96, 116, 130, 132, 139, 141, 143

Balmbra's Music Hall, 249, 290

Bamburgh, 4, 27, 32, 38, 39, 40, 49, 55, 61, 67, 71, 72, 77, 78, 79, 82, 83, 85, 89, 96, 116, 121, 144, 147, 153, 154, 189, 243

Bar, Hugh Earl of, 122

Barbarian Conspiracy, 24

Barnard Castle, 14, 15, 96, 106, 132, 141, 155, 160, 162, 174, 177, 186, 230, 248, 249, 290

Battle of Carham-on-Tweed, 79

Battle of Corbridge, 65

Battle of Culloden, 190

Battle of Flodden Field, 159, 167

Battle of Gate Fulford, 85

Battle of Hastings, 82, 86

Battle of Hatfield, 34

Battle of Heavenfield, 37

Battle of Hedgeley Moor, 154

Battle of Hexham, 154

Battle of Marston Moor, 177

Battle of Newburn, 172

Battle of Otterburn, 147

Battle of Stamford Bridge, 82, 85

Battle of the Standard, 115

Battle of Towton, 153

Bayeaux, Odo Bishop of, 92

Bayeux, Thomas of, 91

Beamish Museum, 278, 281

Bede, 45, 46, 47, 48, 49, 50, 51, 52, 55, 67, 79, 103, 217

Bedlington, 196, 247

Beeching report, 274

Bek, Anthony, 104, 134, 141

Bell Brothers, 223, 235, 236

Bell pits, 136, 218

Benedict Biscop, 43, 45, 46, 48

Benedictines, 106, 107, 109, 110, 111, 122, 149

Bensham, 184

Benwell, 17, 241, 242

Bernicia, 27, 28, 31, 32, 33, 38, 39, 55, 56, 60, 61, 64, 77

Berwick upon Tweed, 43, 97, 117, 122, 128, 132, 141, 142, 143, 144, 155, 156, 161, 171, 172, 177, 224, 248, 251

Bessemer Steel, 224

Bewick, Thomas, 192

Billingham, 65, 132, 205, 207, 234, 236, 237, 255, 258, 261, 262, 263, 268, 273, 277

Binchester, 11, 14, 15

Birdoswald, 12, 19, 26

Bishop Auckland, 14, 79, 94, 132, 159, 160, 174, 178, 189, 213, 289, 290

Blackett family, 217

Blackgate, 126, 129

Blair, Tony, 294, 298

Blanchland abbey, 109, 144

Blast furnaces, 138, 185, 223, 224, 225

Blaydon, 172, 217, 219, 249, 273, 281, 290

Blaydon Races, 249, 290

Blenheim, 230

Blood Eagle, 60

Blue Riband, 229, 230

Blyth, 174, 183, 185, 186, 213, 231

Bolckow, Henry, 223, 224, 225, 235, 262

Boldon, 121, 123, 132, 136, 174, 286

Bonnie Prince Charlie, 190

Border Ballads, 167

Border Leicester Sheep, 196

Border Reivers, 163, 164, 165, 167, 168, 172

Boroughbridge, 9, 142

Boroughs, 62, 123, 127

Bost, John, 162

Botany Bay, 191

307

Boudicea, 4

Bowburn, 278

Bowes, 14, 15, 122, 128, 162, 184, 201, 217, 230, 249

Bowes Railway, 201

Brancepeth, 147, 161, 162, 184, 185, 278

Braveheart, 141

Breweries, 237

Bridge building, 226, 255, 256, 261

Brigantes, 3, 4, 5, 8, 9

Britons, 3, 5, 25, 26, 27, 28, 31, 32, 195

Bronze Age discovery, 248

Bruce, 97, 106, 107, 115, 133, 134, 138, 139, 140, 141, 142, 143, 144

Brunner Mond, 236, 261

Burdon, Rowland, 206

Byker, 183, 186, 217

Byland, 106, 142

Byron, Lord, 199

Cade's Road, 14, 18

Caedmon, 45

Caedwalla, 34, 37

Caldecoates, 133

Caledonia, 4, 5, 8, 9, 11, 23, 28, 31, 42, 45, 49

Camboglanna, 19

Canada, 247

Canals, 185, 199, 205

Candymen, 213

Canterbury, 26, 28, 52, 71, 91, 97, 103, 111, 116

Canute, 76, 77, 78, 79, 80, 82

Car chase, 251

Caractacus, 3, 4

Cargo Fleet, 133, 235

Carileph, William, 94, 95, 96, 101, 109, 296

Carl the Hold, 82

Carlisle, 5, 20, 61, 62, 95, 98, 115, 116, 117, 121, 142, 167, 208

Carmelites, 110

Carrawburgh, 19

Carthusians, 107, 111

Cartimandua, 3, 4

Castle Eden, 206, 207, 229, 273

Castles, 89, 96, 116, 122, 134, 147, 154, 164

Castlesteads, 19

Catterick, 15, 31, 39, 55, 56, 217, 290

Causey Arch, 182, 183

Cellnet Riverside Stadium, 296

Celts, 3, 19, 23, 26, 27, 31, 32, 33, 37, 42, 45, 49, 51

Cenred, King of Northumrbia, 51

Ceolfrith, abbot of Jarrow, 46, 48, 49

Ceolwulf, King of Northumbria, 51, 52, 55

Cerebos, 236, 255

Chaldrons, 183, 201

Chamberlain, Neville, 267

Charcoal, 138, 195

Charlemagne, 56, 57

Charles I, 170, 171, 172, 292

Charles II, 179

Charltons, 164, 165, 168, 189, 277

Charters, 121, 123, 132, 133, 138

Chartershaugh Colliery, 184

Chemical Industry, 186, 233, 235, 236, 237, 258, 261, 263, 267, 274, 277

**Chester-le-Street**, 9, 11, 14, 32, 62, 65, 67, 72, 73, 77, 83, 95, 101, 132, 171, 174, 191, 211, 289, 290

**Chesters**, 19, 20, 56

**Cholera**, 206, 248

**Christianity**, 23, 27, 28, 31, 33, 34, 37, 38, 42, 45, 49, 51, 55, 78, 124

**Cinemas**, 264

**Cistercians**, 106, 107, 109, 111

**Civil War**, 3, 171, 177, 179, 292

**Clarence Railway**, 202, 207

**Clarke Chapman**, 230, 242

**Clasper, Harry**, 290

**Claudius**, 2, 3

**Cleveland**, 85, 91, 97, 106, 141, 172, 191, 196, 224, 225, 256, 281, 292

**Cleveland Bridge and Engineering**, 226, 255, 256

**Coal**, 14, 95, 109, 136, 137, 138, 168, 172, 173, 177, 178, 183, 184, 185, 186, 199, 200, 201, 205, 206, 207, 208, 211, 212, 213, 214, 217, 218, 223, 229, 230, 236, 248, 255, 256, 263, 268, 273, 279, 295, 289, 298, 301

**Coatham**, 133, 134

**Coldstream Guards**, 179

**Colliery disasters**, 184, 211, 213, 256, 267, 268, 273

**Colling, Charles and Robert**, 196

**Comines, Robert**, 89

**Common, Alf**, 289

**Coniscliffe**, 55, 56

**Consett**, 207, 208, 223, 225, 282

**Constantine**, 23

**Cook, Captain James**, 185, 191

**Cookson, Catherine**, 302

**Coquetdale**, 34, 110

**Corbridge**, 5, 10, 11, 15, 19, 20, 55, 57, 64, 65, 127, 141, 174

**Cornforth**, 208, 211

**Corstopitum**, 19

**Cospatric**, 83, 85

**Cotton, Mary Ann**, 249

**Council of the North**, 160

**County Durham**, 11, 14, 15, 17, 56, 62, 65, 72, 77, 83, 92, 95, 116, 127, 148, 179, 190, 195, 200, 205, 206, 207, 208, 211, 223, 247, 256, 261, 268, 273, 278, 281, 282, 285, 286, 295, 296, 298

**Cragside**, 241, 242, 243, 244

**Cramlington**, 274

**Cricket**, 268, 289, 292, 295

**Croft on Tees**, 123, 179

**Cromwell**, 175, 176, 177, 178, 179

**Cuerdale hoard**, 66

**Culley, Matthew and George**, 196

**Cumberland**, 83, 117, 128, 143, 147

**Cumbria**, 10, 20, 26, 28, 31, 32, 42, 56, 61, 62, 64, 67, 68, 73, 91, 117, 128, 141, 160, 164, 165, 190

**Cumin, William**, 115, 116, 117

**Curthose, Robert**, 92, 95, 96

**D'Ainai, Geoffrey**, 106

**Dalden**, 142

**Danes**, 60, 61, 62, 64, 65, 68, 71, 73, 77, 78, 90, 195

**Darling, Grace**, 247

**Darlington**, 3, 4, 15, 56, 78, 82, 94, 110, 116, 121, 123, 124, 132, 133, 156, 160, 162, 171, 174, 179, 185, 186, 191, 195, 196, 199, 200, 201, 205, 223, 224, 225, 226, 249, 251, 255, 256, 274, 282, 290

David, King of Scotland, 97, 106, 114, 115, 116, 117, 141, 143, 144, 285

Davison, Emily, 257

Davy Lamp, 199

Defoe, Daniel, 189

Deira, 27, 28, 31, 32, 33, 37, 38, 39, 55, 60

Delaval family, 185

Denmark, 23, 24, 25, 26, 74, 78, 79

Dere Street, 5, 8, 11, 14, 15, 20

Derwent Iron Company, 223, 225

Dixieland, 190

Domesday Book, 95, 121, 123

Dominicans, 110, 134

Doncaster, 33, 34, 90, 124, 290

Dorman Long, 225, 257, 262, 263, 277

Doxfords, 229, 255

Dublin, 58, 62, 64, 65, 67, 68, 72

Dudley, John Earl of Warwick, 160

Dunstanburgh, 142, 147, 153, 154

Dunston on Tyne, 183, 211, 295

Durham, 15, 26, 55, 61, 64, 65, 77, 78, 79, 80, 82, 83, 89, 90, 91, 92, 94, 95, 96, 97, 98, 101, 102, 103, 104, 106, 109, 110, 111, 115, 116, 117, 118, 121, 122, 123, 127, 128, 129, 130, 132, 133, 134, 136, 137, 138, 141, 142, 143, 144, 147, 149, 150, 156, 159, 161, 162, 164, 165, 168, 171, 173, 174, 177, 178, 179, 180, 183, 194, 196, 199, 200, 201, 207, 208, 211, 213, 214, 217, 225, 247, 248, 249, 251, 255, 256, 257, 261, 264, 268, 273, 274, 277, 281, 285, 290, 292, 295, 296, 298, 302

Durham Castle, 91, 92, 95, 117, 156, 179, 268

Durham Cathedral, 15, 95, 96, 98, 99, 101, 102, 103, 104, 109, 110, 129, 149, 150, 161, 162, 179, 268, 284, 285, 296, 302

Durham City, 15, 55, 77, 78, 79, 80, 82, 83, 89, 90, 91, 95, 96, 98, 115, 116, 117, 121, 122, 129, 133, 143, 144, 149, 150, 156, 161, 162, 174, 179, 255, 256, 257, 268, 273, 285, 290, 295, 296, 298

Durham Light Infantry, 257, 277

Durham Ox, 194

Durham University, 178, 207, 251

Eadulf Cudel, 79, 82

Eadulfsons, 77, 78

Earthquakes, 123, 192

Easington, 174, 273, 296

East Anglia, 4, 25, 32, 33, 60

Ebchester, 11, 15, 174

Ecgfrith, 42, 43, 45

Eden, Anthony, 273

Edinburgh, 4, 27, 31, 38, 45, 72, 79, 144, 156, 262, 282

Edison, Thomas, 241, 242

Edward the Confessor, 82, 83, 85

Edward I, 130, 133, 138, 141

Edward II, 133, 141, 142

Edward III, 138, 143

Edward IV, 153, 154, 155

Edward VI, 161

Edward VII, 251, 255

Edward VIII, 264

Edwin, 31, 32, 33, 34, 37, 38, 39, 85, 89, 101

Egbert, 52, 58, 60, 61

Egglescliffe, 134, 206, 235

Egglestone Abbey, 106

Electric light, 241, 242

Elizabeth I, 157, 158, 159, 161, 162, 169, 172

Elizabeth II, 273

Elmet, 31, 33, 38

Elswick, 137, 217, 224, 231, 257, 262

Engineering, 200, 201, 211, 225, 230, 255, 267

Engineers' Strike, 225

Engines, 183, 199, 208

Eric Bloodaxe, 69, 71, 72

Eric Hlathir, Earl of York, 79

Escomb, 14, 79, 136

Eston, 224, 225

Executions, 49, 89, 91, 107, 142, 148, 160, 161, 162, 164, 165, 167, 168, 172, 177, 178, 179, 180, 189, 190, 191, 249

FA Cup Final, 289

Farne Islands, 43, 46, 247

Fawkes, Guy, 172

Felling, 213, 235

Fenwick, Sir John, 179

Fenwicks Store, 251

Ferryhill, 127, 136, 174, 278

Fertilisers, 206, 235, 236, 261, 262

Finchale, 56, 57, 97, 110, 121, 136

Fires, 55, 90, 101, 129, 133, 144, 150, 171, 183, 189, 190, 201, 248, 285

Fishburn, 189, 282

Fishing, 133, 138, 200, 201, 205, 206, 211

Flambard, Bishop of Durham, 96, 97, 98, 133

Flodden Field, 159, 167

Flooding, 143, 191

Football, 165, 276, 277, 289, 295, 296, 298 302

Forests, 96, 121, 127, 128, 138, 195

Forster, John, 165

Forster, Tom, 189

Forth Banks Power Station, 243

Foster, Brendan, 292

Fountains Abbey, 106, 110, 195

Framwelgate Moor, 98, 190

France, 18, 42, 43, 56, 57, 64, 97, 106, 107, 111, 117, 148, 167

Franciscans, 110, 133

Friaries, 110, 111, 133

Friars Goose, 235

Friction matches, 202

Frisians, 43, 48, 56

Frosterley, 103

Gainford, 57, 61

Galloway ponies, 217

Garmondsway, 80, 208, 211

Gateshead, 14, 39, 61, 92, 121, 123, 137, 161, 162, 179, 184, 185, 201, 206, 235, 248, 263, 264, 278, 281, 282, 286, 290, 295, 298, 301, 302

General Strike, 261

Geordies, 189

George I, 180, 189

George II, 189, 190

George V, 256, 262

George VI, 264

Georgians, 187, 188, 189, 192, 290

Germany, 23, 24, 26, 185, 189, 217, 219, 223, 255, 257, 267, 277

Gilesgate, 117, 174

Gilpin, Bernard, 165

Glass, 43, 103, 183, 186, 233, 235, 237, 238

Golf, 290, 292

Gosforth, 184, 290

Grahams, 165, 167, 168

Grand Allies, 184

Grand Lease Way, 183

Gray, William, 229, 231

Great Fire of Newcastle, 248

Great North Run, 291, 292

Greatham, 130, 138, 236, 255

Greathead, Henry, 192

Grey, Walter de Archbishop of York, 102

Guisborough, 106, 133, 171, 281

Guthfrith, King of York, 67, 68

Guthred, 62

Hackworth, Timothy, 223

Hadrian's Wall, 5, 6, 7, 8, 9, 10, 11, 12, 17, 18, 19, 20, 23, 24, 26, 56

Halfdene, 60, 61, 62

Halidon Hill, 143

Hall, Sir John, 286

Haltwhistle, 18, 19, 20

Harald Hardrada, 85

Harold Godwinson, 82, 83, 85

Harrogate, 171

Harrying of the North, 89, 90

Hart, 138, 171

Hartburn, 123

Hartlepool, 17, 38, 42, 57, 65, 91, 111, 116, 117, 122, 123, 127, 130, 132, 133, 136, 138, 141, 142, 143, 144, 171, 185, 190, 199, 200, 201, 205, 206, 207, 208, 211, 212, 223, 229, 231, 236, 237, 249, 255, 257, 273, 277, 281, 286, 289, 296, 298

Hartley, 186, 213

Harton, 214, 278

Haswell, 213, 214

Hatfield, 33, 34, 147

Haverton Hill, 231, 236

Hawks, William, 185

Hawthorn Leslie, 232, 257, 263

Head Ashby & Co, 225

Heathery Burn cave, 248

Heaton, 243

Hebburn, 210, 217, 231, 232, 257, 263, 290

Hebrides, 130

Hedley, William, 199

Hedleyhope, 273

Hell's Kettles, 123

Hendon, 138, 229

Henry I, 96, 109, 115

Henry II, 117, 118, 217

Henry III, 122, 125, 127, 128, 129, 130, 133

Henry IV, 148, 149

Henry V, 149

Henry VI, 149, 150, 153, 154, 155

Henry VII, 153, 156, 159

Henry VIII, 106, 110, 132, 159, 160, 161, 164, 167, 290

Hepburn, Thomas, 213

Heron, George, 165

Heron, John, 167

Herrington, 286

Herriot, James, 302

Hesleyside, 164

Hett, 136

Hetton, 183, 199, 200, 211, 214, 286

Heworth, 137, 278

Hexham, 18, 19, 20, 37, 43, 45, 46, 48, 49, 51, 56, 58, 61, 104, 106, 109, 111, 134, 141, 142, 144, 154, 190, 217

Holy Island, 28, 49, 58, 137

Holystone, 34

Horse racing, 290

Hotspur, Harry Percy, 145, 147, 148, 149

Houghton, 165, 286

Housesteads, 12, 20

Hudson, George, 225

Hull, 111, 133, 173, 212

Humber, 11, 12, 14, 26, 31, 43, 60, 78, 85, 90

Humbleton Hill, 148

Hunderthwaite, 91

Huntcliff, 15, 24

Hunter, George, 230

Hydrochloric acid, 235

Hylton, 174, 282

Ida the Flamebearer, 27, 28, 32

Imperial Chemical Industries (ICI), 237, 261, 268

Iona, 27, 28, 32, 37, 42, 49

Iraq, 18, 23

Ireland, 24, 31, 37, 38, 42, 45, 58, 61, 62, 63, 64, 65, 67, 68, 73, 167, 172, 230, 242, 248

Iron, 3, 134, 137, 138, 183, 185, 207, 211, 212, 218, 221, 223, 224, 225, 226, 229, 230, 267

Isle of Man, 56, 74, 130

Italy, 111, 289

Ivar the Boneless, 60, 61

Jack the Blaster, 191

Jacobites, 189, 190

James I King of England and Scotland, 172

James I of England and Scotland, 167

James I of Scotland, 148

James II, King of Scotland, 150

James IV of Scotland, 156, 167

James VI of Scotland, 162, 172

Jarrow, 45, 46, 48, 49, 51, 52, 57, 79, 91, 94, 110, 211, 225, 230, 231, 238, 257, 261, 262, 263, 281, 301

Jarrow March, 261, 263, 301

Jenkins, David, 280, 285

Jervaulx Abbey, 107, 160

John of Gaunt, 147, 148

John, King of England, 124, 125, 127, 128, 133, 134

Jolly Rant Disease, 179

Jones, John Paul, 191

Jorvik, 59, 60

Joyous Guard, 27

Keel Row, 168

Keelmen, 137, 167, 168, 183, 190, 200, 290

Kielder 165, 282

Kilhope wheel, 216, 218

Killingworth, 199, 274, 290

Knaresborough, 134, 148

Knopfler, Mark, 302

Lambton, John George, 247

Lancastrians, 142, 147, 148, 149, 150, 153, 154, 155

Lanchester, 11, 15, 213, 278, 290

Lead Mining, 121, 136, 215, 216, 217, 218, 219

Leather industry, 136, 171

Lee, Peter, 256

Leeds, 31, 33, 38, 39, 104, 109, 133, 153, 173, 186, 237, 251

Leslie, General, 172, 174, 178

Levellers, 178

Lightning, 150, 285

Lilburne, John, 178

Lindisfarne, 28, 37, 38, 42, 45, 46, 48, 49, 51, 55, 56, 57, 58, 61, 62, 83, 90, 101, 108, 109

Liulf of Lumley, 92

Liverpool, 212, 224, 289

Locomotives, 197, 199, 201, 202, 214, 223, 225, 255, 262

London, 4, 10, 11, 23, 78, 85, 96, 115, 124, 137, 155, 159, 172, 173, 177, 178, 179, 184, 185, 199, 200, 212, 217, 224, 230, 248, 255, 261, 262, 263, 264

London Lead Company, 217

London North Eastern Railway, 213, 262

Londonderry, Lord, 200, 205, 211, 213

Losh Brothers, 186, 223, 235

Lothians, 27, 31, 32, 38, 72, 83, 143

Lumley, 92, 136, 148, 183, 278

Macbeth, 83

Macdonald, Ramsay, 262

Mackay, Hugh, 255

Macmillan, Harold, 261, 273

Magna Carta, 128

Malcolm, King of the Scots, 68, 71, 78, 79, 80, 83, 91, 95, 97, 114, 117

Manchester, 65

Margaret of Anjou, 153

Markets, 95, 104, 123, 132, 133, 134, 138, 147, 196, 224, 268

Marks and Spencer, 251

Marley Hill, 278, 286

Marley, Elsie, 191

Marley, John, 177

Marston Moor, 177

Marton, 191

Mary I, 159, 161

Mary II, 179

Mary Queen of Scots, 159, 161, 162

Matilda, 115, 116, 149

Mauretania, 230

Medieval towns, 131, 132, 133

Members of Parliament, 179, 180, 190, 206, 226, 261, 262, 273, 298

Mercia, 32, 37, 38, 39, 43, 56, 58, 61, 65, 72, 73, 85, 91

Merman, 172

Merseyside, 12, 64, 290

Methodism, 190

Metro Rapid Transport System, 282, 302

MetroCentre, 286, 302

Meynell, Thomas, 201

Micklegate, 107, 153

Middleham, 15, 91, 122, 130, 134, 153, 155, 290

Middlesbrough, 97, 107, 191, 199, 201, 203, 205, 206, 207, 212, 223, 224, 225, 226, 229, 232, 235, 243, 247, 249, 251, 255, 256, 257, 258, 261, 262, 263, 267, 268, 274, 277, 282, 286, 289, 296, 301, 302

Middleton in Teesdale, 217, 255

Milburns, 165, 289

Millennium, 3, 77, 293, 295, 298

Miners' gala, 213, 275, 285

Mitchell & Co, 230

Mithras, 10, 17, 19

Monasteries, 24, 27, 32, 38, 39, 42, 43, 45, 46, 48, 49, 51, 57, 61, 67, 91, 92, 97, 101, 103, 104, 105, 106, 107, 108, 109, 110, 111, 116, 117, 123, 130, 133, 134, 137, 138, 148, 149, 159, 160, 195, 206, 217, 238, 264

Monck, General, 179

Monkchester, 17, 92, 122

Monks, 32, 42, 51, 52, 55, 58, 91, 94, 96, 104, 106, 107, 109, 110, 111, 116, 129, 136, 298

Monks, 37, 38, 48, 49, 51, 55, 57, 106, 107, 111, 160

Monkwearmouth, 43, 45, 48, 49, 91, 214, 298

Monsanto textiles, 281

Morcar, 85, 89

Morpeth, 96, 110, 128, 134, 156, 164, 289

Motorway, 272, 274, 277

Mount Grace Priory, 107, 111, 112

Mowbray family, 95, 96, 109, 115, 122

Murder, 20, 28, 39, 51, 55, 57, 60, 71, 72, 74, 83, 85, 89, 92, 103, 148, 165, 167, 168, 189, 191, 249

Murton, 267, 295

Neasham Abbey, 110

Neville family, 130, 144, 147, 148, 152, 153, 154, 155, 161, 162

Nevilles Cross, 144

New Towns, 268, 302

New Zealand, 191

Newbottle, 183

Newburn, 89, 171, 172

Newcastle, 9, 14, 17, 18, 19, 26, 88, 92, 95, 96, 101, 104, 109, 110, 116, 121, 122, 123, 124, 127, 128, 129, 130, 135, 136, 137, 138, 141, 142, 143, 144, 147, 148, 149, 156, 161, 162, 164, 167, 168, 171, 172, 173, 174, 177, 178, 179, 183, 184, 185, 189, 190, 191, 192, 201, 208, 212, 213, 217, 223, 224, 226, 229, 237, 241, 242, 243, 247, 248, 249, 251, 255, 262, 264, 267, 268, 273, 274, 282, 289, 290, 292, 295, 302

Newcastle Roads, 183

Newcastle United FC, 276, 289

Newport Lifting Bridge, 263

Newton Aycliffe, 268

Nicholson, Cuthbert, 178

Nissan, 285, 302

Norham on Tweed, 58, 61, 97, 121, 127, 154, 247

Normans, 14, 60, 64, 81, 82, 85, 86, 87, 89, 90, 91, 92, 95, 96, 97, 98, 101, 102, 103, 106, 109, 110, 115, 117, 122, 134, 141, 164, 243, 289

North Eastern Railway, 211, 224

North Sea ferry, 263

North Shields, 109, 137, 138, 172, 190, 231, 256

Northallerton, 90, 115, 134, 156, 248

Northamptonshire, 49, 85, 91, 155

Northern Economic Planning Council, 274

Northumberland, 4, 5, 8, 9, 10, 11, 12, 15, 20, 26, 32, 34, 38, 43, 61, 77, 85, 91, 94, 95, 96, 104, 109, 115, 116, 117, 118, 121, 122, 123, 124, 127, 128, 129, 141, 142, 143, 147, 148, 149, 150, 153, 154, 155, 156, 159, 160, 161, 164, 165, 172, 177, 179, 189, 195, 196, 213, 241, 242, 243, 247, 255, 256, 274, 281, 290, 301

Northumberland Fusiliers, 257

Northumberland Plate, 290

Northumbria, 23, 29, 31, 32, 33, 34, 37, 38, 39, 42, 43, 45, 46, 48, 49, 51, 52, 55, 56, 57, 58, 60, 61, 62, 68, 71, 72, 77, 78, 79, 82, 83, 85, 89, 91, 94, 101

315

Norton, 79, 94, 132, 171, 180

Norway, 57, 58, 64, 65, 71, 73, 79, 82, 85, 86, 117, 130, 195, 263

Nottinghamshire, 60, 62, 128, 162, 177

Offa, 56

Oil, 230, 236, 237, 263, 273, 277

Olaf Ball, 65

Olaf Sihtricson, 72

Old Pretender, 189

Osmotherley, 107, 111

Oswald, King of Northumbria, 32, 35, 37, 38, 39, 73, 101

Oswine, King of Deira, 38, 39

Oswy, King of Northumbria, 38, 39, 42, 45

Oxford University, 130, 161, 178, 267

Palace Green, 133

Palmers, 225, 230, 231, 257, 262

Parkin, John, 207, 229

Parliament, 171, 172, 173, 177, 178, 179, 196, 214

Parsons, Charles Algernon, 230, 242, 243

Paulinus, 34, 37

Pease family, 186, 201, 204, 205, 223, 249

Pele Towers, 142, 159, 164

Pelton, 278

Penda, 34, 37, 38, 39

Pennines, 3, 9, 20, 217

Penshaw, 183, 247

Percy family, 115, 141, 143, 145, 147, 148, 149, 150, 153, 154, 161

Perkin Warbeck rebellion, 156

Peterlee, 268, 302

Petillius Cerealis, 4

Petro-Chemicals, 237

Pickersgill, William, 229

Picktree, 184, 191

Picts, 12, 23, 24, 39, 42, 49, 51

Piercebridge, 4, 12, 15, 17, 174

Pilgrimage of Grace, 107, 159, 160

Place names, 60, 195

Plagues, 42, 46, 78, 128, 160, 171, 179

Plastics, 236, 263

Pons Aelius, 9, 17, 26, 92

Pont L'Eveque, Roger, 101

Pope, 49, 52, 97, 101, 116, 123, 133, 159

Population, 132, 134, 167, 184, 199, 205, 206, 212, 248, 249, 255, 302

Port Clarence, 202

Port of Tyne Autority, 277

Portrack, 205

Ports, 8, 11, 18, 109, 122, 127, 133, 134, 136, 137, 138, 180, 185, 200, 201, 202, 205, 206, 207, 211, 212, 217, 229, 235, 236, 277, 285

Premonstratensians, 106, 109, 111

Press Gangs, 190

Preston, 64, 189, 200

Preston Park, 282

Priestman's shipbuilders, 231

Prime Ministers, 273, 282, 298

Prince Bishop, 91, 93, 94, 95, 104, 116, 121, 123, 195, 207, 217, 296

Protestantism, 159

Prudhoe, 129, 147

Pudsey, Hugh Bishop of Durham, 103, 118, 119, 120, 121, 122, 123, 124, 138

Puffing Billy, 199

Quakers, 205

Quarrington Hill, 174

Raby, 80, 98, 130, 147, 148, 161, 162, 177

Ragnald, 64, 65

Raid of Reidswire, 165

Railways, 211, 213, 223, 225, 267, 274, 282

Railway Stations, 248, 251

Railways, 183, 185, 198, 199, 200, 201, 202, 205, 206, 207, 208, 211, 213, 217, 223, 224, 225, 247, 248, 249, 274, 282, 285, 302

Rainton, 136, 282

Raisbeck, Leonard, 199

Redcar, 133, 134, 247, 277, 290, 292

Redesdale, 147, 165, 168

Rheged, Kingdom of, 28, 31

Richard I, 123, 124, 127, 128

Richard II, 147, 148

Richard III, 152, 155, 156

Richard, Duke of York, 153

Richardson, Thomas, 207, 229

Richmond, 89, 91, 111, 122, 134, 192, 290

Ridley, Geordie, 249, 290

Ridley, Nicholas, 161

Ridleys, 165

Rievaulx Abbey, 106, 107, 117, 160

Riots, 189, 190, 200, 201, 290

Ripon, 42, 48, 49, 67, 71, 77, 101, 104, 290

Rising of the North, 159, 161, 162, 165

Robin Hood, 128

Robsons, 164, 165, 168

Roker Park, 277

Romans, 1, 3, 4, 5, 8, 9, 10, 11, 12, 13, 14, 15, 17, 18, 19, 20, 23, 24, 25

Roman Catholocism, 159, 160, 161, 161

Rome, 3, 5, 8, 9, 10, 11, 18, 24, 25, 28, 43, 46, 49, 55, 97, 101, 111, 116, 118, 121, 159

Rookhope, 165, 218, 219, 220

Roseberry Topping, 171, 191

Rothbury, 243

Rowing, 290

Royal Border Bridge, 224, 248

Royalists, 173, 174, 177

Russells of Brancepeth, 184

Sacriston, 286

Sadberge, 61, 95, 116, 123

St.Abbs Head, 43

St.Aidan, 31, 35, 36, 37, 38

St.Augustine, 28, 111

St.Barbara, William 116, 121

St.Cedd, 39

St.Columba, 27, 28

St.Cuthbert, 14, 38, 41, 42, 43, 44, 45, 46, 48, 51, 58, 61, 62, 64, 67, 72, 77, 78, 80, 90, 96, 103, 115, 133, 149, 150, 290, 298

St.Godric, 97, 110, 121

St.Hilda, 38, 42, 45, 107, 123, 206

St.John Lee, 103

St.Ninnian, 24

St.Olaf's church, York, 83

St.Wilfrid, 41, 42, 43, 45, 46, 48, 49, 51, 71, 109

St.William Fitzherbert of York, 103

Salt, 138, 183, 185, 235, 236, 255

Saltburn, 15, 24, 109, 249

Scarborough, 24, 73, 98, 111, 118, 142, 172, 190, 257

Scone, 83, 141, 143

Scotch Corner, 4

Scotland, 5, 8, 9, 10, 15, 23, 24, 25, 26, 27, 31, 32, 38, 39, 49, 61, 64, 67, 68, 71, 72, 73, 77, 78, 79, 80, 82, 83, 89, 91, 92, 95, 97, 106, 110, 113, 115, 116, 117, 118, 121, 122, 127, 128, 129, 130, 132, 133, 134, 137, 141, 142, 143, 144, 147, 148, 149, 150, 153, 154, 155, 156, 159, 160, 161, 162, 164, 165, 167, 168, 171, 172, 173, 174, 177, 178, 179, 189, 190, 195, 196, 223, 248, 290

Scrope, Richard Archbishop of York, 148

Seaham, 142, 199, 200, 205, 206, 211, 213, 262, 286, 296

Seal Sands, 236, 261, 274, 281

Seaton Carew, 249, 257, 292

Seaton Delaval, 185

Sedgefield, 14, 79, 132, 192, 289, 290, 298

Septimius Severus, 10

Shafto, Bobby, 190

Sharp, Sir Cuthbert, 200, 207

Sheep, 164, 165, 168, 195, 196

Sheffield, 58, 224, 225, 262

Shildon, 201, 202, 223, 273, 278, 285

Shildon Wagon Works, 285

Shincliffe, 15

Shipbuilding, 134, 137, 189, 207, 211, 223, 227, 229, 230, 231 229, 230, 231, 232, 255, 262, 263, 277, 282, 283, 286, 301

Shotley Bridge, 185

Sihtric, 64, 65, 67

Silver mining, 217, 218, 219

Sir Lancelot, 27

Siward, Earl, 82, 83, 115

Skelton, 97, 106, 141

Skinningrove, 172

Skirlaw, Walter, 102, 134

Slum clearance, 277, 301

Smith, T.Dan, 274, 302

Smiths Dock, 231, 232, 256, 286

Soap making, 235

Sockburn, 56, 79

Soda making, 186, 235

Solingen, 185

Solvay process, 235

South Bank, 224, 256, 267, 286

South Hetton, 286

South Moor, 278

South Shields, 8, 18, 23, 24, 138, 174, 185, 191, 192, 206, 208, 212, 214, 230, 236, 238, 281, 290, 292, 296

Southwick, 186

Spain, 8, 17, 24, 121, 219, 225

Spas, 171, 172, 179

Special Areas Act, 263

Spectacle making, 186

Spennymoor, 136, 282

Spitfires, 266

Sport, 287

Spur in the Dish, 164, 166

Stadium of Light, 297

Staindrop, 80, 147, 278

Stainmore, 17, 71, 72, 73

Staithes, 183, 200, 206, 207, 211, 212, 295

Stanegate, 5, 11, 19, 20

Stanhope, 200, 208, 219

Stanley, 268, 278

Stanwick, 3, 4

Stars and stripes, 123

Stead, W.T, 256

Steam Naptha process, 237, 273

Steel, 18, 224, 225, 226, 229, 230, 258277, 282, 298

Stephen, King of England, 115, 121

Stephenson, George, 199, 200, 201, 202, 214

Stephenson, Robert, 201, 223, 224, 225, 248, 255

Sting, 302

Stitchill, Bishop of Durham, 130

Stockton, 79, 116, 123, 134, 136, 142, 177, 179, 180, 185, 188, 190, 192, 199, 200, 201, 202, 205, 206, 208, 211, 212, 217, 223, 225, 229, 231, 251, 261, 273, 277, 282, 290, 296

Stockton and Darlington Railway, 185, 198, 199, 200, 201, 205, 223, 282

Storms, 150, 178, 179, 180, 190, 192, 201, 249

Strikes, 210, 213, 225

Stuarts, 169, 171, 177, 189

Suffragettes, 257

Sunday School, 180

Sunderland, 43, 45, 48, 65, 67, 91, 97, 110, 123, 130, 136, 138, 172, 174, 177, 178, 179, 183, 184, 185, 186, 200, 201, 206, 207, 208, 211, 212, 224, 225, 229, 230, 231, 232, 237, 238, 241, 242, 248, 251, 255, 264, 274, 277, 281, 285, 286, 289, 290, 295, 296, 297, 298, 302

Sunderland FC, 289, 297

Sutton Hoo, 22, 33

Swaledale, 91, 142, 217

Swan Hunters, 230, 232, 286

Swan, Joseph, 240, 241, 242

Swein Forkbeard, 74, 77, 78

Swing Bridge, 226

Swordmaking, 185

Sydney Harbour Bridge, 261, 263, 301

Synods, 42, 45, 49, 57

Synthetic ammonia, 236, 258

Tanfield, 183, 278, 290

Team Valley Trading Estate, 263, 301

Tees, 11, 14, 17, 20, 24, 26, 27, 31, 43, 56, 57, 58, 60, 61, 62, 64, 71, 72, 73, 77, 79, 85, 91, 92, 94, 95, 106, 115, 116, 123, 132, 133, 134, 143, 165, 179, 185, 191, 199, 200, 202, 205, 207, 211, 223, 225, 231, 232, 237, 251, 261, 267, 268, 273, 274, 277, 281, 285, 286, 290, 292, 295, 296, 301, 302

Tees and Hartlepool Port Authority, 277, 282

Tees Barrage, 296

Teesdale, 17, 72, 73, 91, 96, 104, 106, 116, 123, 128, 141, 217, 255, 281

Teesside, 17, 201, 206, 207, 224, 225, 226, 229, 235, 236, 237, 257, 267, 274, 277, 281, 282, 285, 286, 295, 296, 301

Teesside Development Corporation, 286, 296

Tennant, Christopher, 206, 207, 208, 211

Thatcher, Margaret, 282

The Northern Echo, 256

Thirsk, 14, 122, 290

Thornaby, 60, 223, 225, 229, 277

Thornley, 117, 278, 282

319

Thrislington, 136, 278

Thurstan, Archbishop of York, 97, 106, 115

Titanic, 256

Tons, 137, 172, 185, 195, 206, 230, 248, 258

Tostig, 82, 83, 85, 89

Tourism, 247, 249

Tower of London, 96, 155

Town Moor, 137, 178, 191, 213, 290

Transhumance, 195

Transporter Bridge, 256, 267, 301

Treaties, 115, 116, 128, 142, 144, 149, 161

Trevelyan, G.M, 167

Trevithick, Richard, 199

Trimdon, 211, 213, 278, 298

Trimontium, 5, 15

Trinity House, 137

Tuda, 42

Tudors, 153, 156, 157, 159, 164, 196

Turbines, 242

Turbinia, 230, 243

Turgot, 97, 110

Tyne, 3, 4, 5, 9, 10, 11, 17, 18, 19, 20, 23, 26, 39, 61, 62, 64, 92, 94, 95, 96, 127, 129, 136, 137, 149, 165, 167, 168, 172, 174, 183, 185, 191, 199, 211, 214, 219, 223, 230, 231, 235, 236, 248, 255, 262, 263, 267, 273, 274, 277, 281, 286, 290, 295, 296, 301, 302

Tyne and Wear, 281, 286

Tyne Bridge, 26, 129, 226, 246, 260, 301, 303

Tyne Tunnel, 277

Tynedale, 20, 23, 118, 121, 128, 142, 162, 164, 165, 168, 208, 217, 282

Tynemouth, 39, 57, 61, 95, 96, 109, 137, 138, 148, 177, 206, 247, 282

Tyneside, 8, 18, 51, 52, 57, 136, 168, 172, 183, 186, 190, 211, 217, 223, 225, 230, 232, 235, 236, 238, 241, 242, 243, 248, 249, 252, 256, 257, 262, 263, 268, 274, 277, 278, 281, 282, 285, 290, 292, 296, 301, 302

Uhtred, Earl of Northumbria, 77, 78, 79

Umfraville, Robert, 149

Unemployment, 261, 262, 263, 301

United States of America, 123, 190, 191, 219, 241, 242, 264

Universities, 130, 207, 249, 264, 274, 295

Urban regeneration, 301

Urien, 28

Urlay Nook, 206, 235

Uttan, of Gateshead, 39

Van Mildert, William, 14, 207

Vanbrugh, John, 180

Vaughan, John, 222, 223, 224, 225, 235, 262

Vaux Breweries, 237

VE Day, 268, 270

Venutius, 3, 4

Vercovicium, 20

Vesci, Ivo de, 98

Vici, 11

Victoria Falls Bridge, 255

Victoria Hall Disaster, 251

Victoria, Queen, 247, 251

Victorians, 245, 246, 250, 252

Vikings, 55, 57, 58, 60, 61, 62, 64, 65, 67, 68, 72, 73, 74, 77, 78, 79, 106, 117, 130, 195

Vindolanda, 11, 19, 20

Vortigern, 26

Votadini, 4, 27, 31

Wagonways, 183, 199

Walcher of Lorraine, Bishop of Durham, 91, 92, 110

Wales, 12, 31, 32, 73, 248

Walker on Tyne, 223, 230, 235

Walker, John, 202

Wallace, William, 141

Wallington, 164, 252

Wallsend, 18, 213, 230, 232, 243, 278, 286

Waltheof, 91

Ward Jackson, Ralph, 208, 211

Wark castle, 97

Warkworth, 143, 146, 147

Wars of the Roses, 150, 151, 153, 154

Warwick the Kingmaker, 155

Washington, 123, 178, 183, 211, 254, 256, 274, 278, 282, 285, 302

Washington New Town, 274

Washington, George, 123

Watson, Tom, 289

Watt, James, 183

Wear Glass Works, 238

Weardale, 79, 103, 121, 128, 138, 143, 162, 165, 195, 200, 208, 217, 218, 219, 223, 247, 248

Wearmouth, 45, 46, 94, 97, 110, 123, 130, 138, 238, 296, 298

Weather, 150, 179, 180, 190, 192, 201

Weddell, George, 236

Welsh, 3, 19, 31, 32, 34, 37, 39

Wensleydale, 15, 91, 107, 122, 130, 155, 161

Wessex, 26, 33, 34, 58, 61, 62, 65, 67, 68, 71, 72, 77, 83, 90

West Auckland, 249, 278, 288, 289

West Hartlepool, 211, 212, 229, 277

West Stanley, 256

Westoe Colliery, 296

Whickham, 18, 136, 137, 183, 290

Whitburn, 278

Whitby, 42, 45, 57, 97, 107, 109, 137, 138, 160, 185, 223, 224, 257

Whitley Bay, 109

Whitworth, Robert, 185

Wickwane, Archbishop of York, 104

Wight, Alf, 302

William I the Conqueror, 82, 86, 89, 90, 91, 92, 121

William II Rufus, 95, 96, 107

William III of Orange, 179, 180

William IV, 202

William, King of Scotland, 122

Wilson, Isaac, 223

Wilson, Robert, 206, 235

Wilton, 236, 268

Windermere, 56

Windlestone Hall, 273

Windsor, 96, 121, 124, 217

Wingate, 256, 278

Winlaton, 137, 185

Witches and Witch Trials, 171, 178

Witton, 223, 278, 290

Wolsey, Thomas, 159, 164

Wolsingham, 121

**Wool industry**, 133, 186

**Wooler**, 34, 148, 149, 154, 196

**World Cup**, 277, 289

**World War One**, 219, 236, 253, 255, 257, 261

**World War Two**, 265, 267, 268

**Wouldhave, William**, 192

**Wulfstan, Archbishop of York**, 71, 72, 78, 79

**Wycliffe, John**, 159

**Wylam**, 199, 223

**Yarm**, 111, 132, 134, 171, 185, 199, 200, 201, 206, 211, 229, 296

**Yeavering**, 30, 34, 149

**York**, 4, 5, 8, 9, 10, 11, 12, 15, 18, 23, 24, 31, 34, 37, 38, 42, 43, 45, 51, 52, 54, 55, 56, 57, 58, 59, 60, 61, 62, 64, 65, 67, 68, 71, 72, 73, 74, 78, 79, 82, 83, 85, 86, 89, 90, 91, 97, 99, 100, 101, 102, 103, 104, 106, 107, 109, 110, 111, 115, 116, 118, 121, 122, 124, 128, 130, 132, 134, 137, 141, 142, 148, 150, 153, 154, 155, 156, 159, 160, 162, 172, 173, 174, 177, 189, 195, 225, 263, 267, 285, 290

**York Minster**, 34, 55, 89, 90, 97, 99, 101, 102, 103, 104, 134, 285

**Yorkists**, 153, 154, 155, 156

**Yorkshire**, 3, 4, 10, 14, 15, 24, 26, 27, 28, 31, 32, 33, 34, 38, 39, 42, 49, 51, 56, 60, 61, 62, 64, 65, 68, 71, 72, 73, 74, 77, 78, 79, 82, 85, 90, 95, 104, 106, 115, 117, 118, 122, 128, 142, 147, 148, 149, 153, 155, 156, 159, 160, 173, 180, 186, 189, 195, 196, 217, 257, 277, 281, 292, 302

**Yorkshire Ridings**, 61

**Zeppelin**, 257